VISUAL QUICKSTART GUIDE

ACCESS 2000

FOR WINDOWS

Deborah S. Ray
Eric J. Ray

 **Peachpit Press**

Visual QuickStart Guide
Access 2000 for Windows
Deborah S. Ray and Eric J. Ray

Peachpit Press
1249 Eighth Street
Berkeley, CA 94710
(510) 524-2178
(800) 283-9444
(510) 542-2221 (fax)

Find us on the World Wide Web at
http://www.peachpit.com

Peachpit Press is a division of Addison Wesley Longman

Copyright © 1999 by Deborah S. Ray and Eric J. Ray

Editor: Becky Morgan
Copy editor: Mark Nigura
Production coordinator: Kate Reber
Compositors: Lisa Brazieal, Melanie Haage
Cover design: The Visual Group
Indexer: Cheryl Landes, Tabby Cat Communications

Notice of rights
All rights reserved. No part of this book may be reproduced or transmitted in any form or by any means, electronic, mechanical, photocopying, recording, or otherwise, without the prior written permission of the publisher. For more information on getting permission for reprints and excerpts, contact Gary-Paul Prince at Peachpit Press.

Trademarks
Visual QuickStart Guide and its marks are registered trademarks of Peachpit Press. Throughout this book trademarked names are used. Rather than put a trademark symbol in every occurrence of a trademarked name, we state that we are using the names only in an editorial fashion and to the benefit of the trademark owner with no intention of infringement of copyright.

Notice of liability
The information in this book is distributed on an "As is" basis, without warranty. While every precaution has been taken in the preparation of the book, neither the author nor Peachpit Press shall have any liability to any person or entity with respect to any loss or damage caused or alleged to be caused directly or indirectly by the instructions contained in this book or by the computer software and hardware products described in it.

ISBN: 0-201-35434-9

9 8 7 6 5 4 3 2

Printed and bound in the United States of America

♻ Printed on recycled paper

Acknowledgements

This book came together with the help and effort of many talented people. First, a special thanks to Simon Hayes for his confidence and enthusiasm in getting this project rolling. This project could never have happened without the hard work and effort of Curtis D. Frye, who put in many long days and nights helping with all parts of this book. Becky Morgan's patience and understanding, as well as skillful editing, helped tremendously to make this book what it is. Thanks also to Marjorie Baer for her comments, Mark Nigara for copyediting, Cheryl Landes for indexing, and Kate Reber in production for bringing it all together.

TABLE OF CONTENTS

TABLE OF CONTENTS

INTRODUCTION

Microsoft Access 2000 (*Access* from here on), a component of Microsoft Office, is a powerful database program you can use to store, organize, and analyze information about the people, places, and things in your life.

This Visual QuickStart Guide will help you gain control over the Access environment using easy-to-understand instructions, lots of illustrations, and helpful tips to guide you past the pitfalls new users encounter when creating, using, and administering databases.

You can read this book cover to cover or flip through it. Use the table of contents, index, or thumb tabs to find the topics you're interested in. If you're new to Access or databases in general, be sure to read the first two chapters. Chapter 1 introduces databases and their components, and gives you a detailed view of the main Access window. Chapter 2 covers designing a database and using Access tools (or *wizards*) to create your databases with a minimum of effort.

Access is a powerful program with a lot of options and controls, but don't be intimidated by it. This Visual QuickStart Guide will have you up and running confidently in no time.

Why Access?

Why should you use Access? There are quite a few reasons, the first being that Access is a feature-rich program that can handle any database-related task you have. You can create places to store your data, build tools that make it easy to read and modify your database's contents, and ask questions of your data. You can create your database tools from scratch or by using wizards, which not only step you through the process of building your objects, but actually supply many of the necessary components of a database.

Another reason Access makes it easy to work with your data is that Access is a *relational* database, a database that stores information about related objects. For instance, a sales database contains information about customers, suppliers, sales reps, products, and orders. Because each order is placed by a customer, it makes sense to store your customer data in one table, and your order data in another table, and *relate* the two tables by a common field. In this case, you can use a customer's unique identifier in the Customer table to relate information about that customer to an order in the Orders table.

Another good reason to use Access is that it's a component of the overwhelmingly popular Microsoft Office software suite. You can share Access data with other Office applications, such as Microsoft Excel, Microsoft Word, and Microsoft PowerPoint seamlessly.

Finally, Access makes it easy to publish your information to the Internet via the World Wide Web. You can save your database objects as HTML documents, Active Server Pages, or even as Data Access Pages, which are HTML documents that offer nearly the same power as Access itself.

Who Are You?

A lot of folks can benefit from using Access. Maybe you're an entrepreneur who needs to maintain a list of contacts, complete with addresses and phone numbers. Or a researcher collecting survey data. Perhaps your company has asked you to create a database to track product sales and warranty data. Or you might be a home user who wants to keep track of the books in your library. In short, you're someone who can benefit from using Access to store and manage your data.

What You Need to Know

We assume you have a bit of experience using computers in general and Microsoft Windows in particular. Specifically , you'll need to be familiar with:

◆ Opening, closing, and saving files

◆ Navigating to folders and files using My Computer or Windows Explorer

◆ Printing files

◆ Starting and closing programs

◆ Minimizing, moving, resizing, restoring, and closing windows

◆ Cutting, copying, and pasting information

◆ Using a Web browser

If you need additional information about using Windows 98, refer to *Windows 98: Visual QuickStart Guide,* by Steve Sagman, published by Peachpit Press.

Anything Else You Should Know?

Yup! Feel free to contact us at accessvqs@raycomm.com. We welcome your input and suggestions as well as questions related to this book. Thanks, and we look forward to hearing from you.

GETTING STARTED WITH ACCESS

Access is a powerful, full-featured program. If you're new to databases in general, or Access in particular, it can take a little time to get a feel for the features at your disposal. This chapter helps you learn about Access by explaining how databases work, and what makes them different from other data-storage and -analysis tools. It also introduces you to the components of an Access database.

What Is a Database?

Simply put, a *database* is a program that manages a collection of information. What sets databases apart from other data management tools (like spreadsheets) is their ability to present that information in a variety of formats.

Access stores its data in *tables*, which are in turn made up of *fields* and *records*. A field is the basic unit of a database—it stores a particular piece of data. For instance, a bibliographic database might contain a table listing technology books. That table might have fields for each author's first name, last name, the book title, the ISBN, the copyright year, and the publisher. Fields correspond to the *columns* in a table (**Figure 1.1**). The *rows* in a table contain information about a single entity described by the table. In this case, each row, or record, describes a book (**Figure 1.2**).

Databases present your data in a variety of ways. For instance, if you maintain a set of addresses in a database, Access allows you to print mailing labels based on those addresses. You can also ask questions of the data by searching for specific values in a record. For instance, you can find every book you own that was published in 1996 or see if anyone you know lives in Hawaii.

Spreadsheet programs, such as Microsoft Excel, are much better for financial and numerical information than for maintaining lists of addresses and books. Spreadsheets have a wide range of built-in operations that they can perform on numerical data, so it's almost always easier to do strictly financial or numerical work with Excel than Access.

Fortunately, you can easily share data between the two. You can also share data with Microsoft Word, the word processing program in the Microsoft Office suite.

Copyright Year	ISBN Number	Publisher Name
1995	20130856	Macmillan Publi
1997	312166907	St. Martin's Pre
1993	805368299	Benjamin/Cumn
	471012734	Wiley
1983	895030365	Baywood Pub C
1997	205260772	Allyn & Bacon
1993	23060956	Prentice Hall
1990	471622605	Wiley
1995	471058467	Wiley
	1558514775	M&T Books
1996	471149292	Wiley

Figure 1.1 In a table, fields are represented by columns.

Book ID	Title	Copyright Year
109	(The) Elements of Technical Writing	1995
110	Handbook of Technical Writing	1997
111	How to Communicate Technical Information : A Handbook of Software	1993

Figure 1.2 The rows in a table represent individual records.

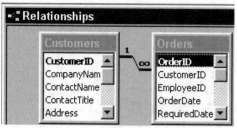

Figure 1.3 Tables that have an identical field are related.

Database Relationships

There are four types of relationships between tables. The most common is the *one-to-many* relationship, in which one record in one table corresponds to one or more records in another table. A customer can place more than one order, which means that that customer's identifier will probably occur more than once in an orders table. The opposite of the *one-to-many* relationship is the *many-to-one* relationship, in which multiple records in one table are related to a single record in another table.

In *one-to-one* relationships, each record in one table corresponds to exactly one record in another table. One-to-one relationships are rare, but they can occur. For example, you might create a table listing customers' billing addresses, in cases when they are different from main mailing addresses; the relationship between the billing address and the customer's identifier would be one-to-one.

The final type of relationship is the *many-to-many* relationship, in which multiple records from one table are related to multiple records in another table. For instance, screenplays often have more than one author. A table of screenplay titles and a table of authors would have a many-to-many relationship.

What Is a Relational Database?

Databases store data that occurs in a particular context. For instance, a sales database contains information about your customers, products, orders, suppliers, and sales representatives. If you stored that information in a spreadsheet program like Excel or a *flat-file* database program, the program would make no connection between a customer (stored in one place) and that customer's orders (stored in another place).

Access, however, is a *relational* database, which means that you can define relationships among the data it contains. If you construct a relational database with tables listing customers and customer orders, you can define a connection between those tables based on a common field (in this case, probably a customer's identification number) (**Figure 1.3**).

Relational databases are superior to flat-file databases because you can store discrete information, such as customer contact information and orders by that customer, in separate locations and bring that information together as needed. To do the same in a flat-file database, you'd need to include all of the customer's information in every order record, needlessly expanding your tables.

WHAT IS A RELATIONAL DATABASE?

Starting Access

To use Access, you need to launch the program. Launching the program loads it into your computer's memory so you can use it.

To launch Access from the Start menu:

1. Click the Start button on the Windows taskbar and choose Programs > Microsoft Access (**Figure 1.4**).

   The Microsoft Access dialog box appears. The default setting is to open an existing Access file (**Figure 1.5**).

2. Click the file you want to open and click OK.

   or

   Click More Files and click OK.

   The Open dialog box appears (**Figure 1.6**).

3. Navigate to the directory containing the file you want to open, click the file's name, and click Open.

   Your database appears in the main database window (**Figure 1.7**).

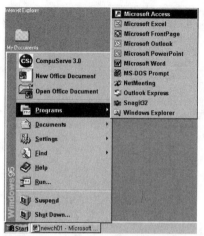

Figure 1.4 Click the Start button and choose Microsoft Access from the menu that appears.

Figure 1.5 The initial Access dialog box appears.

Figure 1.6 Select the file you want to work with from the Open dialog box.

Figure 1.7 Your database appears in the main database window.

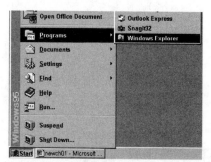

Figure 1.8 Click the Start button and choose Windows Explorer from the Start menu.

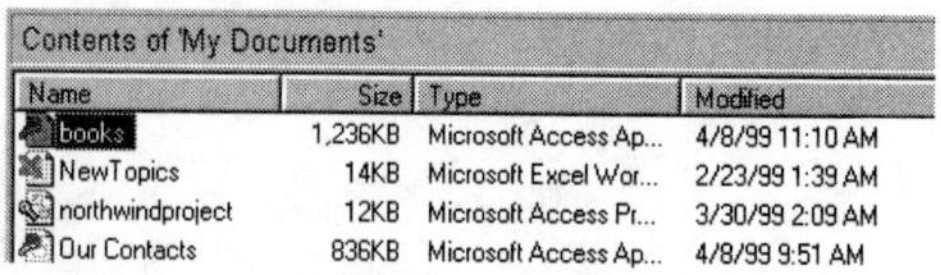

Name	Size	Type	Modified
books	1,236KB	Microsoft Access Ap...	4/8/99 11:10 AM
NewTopics	14KB	Microsoft Excel Wor...	2/23/99 1:39 AM
northwindproject	12KB	Microsoft Access Pr...	3/30/99 2:09 AM
Our Contacts	836KB	Microsoft Access Ap...	4/8/99 9:51 AM

Contents of 'My Documents'

Figure 1.9 Double-click the file's icon once you've opened the directory where it's stored.

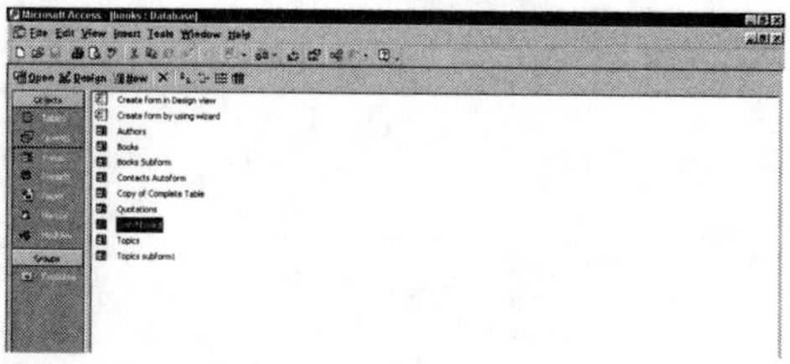

Figure 1.10 Your database appears in the active window.

To open an Access file from Windows Explorer:

1. Click the Start button on the Windows taskbar and choose Programs > Windows Explorer (**Figure 1.8**).

2. Navigate to the directory containing the Access file you want to open and double-click the file's icon (**Figure 1.9**).

   Access launches with the database you chose in the active window. (**Figure 1.10**).

✔ Tip

■ You can also navigate to an Access file you want to work with by double-clicking the My Computer icon and opening the folder containing the file.

Looking at the Access Database Window

Here's a quick tour of the main Access database window (**Figure 1.11**). Don't be overwhelmed...it's actually quite well organized and easy to use.

1 Menu bar

The menu bar appears at the top of the Access window and makes all of the program's commands available, such as saving your work, printing your database's contents, and checking spelling.

2 Database toolbar

The Database toolbar presents buttons for many basic commands like saving and printing your files.

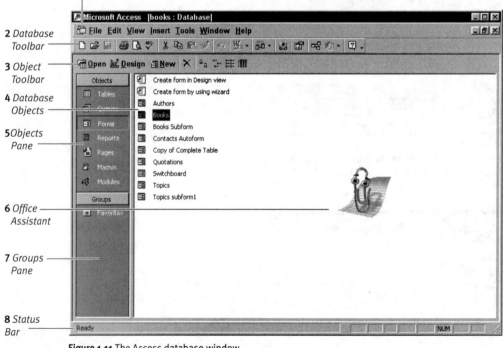

1 *Menu Bar*

2 *Database Toolbar*

3 *Object Toolbar*

4 *Database Objects*

5 *Objects Pane*

6 *Office Assistant*

7 *Groups Pane*

8 *Status Bar*

Figure 1.11 The Access database window.

3 Object toolbar

The Object toolbar offers buttons that allow you to view existing database objects or create new ones. The toolbar changes based on the type of object you are viewing.

4 Database objects

These are the objects and wizards of the type you've selected. The objects in the window represent pre-existing items of a particular type. Double-click objects to open and work with them. Wizards are tools that allow you to create new objects. The wizards available depend on the type of object shown in the database window.

5 Objects pane

The objects pane lets you choose the type of object (and associated wizards) you want to display in the main database window.

6 Groups pane

The groups pane lets you display the contents of any groups of objects you've created.

7 Office Assistant

The Office Assistant helps you perform tasks in Access.

8 Status bar

The status bar displays messages from Access about what's happening in your database and the progress of any jobs you've started.

LOOKING AT THE ACCESS DATABASE WINDOW

Access Database Objects

Access databases are made up of *objects* that store your data, allow you to enter and view data, ask questions about the data in your database, and present your data in an easily understood format. The four primary object types in an Access database are: *tables, forms, queries,* and *reports.*

Tables

Tables are the objects Access uses to store your data. Each table consists of *fields*, which store a specific piece of information (like a person's last name or the city they live in), and *records*. A record is a complete set of information about a specific entity.

You can open tables in one of two *views*, or interfaces. Opening a table in *Design view* allows you to change the structure of your table; you can add fields, include comments about each field, or change the type of information stored in each field (for example, numbers, text, dates, and so forth).

Datasheet view displays the data in your table in a spreadsheet-like grid. Each column in the datasheet represents a field, while each row represents a record.

Forms

You can use forms to present information in your database in a user-friendly format. Unlike tables, which can be viewed only in a datasheet format, forms let you include explanatory text to give the user more information than is offered by field names. You can also add graphics and arrange the fields displayed in your form to present your data most effectively.

You can open forms in three views: *Form view*, which displays the form and the active record or records; *Design view*, in which you can change the layout and the data displayed in your form; and *Datasheet view*, which presents the data from your form in a datasheet.

Queries

Queries are database objects that you can use to find specific information in your database. For instance, you can search a Books table to find every book in your library put out by a particular publisher.

You can open queries in three views: *Datasheet view*, which displays the data your query finds; *Design view*, in which you can change the fields included in your query, the calculations performed on the results, and even what type of query you've created; and *SQL view*, which displays your query as a statement in the Structured Query Language.

Reports

Reports are a bit like forms in that they display the data in your tables and queries. Unlike forms, you can't use reports to enter data into your tables, but you can use the report wizards to create mailing labels or charts based on your table and query data.

You can view reports in two views: *Design view*, in which you can change the layout of your report; and *Print Preview*, which displays what your report will look like when it's printed.

STARTING A DATABASE

Creating a database takes a bit of planning. You need to determine what information you want to store, how that information will be arranged, and what relationships will exist between the data in the database.

Planning a database takes some time, but the energy you put into setting it up is paid back when you create the database. Planning not only makes it easier to create the database, but also makes it less likely that you'll need to make changes because you left something out or stored the same information twice.

This chapter will show you one way to plan and create your database, but there are many others. The most important lesson you'll learn is that a few minutes of planning can save you many hours or days of modifying or re-creating a poorly designed database.

In this chapter, we'll plan and create a contact-management database to store information about people we've contacted for business and personal reasons. This type of database is extremely useful—you can use it as an address book, to keep track of calls for a charitable organization, or to maintain a record of your sales calls.

Planning Content

Before you begin building your contact-management database, you should plan your content. By doing so, you can ensure that your database meets your intended needs, that it includes all the necessary objects and information, and that it won't require extensive changes after the database is in place. It's best to plot this stage of database planning on paper.

To plan database content:

1. Determine the categories of information you want to include.

   Figure out the general types of information you'll be storing. For example, in our contact-management database, we'll want to store information about our contacts, the calls we've made, and what type of contact it is.

2. Break these categories into smaller subcategories. Determine the data items you'll include for each kind of information planned in Step 1.

   For example, you need to determine exactly what your contact information includes, such as first names, last names, middle initials, street addresses, phone numbers, and so on.

3. Reduce the information to the smallest increments possible. Break down each subcategory again, into the smallest pieces possible. For example, you can break down street addresses into fields such as street name and number, city, state, ZIP, country, and apartment or suite number.

4. Check carefully for duplicated information. Duplicated information in a database design indicates that your design may not be the most efficient.

Planning Structure

After determining the database content, you should decide where the information goes in the database.

This process is less important if you're using an Access wizard to create a database—wizard-created databases are well-planned and ready to run, so your information should slip right into the database objects. If you create a database from scratch, or use a wizard-created database as a foundation for a new database, you will need to plan your database more carefully and include elements created by the wizard. Refer to the information you determined in the previous section.

◆ Each of the general categories (contacts' personal information, details of each call, and the type of contact) will become a *table*.

◆ Each set of subcategories, such as names and addresses, will be a *record*.

◆ Each of the pieces of information will become a *field* (first name, last name, and so on).

Be sure to create as many tables, fields, and entries as you anticipate being necessary. Just as you broke down the content in the previous section, you should also structure it as precisely as possible. Make sure that you're not duplicating information unnecessarily. Each table should represent a single type of item, though fields can refer to records in other tables. For example, a record of a contact can include a reference to the table listing contact types.

Planning Relationships

Tables in a database don't exist in isolation; records in one table often *relate* to records in another table. Relationships are covered in more detail in Chapter 8.

The Contact-Management database we're creating has three tables: Contacts, Calls, and Contact Type. Contacts and Calls are directly related: everyone you call is listed in your Contacts table.

The Contact Type table is also related to the Contacts table. Everyone listed in your Contacts table will be (for example) either a business or personal contact.

Because the Calls and Contact Type tables are both related to the Contacts table, the tables are *indirectly* related to each other.

If you create a database using a wizard, Access creates relationships between its tables automatically.

To plan relationships:

1. Sketch out the tables you created in the previous sections.

   If you suspect that a table will be related to a number of other tables, place that table near the middle of the diagram.

2. Draw lines to connect related tables.

   Relationship lines indicate that the current table uses information from another table. For instance, the Calls table would have a Contact Type field, which also occurs in the Contact Type table (**Figure 2.1**).

✔ Tip

■ When you plan relationships, note whether any tables stand apart from the others; if so, they belong in another database.

Figure 2.1 Relationships between tables in your contact management database.

Figure 2.2 In the opening dialog box you can choose whether to work with an existing database or create a new one.

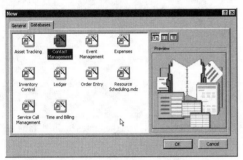

Figure 2.3 The database tab shows the wizards you can use to create a new database.

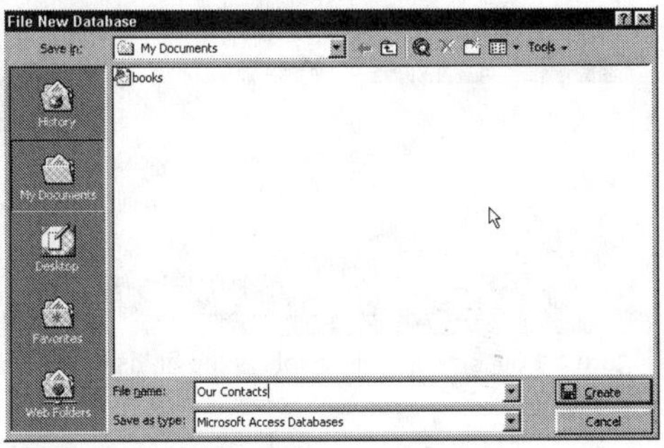

Figure 2.4 The File New Database window.

Creating a Database Using a Wizard

Access makes it easy to create a database by providing *wizards*, or tools that allow you to create a database from a series of templates included with the program. You can create a database from scratch, but the comprehensive selection of wizards makes it unlikely that you'll need to do so.

The database wizards at your disposal create a wide range of databases, from contact managers to inventory control to expense reports. On the business side, you can create a database with tables to record orders, maintain employee data, and track invoices and payments. You can also create tables for personal use, such as keeping track of your books and recipes, or to even maintain an exercise log.

Explore the wizards available to you so you don't spend hours planning and building a database from scratch that you could create almost immediately with a wizard.

To create a database using a wizard:

1. Launch Microsoft Access.

2. In the opening dialog box (**Figure 2.2**), click the "Access database wizards, pages, and projects" option button and click OK.

   The New window appears. If the Databases tab isn't selected, click it now (**Figure 2.3**).

3. Select the wizard you want to use to create your database and click OK.

   For this example, we've chosen the Contact Management Wizard.

4. In the File New Database window (**Figure 2.4**), type a name for your new

(continued on next page)

database in the File Name text area and click Create.

The Database Wizard appears with a description of the database you chose (**Figure 2.5**).

5. Click Next.

The next wizard screen shows a list of the tables in the database and the fields those tables contain (**Figure 2.6**).

6. Select the name of the table you want to examine.

Access highlights the name of the table you clicked and displays its fields in the Fields in the table pane (**Figure 2.7**).

7. Select or clear the checkboxes next to the fields you want to include or exclude from your tables. Click Next when you're done.

For this example, simply accept the default tables.

8. In the next wizard screen (**Figure 2.8**), select the style you want Access to use for your database and preview your choice. Click Next to continue.

9. In the next screen (**Figure 2.9**), choose the style you want Access to use for your printed reports. Click Next.

10. Type a name for your database in the text box at the top of the screen and then click Next (**Figure 2.10**).

11. When the final database wizard screen appears, click Finish.

The switchboard for your new database appears (**Figure 2.11**). The switchboard is a form that allows you to get at the common functions for that type of database (see Chapter 14).

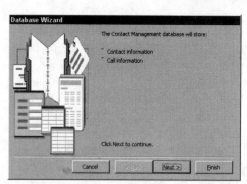

Figure 2.5 Access presents information about the database you've chosen to create.

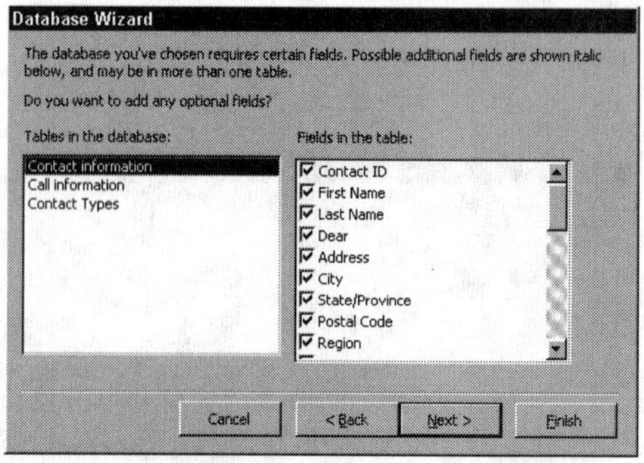

Figure 2.6 Access displays the tables in the database.

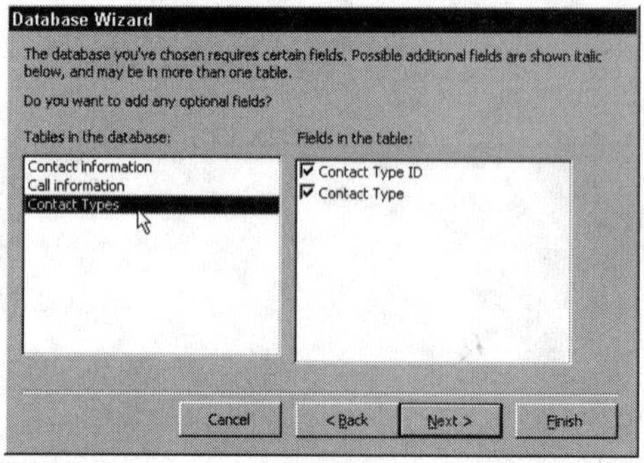

Figure 2.7 Clicking a table displays the fields in the table.

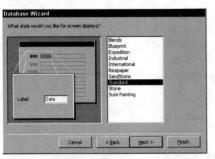

Figure 2.8 Select a style for the objects in your database.

Figure 2.9 Choose a style for your reports.

Figure 2.10 Type a name for your database in the space provided.

Figure 2.11 The switchboard gets you up and running with your new database.

✔ Tips

■ You can click the Finish button to create your database at any time. Access will use its default selections to fill in the choices from any screens you haven't visited.

■ You can revisit any of your choices in a wizard by clicking the Back button.

Saving Databases

Saving your work frequently is one of the best habits you can cultivate. If you save your work every five minutes, the worst that can happen if your power fails is that you'll lose five minutes' worth of work. If you save once an hour, you'll spend a considerable amount of time replacing the work you did since your last save.

Access automatically saves your database whenever you create or delete an object (like a form or report) or whenever you add or delete data. The program does not, however, save changes to your objects automatically. You can (and should) save your work in progress.

To save a database:

◆ Choose File > Save (**Figure 2.12**).

✔ Tip

■ The best time to save your work is whenever you think about it; saving takes less than a second but prevents the loss of a significant amount of work.

Figure 2.12 Choose File > Save to save your work

Starting from Scratch

Occasionally, the Access wizards may not meet your needs. You may choose to develop a database from scratch if you:

◆ Want to learn all the ins and outs of Access.

◆ Want to copy the field names and configuration of an existing database.

◆ Want to create a *very* simple (a few fields you could just as easily enter into a table manually) or a *very* complex database.

To create a database from scratch, choose File > New, select the Blank database option, and then click OK. You can then create tables, forms, queries, and other objects using the skills you'll learn throughout this book.

WORKING WITH TABLES

Once you've created a database, you need to create specialized containers within the database to hold your data. These containers are called tables. In this chapter, you'll learn how to create and modify your tables so you can store your data efficiently.

Looking at Tables

You can view the contents of your tables by opening them in *Datasheet view* (**Figure 3.1**) and change their design by opening them in *Design view* (**Figure 3.3**).

Datasheet view of a table:

1 Menu bar

The menu bar appears at the top of the Access window and makes all of the program's commands available to you.

2 Table datasheet toolbar

The table datasheet toolbar presents buttons for many basic commands like saving, sorting, and printing your table's contents.

1 *Menu bar*

2 *Table datasheet toolbar*

3 *Column (field) selector*

4 *Active row indicator*

5 *Row (record) selector*

6 *Navigation bar*

7 *Status bar*

Figure 3.1 The Datasheet view of a table.

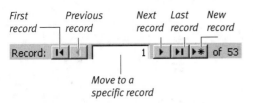

First record —— *Previous record*   *Next record* *Last record* *New record*

Record: 1 of 53

Move to a specific record

Figure 3.2 The navigation toolbar helps you move between records.

3 Column (field) selector

Column selectors show the name of the field that column is associated with and allow you to select every cell in the column with a single mouse click.

4 Row (record) selector

Row selectors allow you to select every cell in the row with a single mouse click.

5 Active row indicator

A right-pointing arrow in the row selector column indicates which record is active.

6 Navigation bar

The navigation bar lets you move from record to record, to the first or the last record, or to the record whose number you enter in the center box. **Figure 3.2** points out which button does what.

7 Status bar

The status bar displays the state of your table and the progress of any jobs you've started.

LOOKING AT TABLES

Design view of a table:

1 Menu bar

The Access menu bar appears at the top of the database window. You can get to all of the commands in Access via the menu system.

2 Data Type column

The Data Type column contains the types of data each field stores, such as text, currency, or dates.

3 Description column

The Description column contains notes about the fields you've created. It's a good idea to write a description for all but the most obvious fields in your tables.

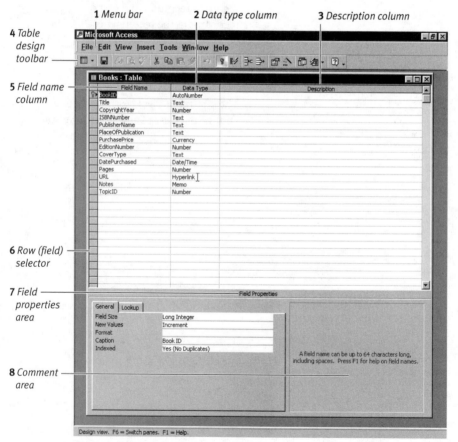

1 *Menu bar* **2** *Data type column* **3** *Description column*

4 *Table design toolbar*

5 *Field name column*

6 *Row (field) selector*

7 *Field properties area*

8 *Comment area*

Figure 3.3 A table opened in Design view.

4 Table design toolbar

The table design toolbar contains buttons to help you work with your table, like adding or removing rows, copying information, and saving your work.

5 Field Name column

The Field Name column of the design grid contains the names of the fields in your table.

6 Row (field) selector

Clicking a row selector highlights that entire row in the table. The selector also indicates (by displaying a key icon) if the field it represents is a *key* field.

7 Field Properties area

The Field Properties area contains information about the field, like the maximum number of characters it can store, whether Access maintains an index of the field's values, and if there is a default value for the field.

8 Comment area

Access uses this area to display information about the property you've selected.

CREATING TABLES WITH WIZARDS

Creating Tables with Wizards

When you use an Access wizard to create a database you can create most, if not all, of the tables you need for the type of database you have. If you forgot to create a table you need, want to expand your database beyond the template, or are creating a database from scratch, you can use Access table wizards to simplify the job.

You can choose either Business or Personal tables. Tables in the Business list focus on transaction tracking–you'll find tables for monitoring payments, tracking invoices, and managing contacts. The Personal list contains tables that are more useful around the house; for example, you can track recipes and catalog books and videos. For this example we're creating a table for videos in our Books database.

To create a table with a wizard:

1. Open the database you want to use. Click Tables at the left side of the Database window. From the list, double-click Create table by using wizard.

   The table wizard launches.

2. Select either the Business or Personal table option (**Figure 3.4**).

   We clicked Personal, which contains the sample table we need.

3. Select the table you want to use as the model for your table.

   When you click a table name, the list of fields in that table appears in the Sample Fields pane. To follow along with this example, choose Video Collection (**Figure 3.5**).

4. To add all of the fields from the sample table to your new table, click the >>

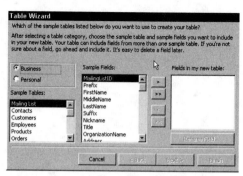

Figure 3.4 You can select fields from two sets of sample tables in the Table Wizard.

Click Personal

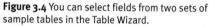

Click Video Collection

Figure 3.5 Once you've selected a table to add fields from, the list of fields in that table appears in the Sample Fields pane.

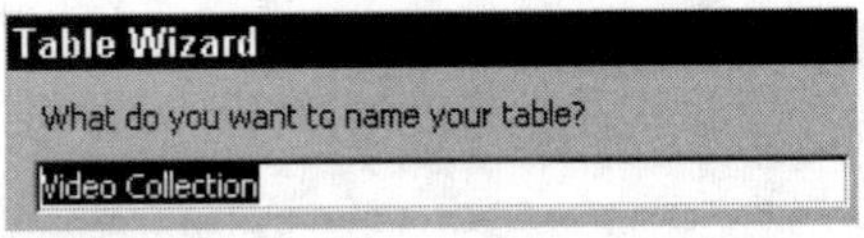

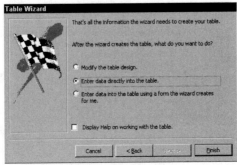

Figure 3.6 Now you're ready to name your table and set a primary key (or have Access do it for you).

Figure 3.7 The final table wizard screen.

button. Click Next when you're done adding fields.

You can add fields one at a time by clicking the > button, remove them one at a time by clicking the < button, or remove them all by clicking the << button.

5. Type a name for your table in the space provided (**Figure 3.6**).

6. Decide if you want Access to assign a primary key to your table. Click Next once you've decided.

   If you added all of the fields from a sample table, it's safe to have Access assign the primary key for you—each sample table contains a primary key field. If you prefer to assign one yourself, click the No option, click Next, and select the field that will contain a unique value for each record in your table. See the discussion of keys in Chapter 9.

   The final table wizard screen appears (**Figure 3.7**).

7. Click Finish to have Access create your table and open it in Datasheet view (Access refers to the view on this wizard screen as "Data-entry mode").

   or

   Click the "Modify the table design" option to open your table in Design view.

   or

   Click the "Enter data into the table using a form the wizard creates for me" option to have Access create (and open) an AutoForm that you can use to enter data into your table. You can find out more about AutoForms in Chapter 4.

✔ Tips

■ You can include fields from more than one sample table in your finished table. Simply select the sample table(s) containing the other fields you want and add them normally.

■ You can rename any field you're adding to your new table while you're still in the first Table Wizard screen (see **Figure 3.4**). Click the field you want to change, click the Rename Field button, and type a new name for the field you selected.

Entering, Editing, and Deleting Data

Once you've created your table you can jump right in and start entering data. You can move between records using the navigation bar; erase, add, or modify values in your records; or get rid of entire records altogether.

To enter data into a table:

1. Open the tables in your database and click the table in which you want to enter data.

2. Click the Open toolbar button (**Figure 3.8**).

   Your table appears in Datasheet view, with the insertion point (represented by a blinking cursor) in the first cell of the first record (**Figure 3.9**).

3. To enter data into a field, type it in. To move to the next field, press Tab. When you reach the end of a record, pressing Tab moves you to the first cell in the next record.

   Access automatically enters values into an AutoNumber field like the Video Collection ID field in the example. Press Tab to move to the next field.

books : Database

Open **Design** **New**

Figure 3.8 Clicking the Open toolbar button opens your table in Datasheet view, in which you can enter, edit, and delete table data.

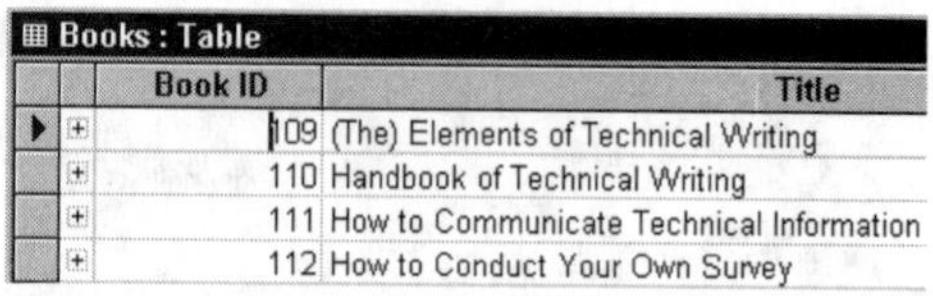

Books : Table

	Book ID	Title
	109	(The) Elements of Technical Writing
	110	Handbook of Technical Writing
	111	How to Communicate Technical Information
	112	How to Conduct Your Own Survey

Figure 3.9 A datasheet is a lot like a spreadsheet.

Navigating Tables

Use these handy navigation shortcuts	
Tab or Left Arrow	Move one cell to the right
Shift + Tab or Right Arrow	Move one cell to the right
Down Arrow	Move one cell down
Up Arrow	Move one cell up
Ctrl + Home	Return to the first field of the first record (top left corner)
Ctrl + End	Go to the last field of the last record (lower right corner)

Delete Record button

Figure 3.10 You can delete an entire record at once by clicking the Delete Record toolbar button.

To edit a field's contents:

◆ To edit a field's contents, click anywhere in the field, position the cursor, and edit the field's contents.

To delete a field's contents:

◆ To delete a field's contents, double-click the field (which highlights the contents) and press Delete.

You can delete an entire record by clicking any field in the record and clicking the Delete Record toolbar button (**Figure 3.10**).

✔ Tips

■ You can go directly to any cell in your table while in Datasheet view by clicking the cell you'd like to work in.

■ For a list of keyboard shortcuts for moving around your datasheet, see the "Navigating Tables" sidebar on page 26.

ENTERING, EDITING, AND DELETING DATA

Formatting Columns and Rows

The default datasheet Access provides for data entry is compact and functional, but it lacks the little frills that make a datasheet a home. Use the Format menu to change your datasheet's appearance and make it easier to enter and read data in your tables. In this example, we'll show you how to change a column's width to make its contents more legible.

To format columns and rows:

1. In Datasheet view, open your table and position your cursor over the column selector of the column you want to reformat. Your curosr appears as a black, downward-pointing arrow when it's in position (**Figure 3.11**).

2. Choose Format > Column Width.

    The Column Width dialog box appears.

3. Enter the value for your column's new width in the dialog box and click OK (**Figure 3.12**).

    The default width (expressed in 1/16ths of an inch) for a column is 15 points. To make your column 2 inches wide, you would type 32 in the dialog box.

✔ Tips

- You can choose a row in the table by clicking its row selector, which is the gray box at the far left edge of the row you want to select.

- You can change a row's height by clicking the row selector, choosing Format > Row Height, and following the steps outlined above. The standard row height is 12.75 points.

Figure 3.11 When your cursor is over a column selector it appears as a black, downward-pointing arrow.

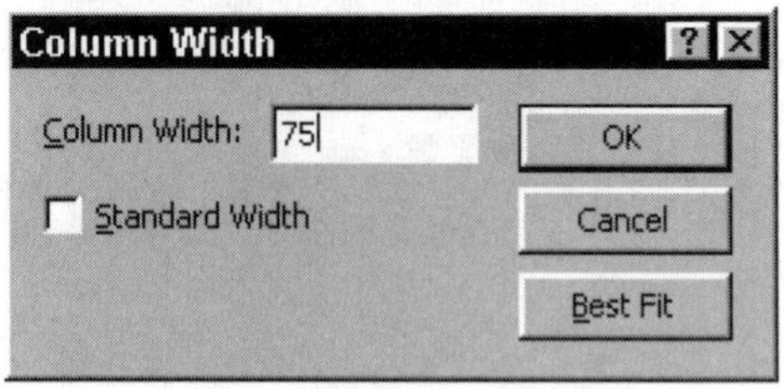

Figure 3.12 You can assign your columns precise widths by entering the value you want.

FORMATTING COLUMNS AND ROWS

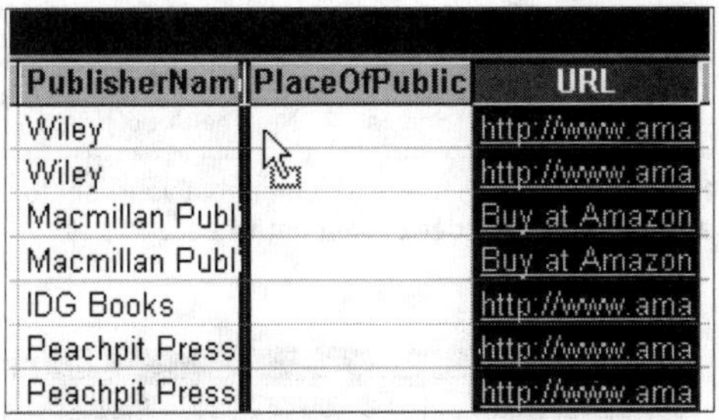

PublisherNam	PlaceOfPublic	URL
Wiley		http://www.ama
Wiley		http://www.ama
Macmillan Publ		Buy at Amazon
Macmillan Publ		Buy at Amazon
IDG Books		http://www.ama
Peachpit Press		http://www.ama
Peachpit Press		http://www.ama

Figure 3.13 You can change a column's position in your datasheet by clicking its column selector and dragging the column to its new position.

Moving Columns

If you don't like where a column appears in your datasheet, you can easily move it to a new position. Changing a column's position in your datasheet doesn't change its position in Design view or in other database objects like forms and reports.

To move columns:

1. Click the column selector of the column you want to move.

   The column's contents are highlighted.

2. Drag the column to its new location (**Figure 3.13**).

✔ Tip

- You can move more than one column at a time by Shift-clicking the column headings of the columns you want to move. The columns must be adjacent to each other to move them together.

Freezing and Hiding Columns

Have you ever scrolled through a datasheet and lost track of which row represented what? Or wished you could hide a column without deleting it from your table completely? You're in luck! Both actions are very easy to pull off in Access.

Freezing a column (or row) means that no matter how far you scroll in a datasheet, you'll always see the frozen column or row. In a Books table, for instance, you can freeze the Title field so you can see which book the data on your screen refers to when you scroll through the table.

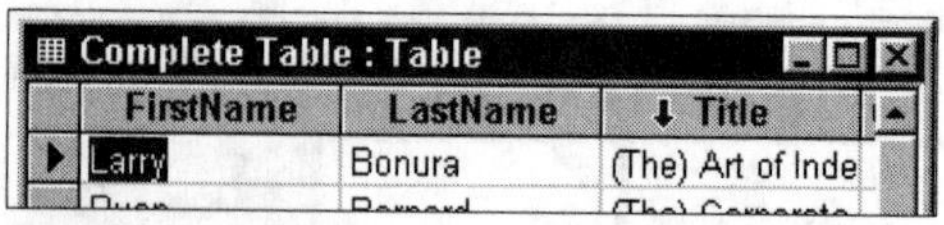

To freeze a column:

1. Click the column selector of the column you want to freeze (**Figure 3.14**).

2. Choose Format > Freeze Columns.

   The column you chose appears at the left edge of your datasheet, regardless of how far you scroll horizontally (**Figure 3.15**).

To hide a column:

1. Click the column selector of the column you want to hide.

2. Choose Format > Hide Columns. Your column disappears from the datasheet.

Figure 3.14 You can freeze a column that you want to appear at the left edge of your datasheet...

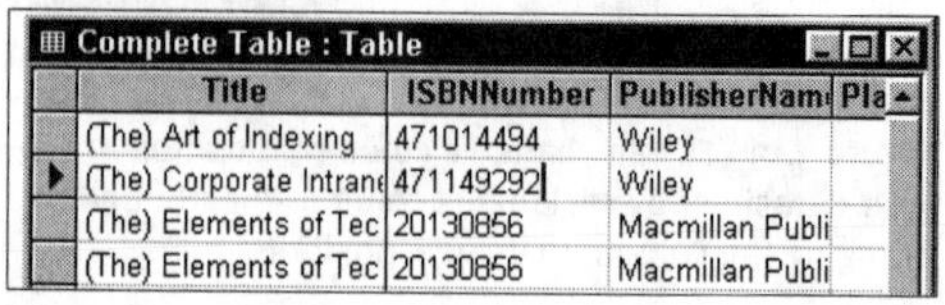

Figure 3.15 ...and it will be there, regardless of how far you scroll.

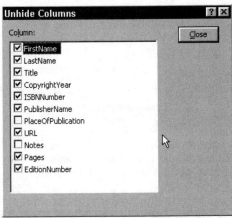

Figure 3.16 Unhiding a column is easy: just display the Unhide Columns dialog box and select the columns you want to reappear.

✔ Tips

- You can hide (or freeze) more than one column by Shift-clicking the column's selectors. The columns must be adjacent to each other in the datasheet.

- You can unfreeze a column by clicking its column selector and choosing Format > Unfreeze All Columns.

- To unhide a column, choose Format > Unhide Columns to display a dialog box with a list of columns in your datasheet. Click the checkbox next to the column(s) you want to unhide and click OK (**Figure 3.16**).

Adding Fields

You should add a field to your table whenever you spot a gap in your information. One common reason to add a field is to give you a place to enter comments that will explain or give insight into a record. Keep the basic information in other fields, but adding a comment field allows you to enter information that may not fit elsewhere.

To add a field:

1. Display the tables in your database and select the table you want to open.

2. Click the Design toolbar button (**Figure 3.17**).

   Your table appears in Design view (**Figure 3.18**).

3. Add a field to your table by typing its name in the first open Field Name cell. Press Tab to move to the Data Type cell.

4. Click the drop-down menu that appears in the Data Type cell and select a data type for your new field. Press Tab.

5. Type a description for your new field in the space provided.

6. Choose File > Save to save your changes.

✔ Tips

- You also use Design view to create a new table from scratch. Display the tables in your database and double-click Create table in Design view (**Figure 3.19**). A blank table design grid appears. You can use the skills you learn in this section to create a new table.

- If you want to switch between views of your table, choose View and select the name of the view you want to switch to.

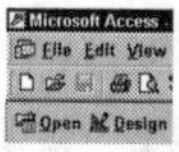

Figure 3.17 Clicking the Design button opens a table in Design view.

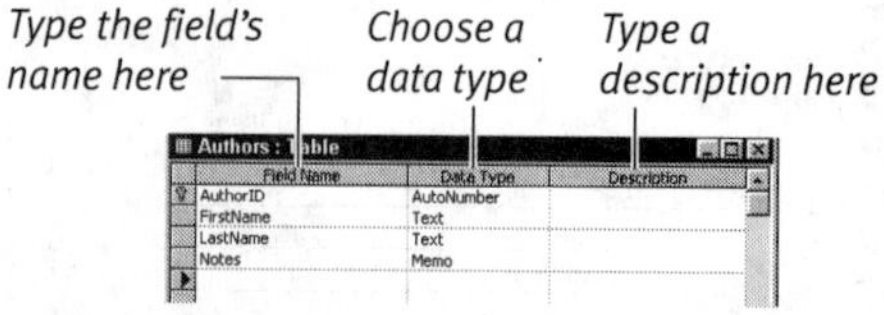

Type the field's name here   Choose a data type   Type a description here

Figure 3.18 Once you've opened your table in Design view, you can start adding fields and comments.

Figure 3.19 Double-click Create a new table in Design view to create your table from scratch.

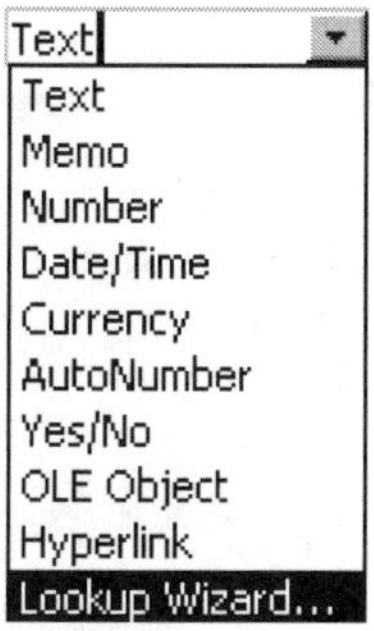

Text
Text
Memo
Number
Date/Time
Currency
AutoNumber
Yes/No
OLE Object
Hyperlink
Lookup Wizard...

Figure 3.20 Select your fields' data type from this drop-down menu.

Understanding Data Types

When you create a field, it's important to select the most appropriate *data type* for the information you want to store in that field. Data type refers to the particular class of information. For instance, text information can be letters, numbers, or any other combination of characters on a keyboard. Fields with a number data type, however, can only contain numerical data. This allows Access to perform calculations on the data in number fields, which isn't possible for the numbers in text fields—just try finding the sum of a number and a name.

Access gives you a variety of data types to choose from, each with its own unique properties. You should have no trouble finding the best data type for your fields. **Figure 3.20** shows the menu used to set a field's data type while the table is in Design view.

For more details on the these data types and their variations, see Appendix B.

Text Text fields can contain alphanumeric characters (A–Z and 0–9) plus special characters such as !, @, and %. Text fields have a maximum length of 255 characters.

Memo Memo fields also contain alphanumeric characters, though memo fields can store much more data than text fields—up to 64,000 characters.

Number Number fields store numbers. The range of numeric values they can store depends on which value you select from the Field Size property's drop-down menu. For information about number data subtypes, see Table B2 in Appendix B.

Date/Time Date/Time fields store calendar data. You can display the date and time

(continued on next page)

UNDERSTANDING DATA TYPES

together or either one separately, in a variety of formats.

Currency Currency fields are designed to hold monetary data, though you can also set a currency field to hold percentages or numbers written in scientific notation.

AutoNumber This data type starts with a number for the first record (Access automatically starts at 1, though you can choose another value) and increases the number by a set amount in subsequent records. You can also change the increment, which is initially set at 1.

Yes/No Yes/No fields allow users to make a choice between Yes and No, True and False, or 1 and 0.

OLE Object OLE (short for Object Linking and Embedding) technology allows you to include non-Access objects like picture, video, and sound files in your tables.

Hyperlink Hyperlink fields contain addresses for information that, when clicked, display the object associated with the address. You can link Web sites, files on your computer, or other objects in your database with a hyperlink.

Lookup Wizard Lookup Fields can take the form of text boxes, list boxes, and combo boxes, all of which you will encounter in Chapter 4. Users can select a value from the list you set, or in the case of combo boxes and text boxes, they can enter their own value.

✔ Tips

- Text and memo fields can store hyperlinks and other Internet addresses, as well. Hyperlink fields are simply "live" links that you can click to go to the object referenced by the hyperlink.

- Access makes sure users enter the proper type of data into each field. If you attempt to enter text into a number field, for instance, Access alerts you to the error and requires you to enter the proper type of data.

UNDERSTANDING DATA TYPES

Printing Tables

Sometimes having your data in electronic format isn't exactly what you need. Whether you want to create a hard copy backup of your data or to include your tables in a company memo, printing your tables is handy.

Figure 3.21 Clicking the Print toolbar button prints the entire contents of the object in the window.

To print a table:

1. In Datasheet view, open the table you want to print.

2. Choose File > Print.

   The Print screen you see depends on the type of printer you have. Choose the number of copies, page range, and quality of the print job and click OK.

To print selected table records:

1. In Datasheet view, open the table containing the records you want to print.

2. Select the records you want to print.

   The records to be printed must be adjacent to each other in the datasheet.

3. Choose File > Print.

   The Print dialog box appears. Click OK.

✔ Tip

■ If you want to print a table in its entirety, you can simply click the Print toolbar button (**Figure 3.21**).

WORKING WITH FORMS

This chapter will get you started working with forms, those database objects that let you input data into your tables and step through your records one at a time. Although you can enter data directly into a table, forms provide an easy-to-use interface for entering information, making it easier to *validate* data as you enter it (that is, ensure that the data is of the proper type and in the proper format). With forms, you can also view and change existing data.

Your forms can be as simple or as complex as you like. Access has a number of wizards you can use to create basic forms, but you can create them from scratch, too. In either case, you can modify your forms after you've built them.

Forms are made up of *controls*, or items on your form's background. In its broadest sense, a *control* is any object in a form or report. When you create a form with a wizard, Access automatically creates controls where you can enter and peruse the data in your tables.

Look at Forms

You can open your forms in *Form view* (**Figure 4.1**), *Design view* (**Figure 4.2**), and *Datasheet view*.

1 Form objects

These objects (including text boxes, check boxes, and list boxes) allow you to enter or modify your table's data.

2 Menu bar

The menu bar appears at the top of the Access window and makes all of the program's commands available to you.

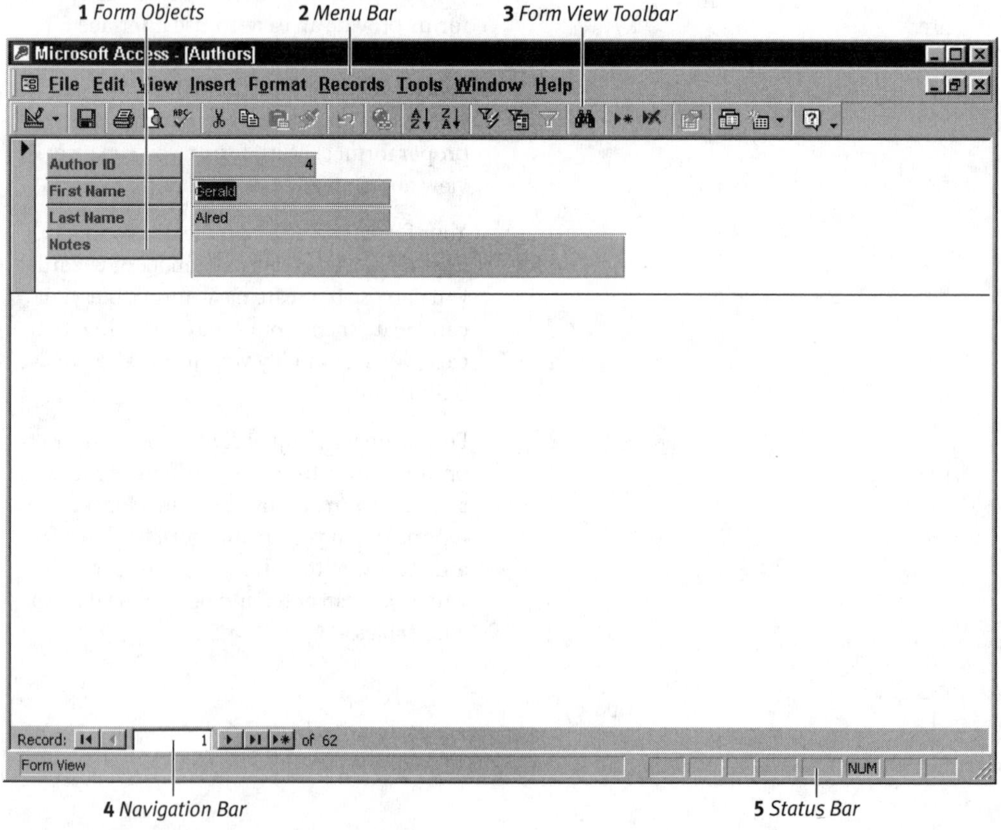

1 *Form Objects* **2** *Menu Bar* **3** *Form View Toolbar*

4 *Navigation Bar* **5** *Status Bar*

Figure 4.1 A form in Form view.

3 Form view toolbar

The form view toolbar presents buttons for many basic commands like saving, sorting, and printing your form's contents.

4 Navigation bar

The navigation bar lets you move from record to record, to the first or last record, or to the record whose number you enter in the center box.

5 Status bar

The status bar displays the state of your form and the progress of any jobs you've started.

LOOK AT FORMS

Design View of a Form

1 Menu bar

The menu bar lets you get to all of the commands in Access.

2 Form header

The form header is a great place to add text describing the contents of your form, graphics that identify you and your company, controls to print the contents of your form, and the current date and time.

3 Form Detail section

The form detail section contains the fields you've used to create your form as well as any controls that relate to the fields in the section.

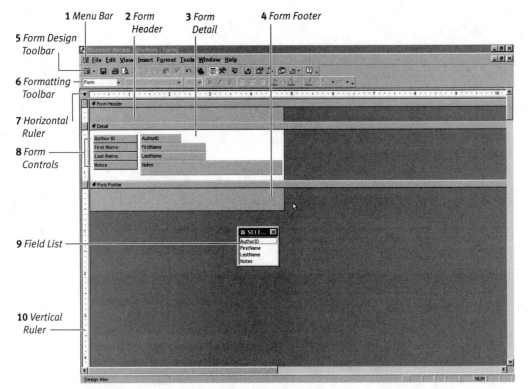

Figure 4.2 The Design view of a form.

4 Form footer

The form footer is the place to put any items you'd like to appear at the bottom of each page when your form is viewed or printed.

5 Form Design toolbar

The Form Design toolbar contains buttons to perform common tasks like saving your work, printing a form, and copying controls.

6 Formatting (Form/Report) toolbar

The Formatting (Form/Report) toolbar lets you change text's font and color, the color and pattern of lines you draw, and the color used to fill controls in your form.

7 Horizontal ruler

The horizontal ruler shows where your objects (and mouse pointer) are in your form.

8 Form controls

Form controls contain data from your fields, labels for those fields, and other controls you create (like the command button to output your product list to an HTML document).

9 Field list

The field list shows which fields you've included in your form.

10 Vertical ruler

The vertical ruler shows where your controls (and the mouse pointer) are located on your form.

DESIGN VIEW OF A FORM

Viewing Forms

Select from a list of forms (**Figure 4.3**), and open the form to view the data in it (**Figure 4.4**).

To view a form:

1. Open the database you want to use.

2. Click Forms at the left side of the database window.

   You will see a list of available forms, along with links to Create form in Design view, and Create form by using wizard (**Figure 4.3**).

3. Select a form from the list.

   Some of your forms may end with the name "Subform;" this just indicates that the form exists within a larger form. You also might see something called a Switchboard form. Ignore these for now and work with the other forms that are available. Switchboards are discussed in Chapter 14.

4. Click Open at the top of the Database window to open the form and view the data in it (**Figure 4.4**).

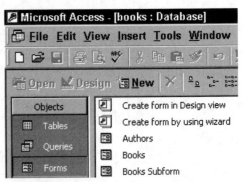

Figure 4.3 Select the form you want to use.

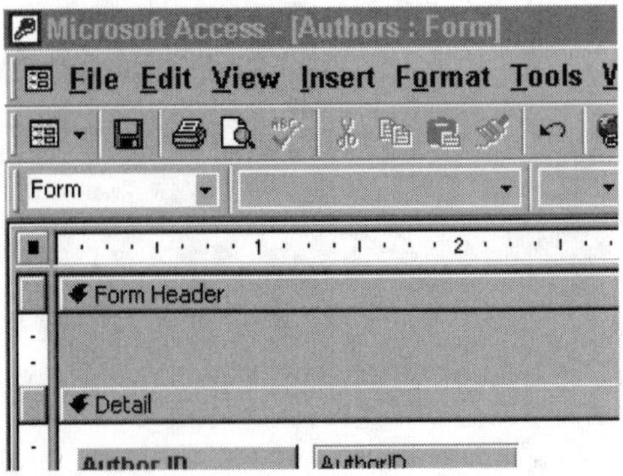

Figure 4.4 Click Open to view the form contents.

Form Navigation Tools

You navigate forms using the navigation tools located at the bottom of the form. Starting at the bottom left (**Figure 4.5**), the buttons are: First record, Previous record, Current record, Next record, Last record, New record.

Record: 14 ◄ | 65 ► ►I ►* of 65

Figure 4.5 Navigate among the records using the navigation toolbar.

Figure 4.6 Click the Open toolbar button to open your form.

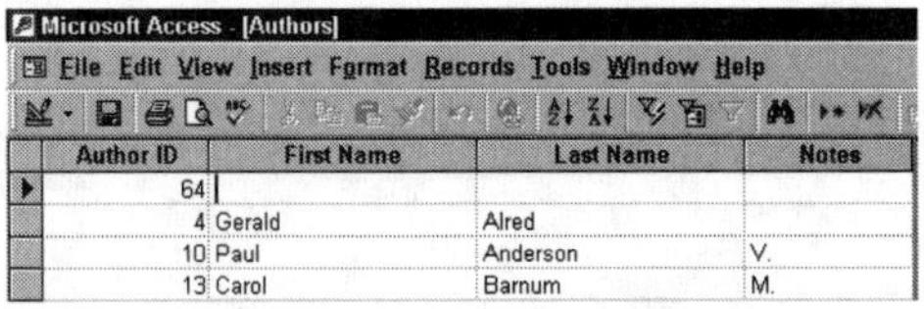

Author ID	First Name	Last Name	Notes
64			
4	Gerald	Alred	
10	Paul	Anderson	V.
13	Carol	Barnum	M.

Figure 4.7 Choose Datasheet View from the View menu to open your form in Datasheet view.

Forms make it easy to view your data one record at a time, which makes it difficult to get a sense for how records relate to one another. Access solves this problem by allowing you to open your forms in Datasheet view, which shows many records simultaneously.

To view your form in Datasheet view:

1. From the list of forms, select the form you want to view and click the Open toolbar button (**Figure 4.6**).

2. Choose View > Datasheet View.

   Your form appears in Datasheet view. (**Figure 4.7**). You can enter, edit, and delete data in your datasheet as you learned to do with tables (see Chapter 3).

✔ Tips

- You can move from record to record with the navigation tools at the bottom of the form. See the "Form Navigation Tools" sidebar for more information.

- Access allows only one opportunity to undo changes in forms. Click Undo or press Ctrl + Z to undo the most recent change you've made.

VIEWING FORMS

Deleting Records from Forms

When you're browsing through your data using a form, you may come across individual records whose presence is no longer required. Perhaps the product has been discontinued, or maybe you lent that book to a friend who moved to Tierra del Fuego. In any event, you should delete the record.

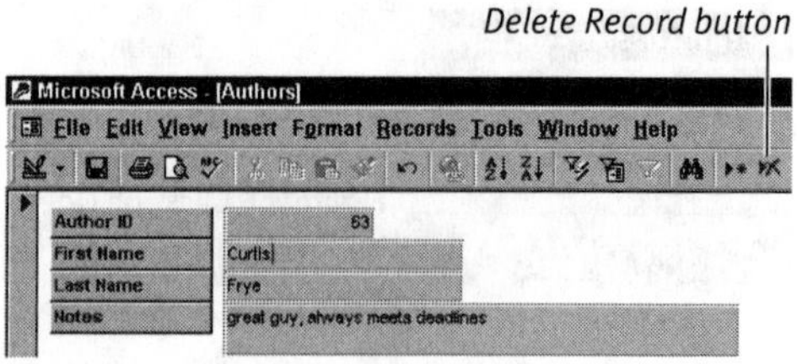

To delete a record from a form:

1. Display the record you want to delete in Form view.

   or

   If you opened your form in Datasheet view, click any cell in the record that you want to delete.

2. Click the Delete Record button on the toolbar (**Figure 4.8**).

   Once you've deleted a record it's gone for good, so Access displays a dialog box asking you to confirm the action.

✔ Tip

■ Unless you're absolutely sure you'll never need a record again, it's probably better to leave it in your database until you've backed up that table.

Delete Record button

Figure 4.8 The Delete Record button.

Figure 4.9 Pressing Ctrl-' copies data from the same field in the previous record.

Copying Data from One Record to Another

The worst part of data-entry drudgery is inputting data that comes in groups—a long list of orders from a single customer, a bunch of folks from the same town, a crate of books from a publisher, and so forth. Forms make it easier to enter this sort of repetitive data into your tables. You can avoid entering the same data over and over again by copying the data from the previous record to a new one.

To copy data from one record to another:

1. Click the field where you want the value from the previous record to appear.

2. Press Ctrl-' (Ctrl + apostrophe).

   Data from the previous record appears in your field (**Figure 4.9**). Wasn't that easy?

✔ Tips

- Other keyboard input shortcuts include Ctrl-Alt-Spacebar (to enter the default value for a field); Ctrl-; (to enter the system date); and Ctrl-: (to enter the system time).

- Keyboard shortcuts for moving around in a form include Ctrl-PageDown (move to the same field of the next record); Ctrl-PageUp (move to the same field of the previous record); Ctrl-Home (move to the first field of the first record); End (last field of the current record); and Ctrl-End (last field of the last record).

Using Autocompletion

When we take messages or write chapters, we like to use a lot of abbreviations. Abbreviations make it easy to write quickly and still understand what's on the page. Access lets you do the same thing when you're entering data by recognizing your abbreviations and completing words automatically.

To use Autocompletion:

◆ To have Access autocomplete your text, just type the abbreviation and press Enter. The replacement text appears immediately.

To add entries to the Autocompletion list:

1. Choose Tools > AutoCorrect to open the AutoCorrect dialog box (**Figure 4.10**).

2. Type your abbreviation in the Replace field.

   We added "sac" as an abbreviation for Sacramento in our list.

3. Type the abbreviation's expansion in the With field and click Add.

   The abbreviation and its full name appear in the Replace/With list (**Figure 4.11**).

4. Click OK when you're done adding abbreviations.

✔ Tip

■ When you add an AutoCorrect entry in one Office program it appears in all the others as well. For instance, our Access "sac" abbreviation now appears in Word as well.

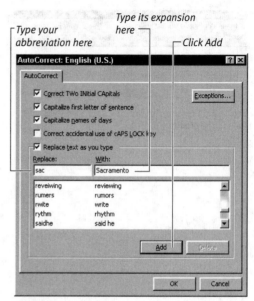

Figure 4.10 You can cut down on your typing by entering abbreviations for commonly used words in the AutoCorrect dialog box.

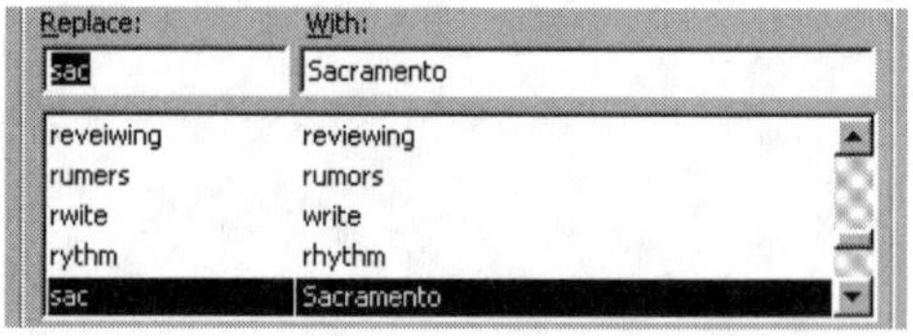

Figure 4.11 Your abbreviation and its full name appear in the list.

Figure 4.12 You can choose tables and queries to supply fields to your new form from the Tables/Queries drop-down menu.

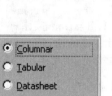

Figure 4.13 The wizard lets you choose which type of form you want to create.

Blends
Blueprint
Expedition
Industrial
International
Ricepaper
SandStone
Standard
Stone
Sumi Painting

Figure 4.14 You can give your form a unique style.

Creating Forms with a Wizard

Although you can create a form from scratch by double-clicking Create a new form in Design view, why not let the powerful Access wizards do most of the grunt work for you? With the Access Form Wizard you can build a variety of forms with the click of a few buttons. You can pick the base you like best and customize it to your heart's content.

To create a form with a wizard:

1. Click the Forms icon in the Objects pane of the main database window.

2. From the list in the right pane, double-click the Create form by using wizard icon.

3. Click the Tables/Queries drop-down menu to select the table or query from which you'd like to add fields (**Figure 4.12**). You can add fields from as many tables and queries as you like.

   Select a field you want to add and click the > button. The field moves from the Available Fields list to the Selected Fields list. If you want to add all of the fields from a table or query, click the >> button. Click Next to continue.

4. The next screen asks what type of form you want to create. Click the option button next to the type of form layout you want and click Next (**Figure 4.13**).

   A preview of the form type appears to the left of the option buttons.

5. Click the name of the style you want for your form and click Next (**Figure 4.14**).

   A preview of the style appears on your screen.

6. Type a name for your form in the text box at the top of the screen. If you created

your form based on a single table, Access puts that table's name in the box.

7. Click the first option button if you want to view or enter data, the second one if you want to modify your form's design. Click Finish.

✔ Tips

■ If you accidentally add a field that you don't want to appear on your table, you can click the < button to remove it. If you've added fields, but want to clear the Selected Fields list and begin adding fields from scratch, click the << button.

■ To accept the default choices for creating forms, click Finish at any time.

Form Types

You should create a *justified form* whenever screen space is at a premium. By contrast, *columnar forms* present one record per page and are best suited for in-depth analyses where the contents of each record counts. *Tabular forms* are a compromise between the two extremes; they require less space than columnar forms but are easier to read than justified forms.

Figure 4.15 Open the Tab Order dialog box and click the control you want to change.

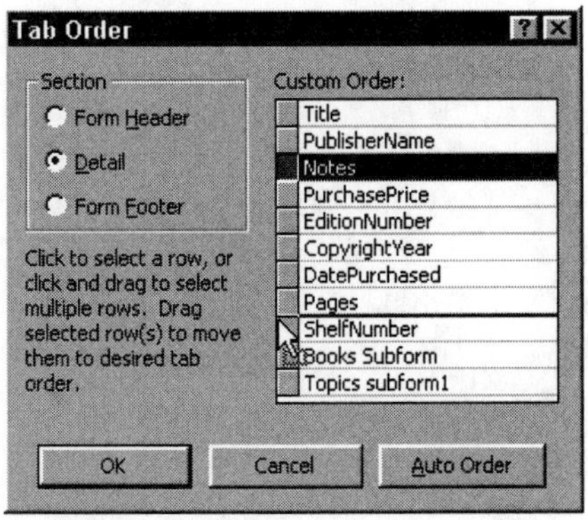

Figure 4.16 Then drag it to its new place in your form's tab order.

Organizing Forms for Efficiency

Most forms will have a natural order in which their fields will be visited; a form in a book-tracking database, for example, would start with the author's name, the title of the book, the publisher, and so forth. If this obvious sequence isn't what you want, you can tell Access what order you'd like to "tab" the fields in.

To establish a tab order:

1. In Design view, open the form in which you want to set a tab order.

   For this example we're using the Books table from the Books database.

2. Choose View > Tab Order.

3. In the Tab Order dialog box, select the row selector of the control you want to move and drag it to the desired position (**Figure 4.15**).

   In this instance, we want to move the Notes field from its current location closer to the end of the tab order. Although most of the other data can be transcribed directly from the book itself, notes require a bit more thought, and should be reserved for the end of the data entry process.

   When you release the left mouse button, the control appears in its new place in the order (**Figure 4.16**).

✔ Tips

- To have Access automatically assign a tab order (based on an up-down or left-right reading of your form), display the Tab Order dialog box and click the Auto Order button.

(continued on next page)

ORGANIZING FORMS FOR EFFICIENCY

- If you have controls in more than one section of your form, click the option button next to the section in which you want to set a tab order.

- You can exclude a control from the tab order by setting its Tab Stop property to "No." To return it to the order, change the Tab Stop property to "Yes." (The control doesn't disappear from the form, it just can't be tabbed to.) For information about setting a control's properties, see "Specifying Properties in Forms," later in this chapter.

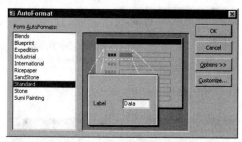

Figure 4.17 Outfit your forms in the latest AutoFormat fashions.

Formatting Forms

If you create a form from scratch, you might be concerned that you won't get to use the nifty AutoFormat features included in the Form Wizard. Don't fret—with Access you can apply a pre-fab format to your form quite easily.

To format a form:

1. Choose Format > AutoFormat to open the AutoFormat dialog box, which contains a list of AutoFormat possibilities.

2. Click the name of the AutoFormat you want to apply to your form. A preview of the formatted form will appear. When you've decided, click OK (**Figure 4.17**).

✔ Tips

- If you want to choose which elements of the AutoFormat to apply (font, color, and border), click the Options button. A set of checkboxes will appear at the bottom of the dialog box. Clear the checkboxes next to the form attributes you don't want to change.

- If you come up with a format you'd like to keep, you can have Access save it. Click the Customize button to display the Customize AutoFormat dialog box and click the Create a new AutoFormat option button. Click OK and your work is preserved.

FORMATTING FORMS

Specifying Properties in Forms

Every element of your form, including the form itself, has a set of attributes, or *properties* that you can modify to change its appearance and/or behavior. Exactly which properties are available depends on the element you're working with.

You can modify a control's properties to change how the control appears or reacts when activated (clicked, double-clicked, right-clicked, and so on). Control properties are divided into four subsets, each with its own tab in the Properties dialog box: Format, Data, Event, and Other. The All tab displays every property for the selected control.

To specify properties in forms:

1. Open your form in Design view and select the element whose properties you want to examine or modify.

2. Click the Properties toolbar button (**Figure 4.18**). When the Properties dialog box appears, click the tab containing the subset of properties you want to examine (**Figure 4.19**).

3. Click the name of the property you want to change. If a drop-down menu button appears, click it to display a list of possible values for that property. If a Build button (a button with three dots on it) appears, click it to launch a tool for building the expression or value for that property.

4. Close the Properties dialog box when you're done.

✔ Tip

■ If you want to display the properties for the form as a whole, click any blank spot in the body of the form before clicking Properties.

Figure 4.18 The Properties toolbar button.

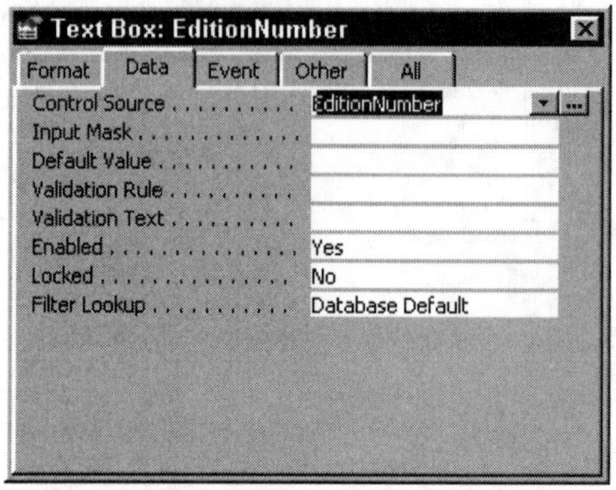

Figure 4.19 The Build button launches tools to create expressions that define your object's properties.

Figure 4.20 Clicking the Toolbox button displays the controls you can add to a form or report.

Adding Controls

When you create a form with a wizard, Access automatically creates controls where you can enter and peruse the data in your tables. Using the Toolbox feature, you can go beyond that basic level of functionality and add other controls, such as labels to describe different areas of your form, text boxes to accept user input, or images to make your form more appealing and easier to use. You can also add list boxes, combo boxes, and command buttons, to make it easier to enter data, run queries related to the data in the underlying tables, print the form, and perform a host of other tasks.

To add a control:

1. Click the Toolbox button on the toolbar (**Figure 4.20**).

2. In the Toolbox, click the icon representing the control you want to add.

    Your mouse pointer changes to a miniature of the icon you chose.

3. Move your pointer to the spot on the form where you want your control to appear and click the left mouse button.

4. A wizard will appear for every control type except labels, text boxes, lines, and rectangles. All you need to do is follow the wizard's instructions to give your control life.

✔ Tips

- You can create labels, text boxes, lines, and rectangles using just the mouse. For instance, to draw a line, click the line icon in the Toolbox, click the starting point for the line on your form, and drag the mouse to the line's endpoint.

- If you want to turn off a control's wizard, click the Control Wizards button on the Toolbox. When the wizards are turned off the button will appear "flat" against the background, rather than recessed.

- If you didn't quite get your control's size right when you created it, you can resize it by clicking the control and grabbing one of the six black boxes that will appear on its border. Just drag the box until the outline on the form is the right size.

Types of Controls in Access

List boxes and combo boxes are two very useful controls to add to your forms and reports. Other common controls include:

- **Labels** contain text you type in when you create a form or report. They're good for identifying different sections of a form or for giving users instructions when they fill out the form.

- **Text boxes** give users a place to enter comments.

- **Option buttons, toggle buttons, and check boxes** let users answer yes/no and on/off questions with a single click of the mouse.

- **Option groups** are sets of option buttons (or toggle buttons or check boxes) that allow a user to pick only one option from the group.

- **Command buttons** you can use to run a macro, Visual Basic code module, or other Windows program.

- **Image and object frames** allow you to include pictures and other OLE-compliant objects in your forms and reports.

- **Tab controls** let you put information on pages accessed by clicking a tab at the top of the control. The Properties dialog box is a tab control.

- **Page breaks** help you to format your forms and make them more readable.

- **Subforms and subreports** let you show the "many" side of a one-to-many relationship based on the contents of the parent form. (You'll learn more about subforms and subreports later in this chapter.)

- **Lines and boxes** are graphical elements you can use to make your forms and reports easier to use and look at.

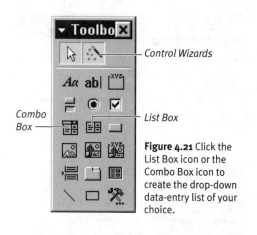

Control Wizards

Combo Box

List Box

Figure 4.21 Click the List Box icon or the Combo Box icon to create the drop-down data-entry list of your choice.

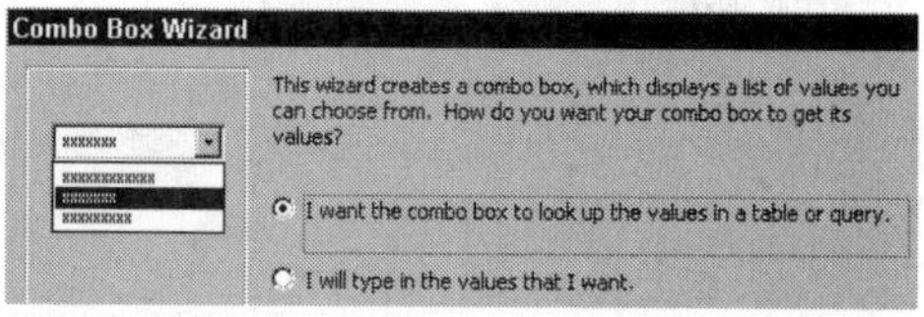

Figure 4.22 You can input your own values for your drop-down list.

Creating a Drop-Down Data-Entry List

Two of the more useful controls in the Toolbox are the List Box and Combo Box. List Boxes present users with a list of values you derive from a table or query. Combo Boxes are, as the name implies, combinations of List Boxes and Text Boxes. Not only can users pick from a list of values, but they can enter their own values as well. The List Box and Combo Box Wizards are very similar, so we've used one procedure to describe them both.

To create a drop-down data-entry list:

1. Click either the List Box or Combo Box button in the Toolbox and click the spot where you want it to appear on your form (**Figure 4.21**).

   Make sure the Control Wizards button is depressed, or you will be when the wizard doesn't start.

2. When the wizard appears, you must choose whether to enter your own values or draw data from a table or query. To get your values from a table or query, click the first option button and click Next (**Figure 4.22**).

   or

   If you want to enter your own values, select the second option and click Next. A screen appears asking you to input the values you want. When you've finished entering the values, click Next and skip to step 7.

3. You can view your queries, tables, or both by clicking the appropriate option button. Click the table or query that you want to provide the contents of your box.

   (continued on next page)

4. From the list of fields that appears (**Figure 4.23**), select the field you want and click the > button to add it to your box. Click Next to continue.

5. The next screen lets you adjust your column width. Drag the edge of the column until it's in the right spot; if you want Access to find the best fit, double-click the right edge. Click Next when you're done. (**Figure 4.24**).

6. Type a name for your box in the space provided and click Finish.

✔ Tips

■ If the values you want to include in your list are scattered among a few tables, you can create a query to gather them in one place (see Chapter 5).

■ To avoid duplicate values in your list, you should pick a key field in the table or query that you choose. You can add more than one field if you want, but one of the fields should be a key field.

■ To change a List Box into a Combo Box, choose Format > Change To. From the Change To submenu, select Combo Box. This technique works to change other objects' types as well; the Change To submenu will display the available types.

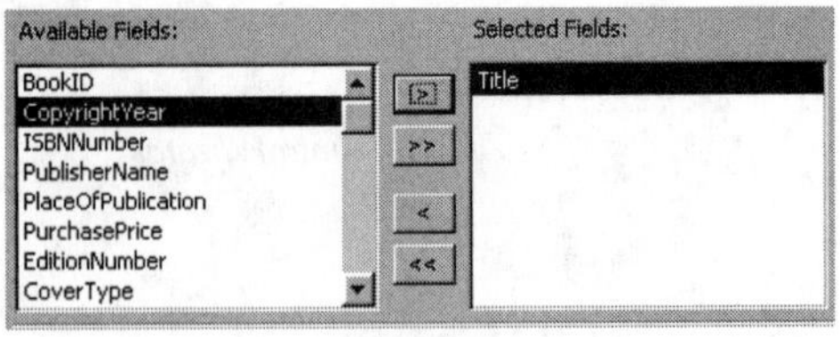

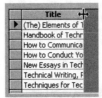

Figure 4.23 Add fields to your list with the >, >>, <, and << buttons.

Figure 4.24 You can resize your list window to make its contents more readable.

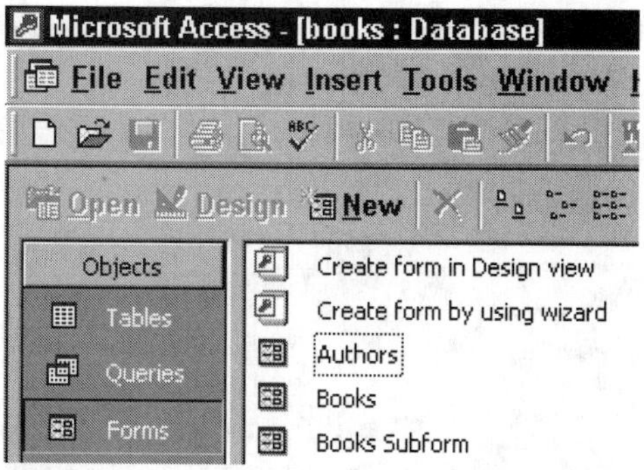

Figure 4.25 Clicking the Forms icon displays the forms in your database.

Figure 4.26 The Design button opens your form to change.

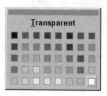

Figure 4.27 Click the toolbar button corresponding to the aspect of the object you want to change.

Figure 4.28 The basic color palette.

Modifying Controls

Access allows you to assign an AutoFormat to your form when you create it with a wizard. If none of the pre-fabricated looks is quite what you're looking for, you can easily customize your controls' appearance with a few mouse clicks.

There are three different ways, for instance, that you can modify the color of your control. Changing a control's fill/back color modifies the control's interior or background color; changing a control's fore/font color changes the control's text; and changing the border/line color changes the outline of the control (or a freestanding line) to the chosen color.

Changing a control's color is just one example of how you can modify your controls, you can also change the font the control's text appears in or the thickness and style of the control's border.

To modify a control:

1. Click the Forms icon in the Objects pane of the main database window (**Figure 4.25**).

2. Select the form you want to modify.

3. Click the Design button on the toolbar (**Figure 4.26**).

4. Click the control you want to change and click the drop-down menu button corresponding to the aspect of the control you want to change (**Figure 4.27**).

5. Click a color from the palette that appears (**Figure 4.28**).

MODIFYING CONTROLS

To pick a custom color:

1. Click the control you want to modify and click the Properties toolbar button.

2. In the Properties dialog box, click the Format tab and click the specific property you want to change.

   For this example, we chose Back Color (**Figure 4.29**).

3. Click the Build button that appears next to the property's text box.

   The Color dialog box appears. The default palette here is larger than the previous one, but you can open an even more powerful color-choosing tool.

4. Click the Define Custom Colors button (**Figure 4.30**).

5. Click the color you want from the color spectrum, and then click OK (**Figure 4.31**).

6. Close the Properties dialog box. Access applies the color to the control.

✔ Tips

- The Fill/Back, Fore/Font, and Line/Border toolbar buttons display the last color applied with that button. To apply the color to another control, simply click the button.

- You can change your color's brightness by clicking the spectrum at the far right of the expanded Color dialog box, which runs from white at the top to black at the bottom. The current brightness is indicated by a left-pointing arrow.

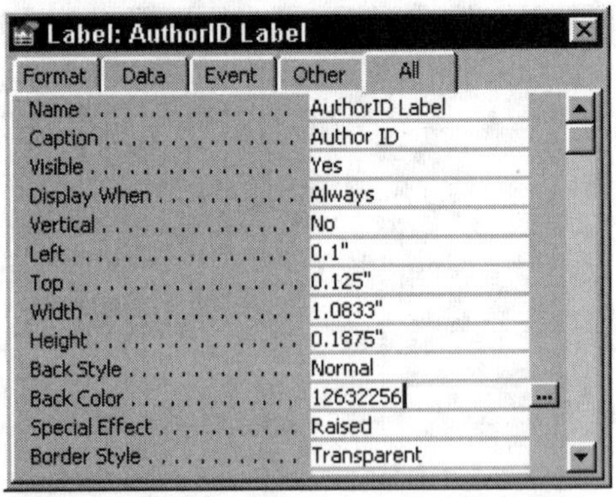

Figure 4.29 Click the property you want to change.

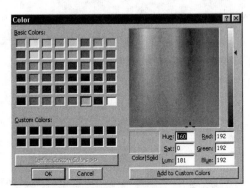

Figure 4.30 Click the Define Custom Colors button to display more than the basic set of colors.

Figure 4.31 Click the color on the spectrum that you want to apply to your object.

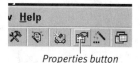

Figure 4.32 Clicking the Properties button gets you to the heart of your control.

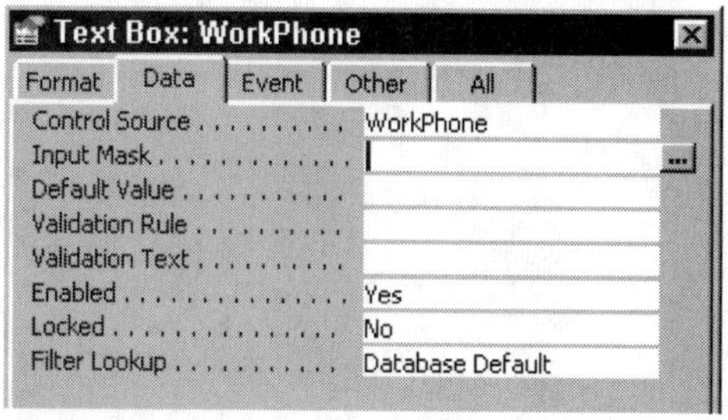

Properties button

Figure 4.33 The Build button next to the Input Mask property launches a wizard that you can use to define your mask.

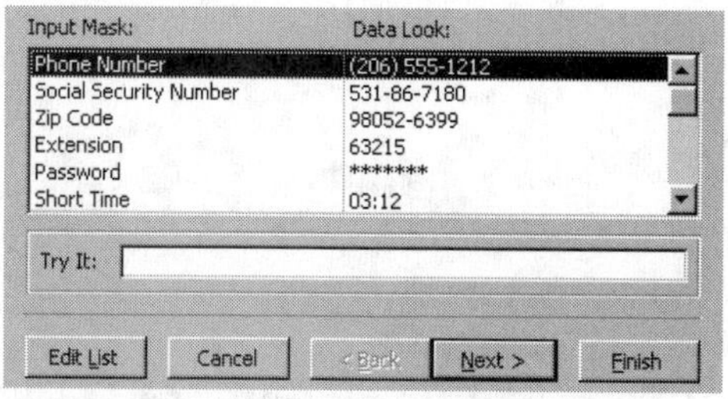

Figure 4.34 Select a mask from the list.

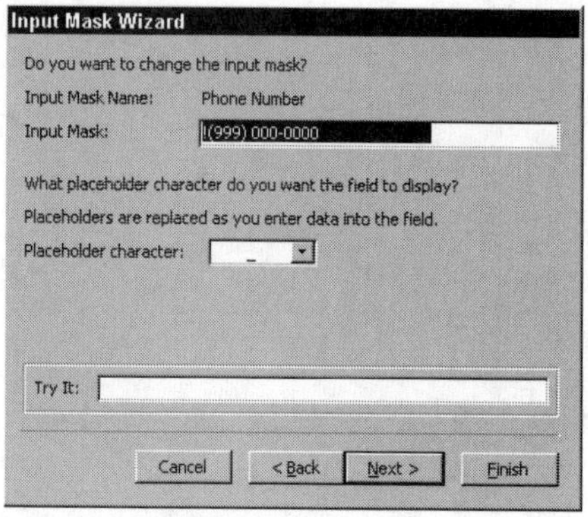

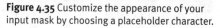

Figure 4.35 Customize the appearance of your input mask by choosing a placeholder character.

Using Input Masks

Wouldn't it be nice if you could make entering data easy? If say, you could set up your telephone number field so that it prompted the user to enter a three-digit area code, a three-digit exchange, and a four-digit identifier? Well you can, and it's not very difficult to do.

An *input mask* is a tool that specifies the format of data entered into a field. To ensure phone numbers are entered in the proper format, for instance, you can create an input mask like (###) ###-####, where each # is a space for a number from 0–9 to be entered.

To use an input mask:

1. Open your form in Design view, click the control corresponding to the field you want to set the input mask for, and click the Properties toolbar button (**Figure 4.32**).

2. In the Properties dialog box, click the Data tab and click Input Mask.

   A Build button will appear to the right of the property (**Figure 4.33**).

3. Click the Build button to launch the Input Mask Wizard.

4. Click the Input Mask you want from the list and click Next (**Figure 4.34**).

   You can modify your input mask here as well as change the placeholder character. Click Next when the mask looks the way you want it to (**Figure 4.35**).

5. Determine how you want to store the field's data and click the appropriate option button. Click the "With the symbols in the mask" option button to store the symbols with the data.

   or

   Click the "Without the symbols in the mask" option button to store the data on its own. Click Next to continue.

(continued on next page)

USING INPUT MASKS

Unless you're short on space, you should probably store the data with the mask characters.

6. You're done! Click Finish to set your field's input mask.

✔ Tips

■ If none of the pre-fab masks are exactly what you want, create your own by clicking the Edit List button to display the Customize Input Mask Wizard.

■ To test drive your input mask before finishing up the wizard, click in the Try It text box, which is available at the bottom of most of the wizard pages.

■ To use the Access Help files to create input masks, ask the Office Assistant about the "InputMask Property."

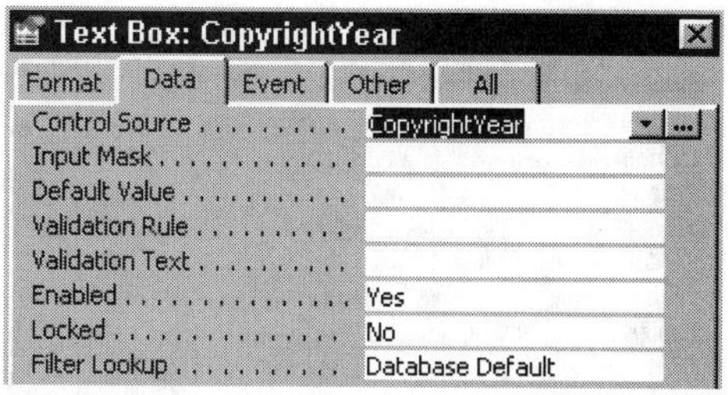

Figure 4.36 Click the Data tab to limit the number of properties displayed in the dialog box.

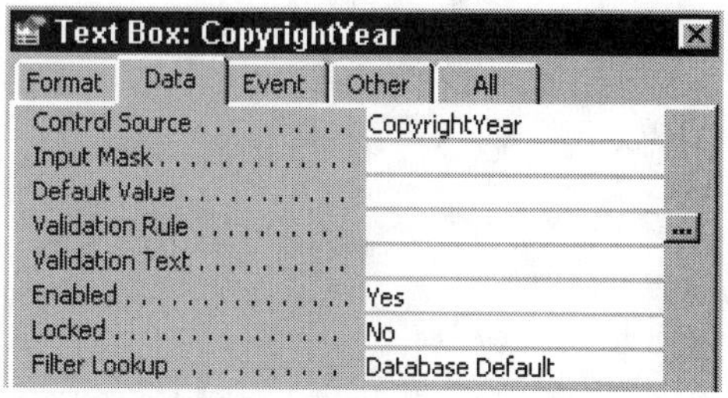

Figure 4.37 Clicking Validation Rule (or the text box next to it) displays the Build button.

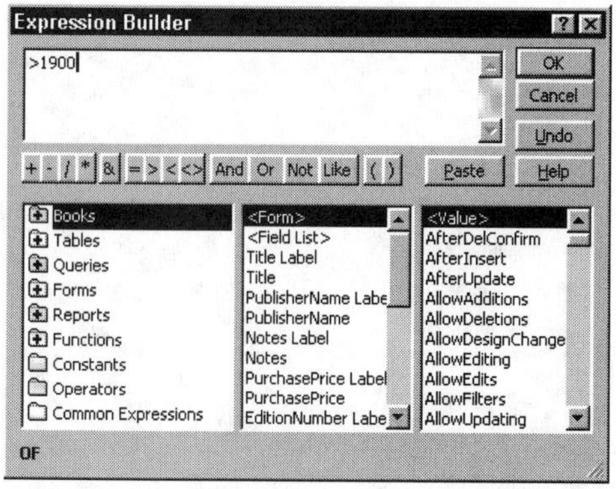

Figure 4.38 The Expression Builder is a powerful and flexible tool you can use to create your validation rule.

Validating Data Entry

Data entry can be a long, tedious process, so it's only natural to expect that an incorrect value will sneak in occasionally, such as a name in a numbers-only field. Rather than blindly accept whatever users type in, you can verify that the data meets certain criteria.

To validate data entry:

1. Click the field in which you want to validate data and click the Properties toolbar button.

   We picked the CopyrightYear field in a database that tracks books in a library.

2. In the Properties dialog box, click the Data tab (**Figure 4.36**).

3. Click Validation Rule, and then click the Build button that appears to the right of the property (**Figure 4.37**).

   The Expression Builder appears (**Figure 4.38**). The Expression Builder helps you create formulas that Access can use to evaluate and calculate data.

4. Enter the expression you want Access to use as your validation rule. Click OK to continue.

   In this case, we entered the rule ">1900" to ensure that we didn't type in an incorrect value. If we owned any books printed before 1901, we would have to modify the rule.

   (continued on next page)

5. Your validation rule appears in the Validation Rule property's text area. Close the Properties dialog box to save your validation rule (**Figure 4.39**).

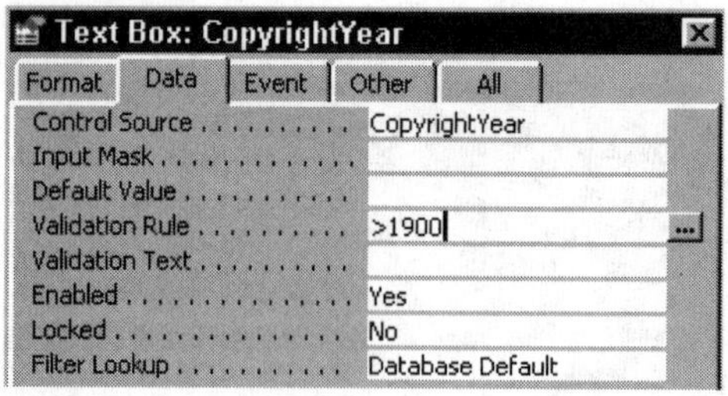

✔ Tips

■ You can choose the message that you want displayed when a user enters incorrect data. To set this message, type it into the Validation Text property's text box.

■ If you click on the property's Build button after you've set a validation rule (if you wanted to edit it, for instance), the rule will appear in the Expression Builder's editing window when it opens.

Figure 4.39 Now everyone can see your expression.

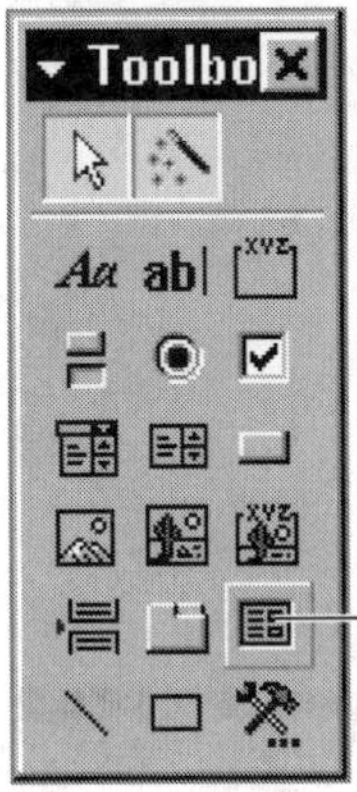

Click the Subform/Subreport Button

Figure 4.40 Open the Toolbox to display the Subform Control Wizard.

Creating Subforms

Records in one table are often related to more than one record in another table. For instance, one author in your Authors table can have more than one book listed in your Books table. Standard forms don't illustrate these *one-to-many* relationships well, but forms with subforms do.

For instance, it's easy to display a list of authors in a form. What you can't do in a simple form is show the books that each author has written. If you add a subform based on a table listing book titles, Access can find the books a specific author has written and display them in the subform.

You should pick the object in your database that contains the fields you want to display in your subform; Access lets you choose the fields you want to show in the subform. Using a query (covered in Chapter 5) includes the fields you've included in your query results, though they can come from more than one table (or another query).

If you use an existing form (as we do in the following example), Access will ask you to give the subform a unique name. This is true for subforms based on tables and queries as well.

To create a subform:

1. Open the form to which you want to add a subform, open the Toolbox if necessary, and click the Subform/Subreport button (**Figure 4.40**).

2. Click the place on the form where you want your subform to appear.

   The best place to put a subform is usually toward the bottom of the form, below the information relating to the record displayed in the main form.

   (continued on next page)

The Subform Wizard launches once you've clicked the target.

3. Select the source for your subform by clicking either the "Use existing Tables and Queries" option button or the "Use an existing form" button. Click Next to continue (**Figure 4.41**).

   The next wizard screen appears, containing a list of the fields in the form and a list of the fields in the subform.

4. Click the name of the field that you want to link your form and subform. Click Next (**Figure 4.42**).

   You can remove fields from the Selected Fields pane by clicking either the < button (to remove one field) or the << button (to remove them all).

5. Type a name for your subform and click Finish.

   You should probably leave the word "subform" in your new subform's name so it will be easier to recognize in your object lists.

✔ Tip

- If you want to use all of the fields in a table, you should check if a form has been created from that table. If one exists, look it over and use it if it fits!

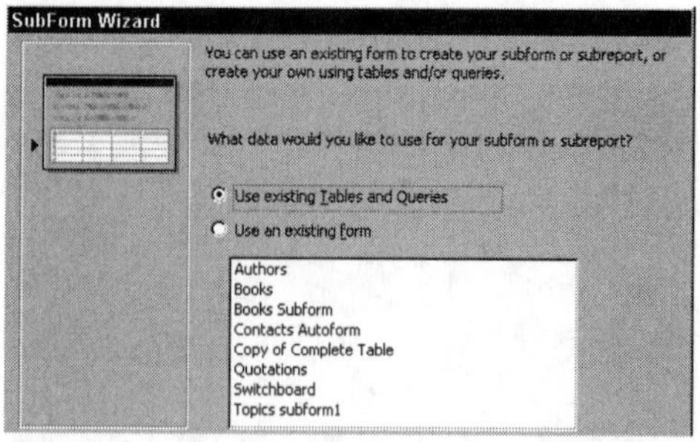

Figure 4.41 Select the source for your subform.

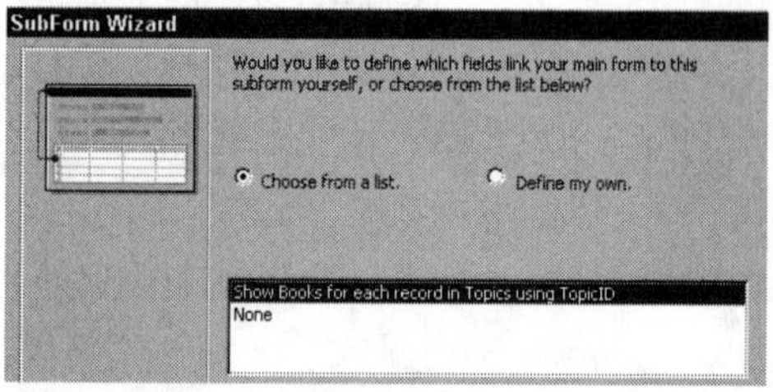

Figure 4.42 You don't need to use all of the fields from a subform's source; you can add only the ones that you want.

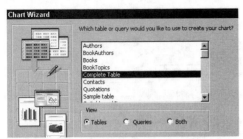

Figure 4.43 Select a table or query to provide your chart's data.

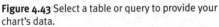

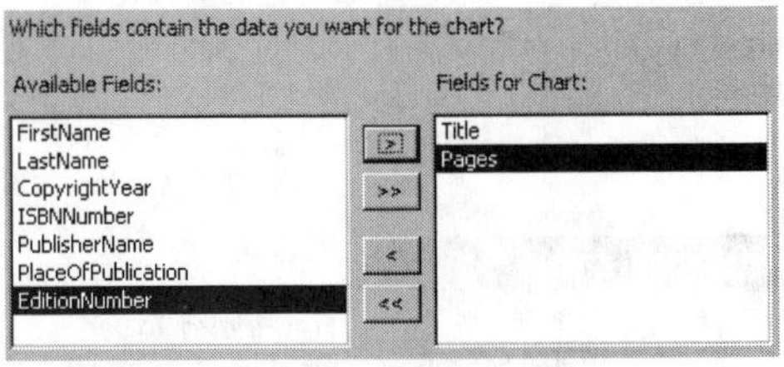

Figure 4.44 Add the specific fields that you want to pull values from.

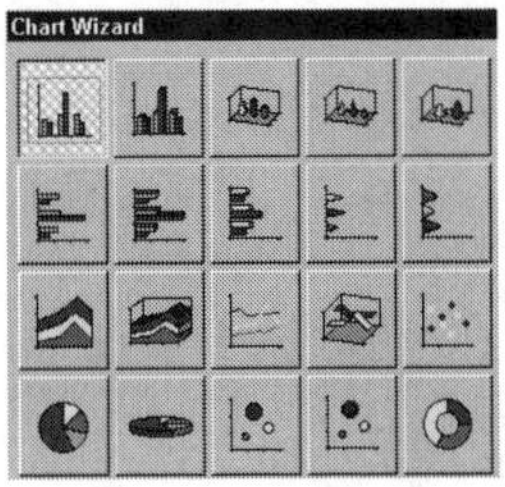

Figure 4.45 Select a chart type.

Creating a Chart in a Form

Lists of data are wonderful for computers, but humans don't do well with long, dry list of numbers. We like pictures, especially pictures that tell stories about numbers. Adding a chart to a form gives viewers a clear summary of the underlying data in that form. When the form is opened, Access draws the data from the table or query behind the chart and presents it to your users in the manner that you specify.

For example, if you want to compare the lengths of books in your library, you can create a chart with the book title on the horizontal axis, a numerical range on the vertical axis, and the number of pages for each book displayed as a bar above the book title.

To create a chart:

1. Open your form in Design view, choose Insert > Chart, and click the spot on the form where you want your chart to appear.

2. Click the name of the table or query you want to supply the data for your chart and click Next (**Figure 4.43**).

3. Add the fields that you want to use in your chart by clicking a field name and then clicking the > button. Click Next when you're done (**Figure 4.44**).

4. Click the type of chart you want to create and click Next (**Figure 4.45**).

   When you click a chart button, a description of the chart and the type of data it summarizes best appears in the lower-right corner of the wizard screen.

(continued on next page)

CREATING A CHART IN A FORM

5. The next screen lets you configure your chart by rearranging the placement of the values from your table (**Figure 4.46**).

To see what your chart will look like, click the Preview Chart button (**Figure 4.47**). Click Next to continue.

6. Type a name for your chart in the space provided and click Finish. That's all there is to it.

✔ Tips

- To change the way your chart summarizes your data, double-click the field name in the chart layout wizard screen; your choices are: None, Sum (the default), Average, Min (minimum), Max (maximum), and Count (the number of entries in the field).

- To edit your chart after you've created it, simply double-click it when it's in Design view. For help, double-click the chart and then choose Help > Help in Microsoft Graph (the helper program that actually creates your chart).

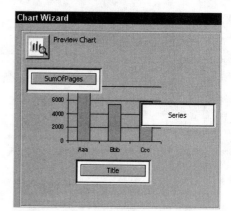

Figure 4.46 If your chart isn't laid out quite right, change it!

Figure 4.47 To see what your chart will look like, click the Preview Chart button.

WORKING WITH QUERIES

Queries are tools built from fields in your tables or in other existing queries that you can use to ask questions about the contents of your database. You can use queries to find records within a single table, and also to combine the contents of several related tables into a single, easy-to-read object.

You can do more than simple record-finding with queries, including performing calculations like finding sums, averages, and even standard deviations in your queries. These calculations can make your results more meaningful and easier to read.

The results of a query are called a *dynaset,* short for "dynamic set" of records. The collection is dynamic because it changes when the query changes—such as when you pull data from different fields or perform different calculations on your results. These changes, however radical, don't affect the data in the source tables or queries.

Looking at Queries

When you design a query, you need to specify which tables and queries you want to use as the query's data sources, pick the fields from those tables and queries that contain the particular information you want, and set a criteria for each field so that Access finds the records you want. You can make these choices in the Query Design Grid (**Figure 5.1**).

1 Menu Bar

The menu bar appears at the top of the Access window and makes all of the program's commands available to you.

2 Query Design toolbar

The query design toolbar presents buttons for many basic commands you'll use when working with your query.

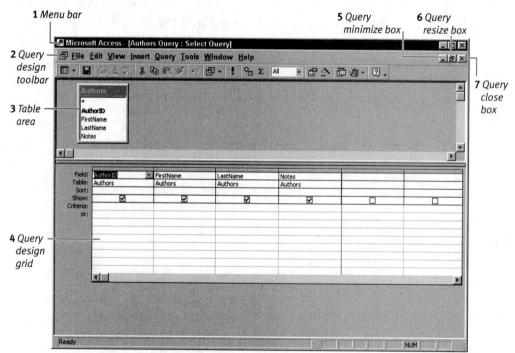

Figure 5.1 A query in Design view.

3 Table area

The table area shows the tables you have chosen to work with in your query.

4 Query design grid

The query design grid is the tool you use to create your query. You enter the name of a field, the table it appears in, how you want the field's contents sorted, whether the field should be shown in your query's results, and what criteria you want to use to select records based on a field's content. The exact configuration of the query design grid changes depending on what type of query you're building. **Figure 5.1** shows a query design grid for a select query.

5 Query minimize box

The query minimize box collapses the query you're working on to a bar within the main database window. The Access window itself does not change size.

6 Query resize box

The query resize box expands your query to fill the entire Access window or shrinks it to its last unexpanded size.

7 Query close box

The query close box closes the query you're working on without shutting down Access.

LOOKING AT TABLES

Creating New Queries with a Wizard

You can create queries quickly and easily using the built-in Access wizards. The most basic query is a Select query, which plucks records from your tables—check out the sidebar on page 72 to find out about the other types of queries you can create with Access query wizards.

With query wizards you can create two different types of queries: *detail* queries, which show every field in the query results, and *summary* queries, which summarize one or more field values by taking the sum, average, maximum or minimum. Summary queries only work with numerical data.

To create a query with a wizard:

1. Click Queries in the Objects pane of the main database window and click New (**Figure 5.2**).

   The New Query dialog box opens. You can choose the type of query you want create in this dialog box.

2. Click Simple Query Wizard and click OK (**Figure 5.3**).

   A brief description of the type of query you will create appears in the far left pane of the New Query dialog box.

3. Select the table or existing query from which you're adding fields by clicking the Tables/Queries drop-down menu and clicking the name of the table or query you want to use (**Figure 5.4**).

4. Add fields to your query using the > (add a field) and >> (add all fields) buttons. To remove fields, use the < (remove a field) and << (remove all fields) buttons. Click Next when you're done (**Figure 5.5**).

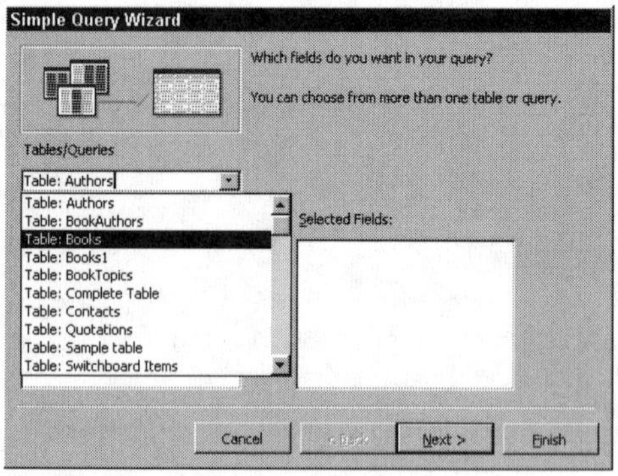

Figure 5.2 Click the New toolbar button to create a brand new query.

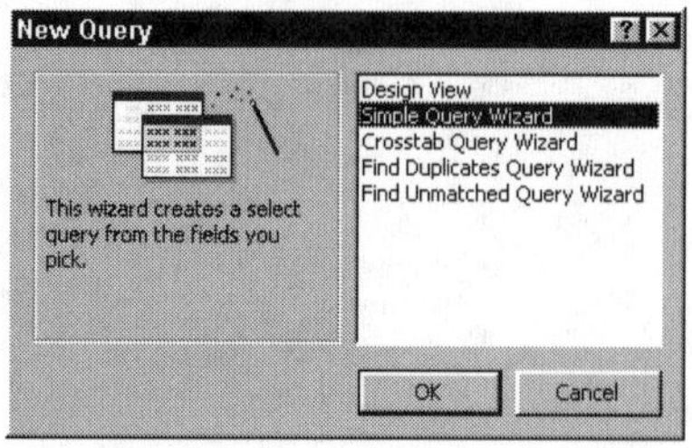

Figure 5.3 Select your task from the New Query dialog box.

Figure 5.4 Use the Table/Query drop-down list to establish a base for your new query.

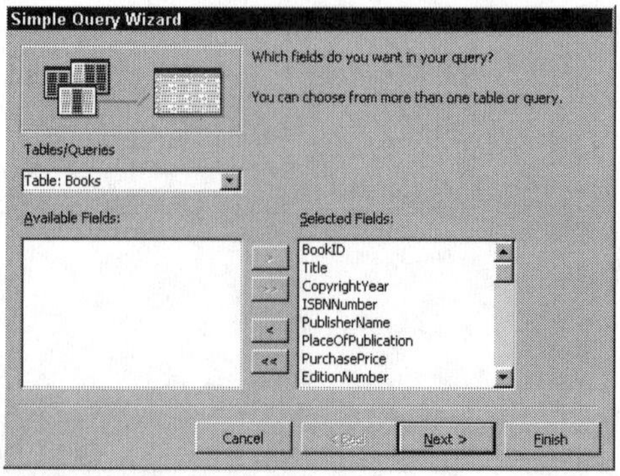

Figure 5.5 Add and remove fields from the Query Wizard through the familiar wizard interface.

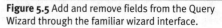

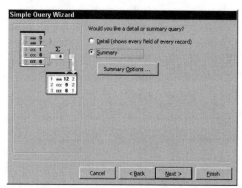

Figure 5.6 You can choose to display every value in your query or to have Access summarize the contents of one or more fields for you.

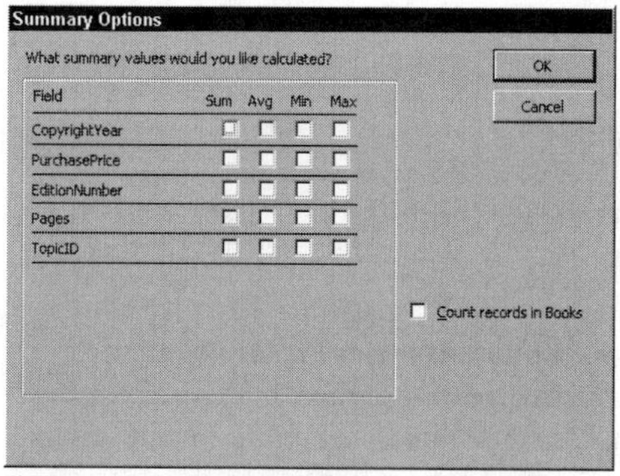

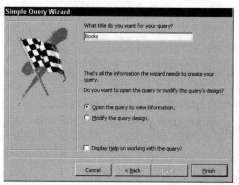

Figure 5.7 Choose which fields you want Access to summarize, and by what method.

Figure 5.8 Type a name for your query and click Finish to create it.

5. Choose whether you want to create a Detail or Summary query (**Figure 5.6**).

6. Access asks you to select which fields to summarize and how (**Figure 5.7**). Click OK to return to the previous wizard screen.

   The Detail/Summary wizard screen only appears if one of the fields you've chosen contains numerical data.

7. Click Next to display the final wizard screen (**Figure 5.8**).

8. Type a title for your query in the space provided at the top of the wizard screen and click Finish.

✔ Tip

- Access can perform more than one summary operation on your query data. For instance, you can find the Minimum *and* Maximum price of the books in your library in the same query. You would need to perform the calculation in two separate fields, however.

Types of Queries

Access lets you go far beyond simple select queries; you won't even need to jump through too many hoops to create different query types. Here's a quick rundown of the query types available to you:

- **Select Queries** The basic query type, select queries find and display the data you want.

- **Parameter Queries** Like select queries, but they prompt you for the criteria (or *parameters*) to use when selecting data.

- **Crosstab Queries** Crosstab queries generate spreadsheet-like output based on data from three or more fields. A standard query's results relate a series of fields (such as Title, Publisher, ISBN) to a single thing (such as a book). A Crosstab query relates a single field (such as Sales) to two things (such as a Publisher and a Book).

- **Delete Queries** Finds records and deletes them. Make sure that's what you want to do!

- **Update Queries** Finds records and changes one or more of their values, such as increasing prices on items from a supplier.

- **Append Queries** Takes records from one (or more) tables and adds them to the end of other tables. Beats typing them in.

- **Make-Table Query** Selects a set of records and makes a table out of them, rather than a dynaset.

- **Find Duplicates Query** Looks for records in a table that have the same value in one or more fields.

- **Find Unmatched Query** Looks for records in one table that have no corresponding records in another table. One example would be a customer with no orders.

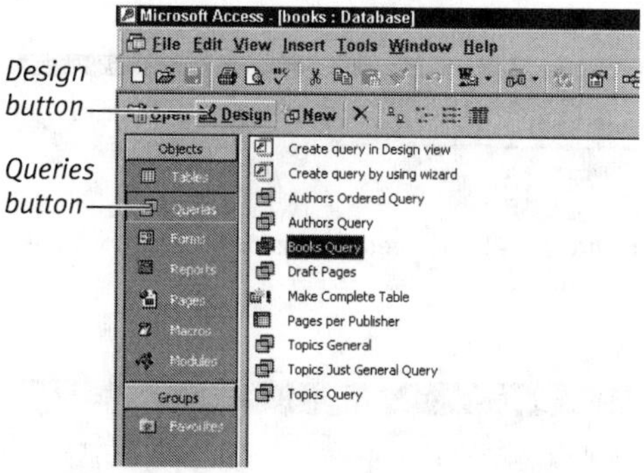

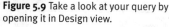

Design button —

Queries button —

Figure 5.9 Take a look at your query by opening it in Design view.

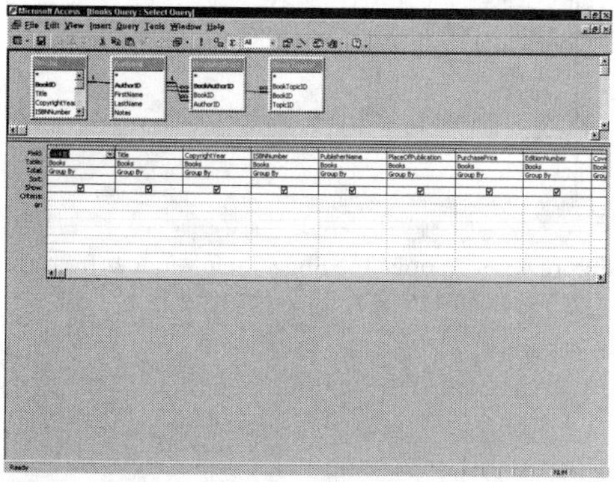

Figure 5.10 Once you've opened your query in Design view, you can examine and modify it.

Viewing Queries in Design View

Working with queries is fairly easy, but it may take a little time to get them working exactly the way you want them to. Plus, if you change the structure of the tables you're querying (by removing a field or moving it from one table to another, for example), you might need to modify your queries to reflect that change.

To view a query in Design view:

1. Display the queries in your database by clicking the Queries button in the left pane of the main database window.

2. Click the icon representing the query you want to view, and then click the Design button (**Figure 5.9**).

   The icon displayed depends on the type of query you selected. (See the sidebar on page 72 for a summary of the different types of queries.)

3. Your query appears in the query design grid, along with the tables used to generate the results (**Figure 5.10**).

✔ Tips

- If you want to modify your query while viewing its results in Datasheet view, you can shift to Design view by choosing View > Design View.

- Remember to hit File > Save—Access doesn't save your work automatically.

Chapter 5

Choosing Which Tables to Query

With your in Design view, you can select the tables you want to have available to select fields from. If you think you might need a field from a table but aren't sure, show that table anyway. You can always hide it later.

For example, say you want to create a query to find all of the books by a certain author and you think you may want to display his or her contact information in the query results. Add the Authors and Books tables to your query, and if you decide that you don't want to show the contact information, you can hide the Authors table.

To choose a table to query:

1. Open your query in Design view, either by clicking the query's icon and clicking the Design button, or by creating a new query in Design view.

2. Click the Show Table button on the Query Design toolbar (**Figure 5.11**).

   The Show Table dialog box appears with a list of the tables in your database.

3. Click the name of the table you want to make available to your query and click Add (**Figure 5.12**).

4. When you're done adding tables, click Close.

✔ Tip

■ To remove a table from the Query Design window, right-click the table's title bar and choose Remove Table from the pop-up menu.

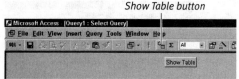

Figure 5.11 All you need to do is click the Show Table button...

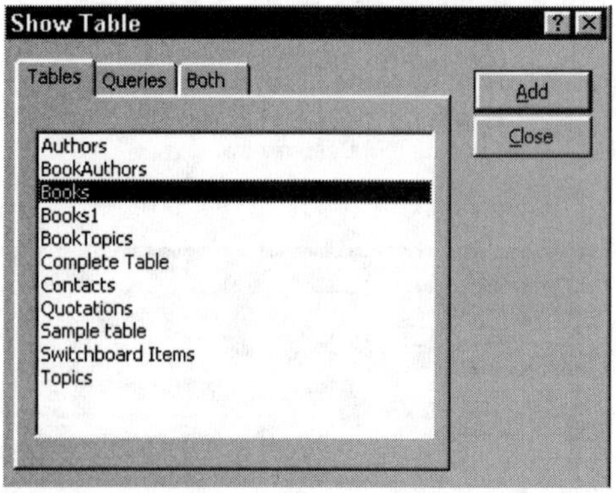

Figure 5.12 ...to open the Show Table window, from which you can add fields to your query.

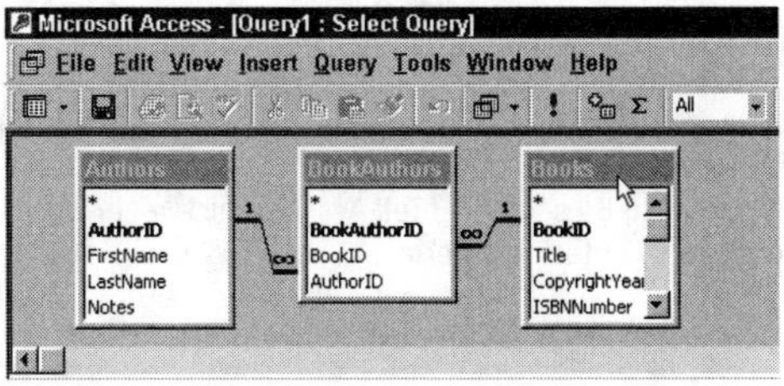

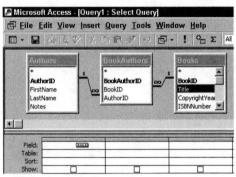

Figure 5.13 Activate a table by clicking its title bar.

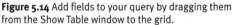

Figure 5.14 Add fields to your query by dragging them from the Show Table window to the grid.

Figure 5.15 Choose the field to use from the drop-down menu

Choosing Which Fields to Query

Adding tables to your query grid isn't much use unless you can use the fields in those tables, right? Access lets you add fields to your query once you've selected the tables you want.

You should add any fields you want to appear in your results or any fields that will help you find the records you want. If you want to find every book by a certain author, for instance, add the book's author and title. Adding the publisher and copyright year is probably a good idea as well.

To choose fields to query:

1. Open (or create) your query in Design view, show the tables from which you want to draw fields, and click the title bar of the table containing the first field you want to add (**Figure 5.13**).

2. Select the field you want to add and drag it to the first open Field cell in the Query By Example grid at the bottom of the Query Design window (**Figure 5.14**). That's all there is to it.

✔ Tips

- If you want to add all of the fields from a table to a query, drag the asterisk ("*") designator from that table's field list to the grid.

- You can also add fields by clicking in an open Field cell, clicking the drop-down menu that appears, and choosing the field name you want from the list that appears (**Figure 5.15**).

Specifying Query Criteria

You're almost done: you've chosen the tables you want and selected the fields that contain the data you want to get at. All you need to do now is tell Access which records to pull from your tables. You do this by using *criteria*.

If you're working with numerical values, simply type in the value you want to use as the base. For instance, if you're working with a table that contains bibliographic information, you can type =1996 in the criteria of the CopyrightYear field to find all of the books published in 1996. You can use other operators, such as > (greater than), < (less than), and <>(not equal to) in your criteria (use the greater-than and less-than keys on the keyboard).

Comparing text strings is also quite simple, but you do need to enclose the string you're looking for in quotes. If you wanted to find all of the books published by Wiley, you would type =**"Wiley"** in the criteria field.

The **<**, **>**, and **<>** operators work for text strings as well. For example, >"Wiley" would return any books by a publisher with a name alphabetized after Wiley. Date comparisons are similar, but you need to indicate that the value in the criteria is a date by typing it in the M/D/Y format and surrounding the date with pound signs: August 2, 1968 would be written as **#8/2/68#**. See **Tables 5.1** through **5.5** for the available operators in Access.

To specify query criteria:

1. In Design view, open the query for which you want to set a criteria and click the cell in the Criteria row in the column representing the field to which you want to assign a criteria.

2. Type the criteria you want to use (**Figure 5.16**).

Figure 5.16 Be selective! Tell Access which records to choose by entering criteria.

Table 5.1

Math Operators in Access

Operator	Description	Example	Notes
*	Multiplication	4*3=12	
+	Addition	4+3=7	
-	Subtraction	4-3=1	
/	Division	4/3=1.333...	
\	Integer Division	4/3=1	The result is truncated, not rounded.
^	Exponentiation	4^3=64	
Mod	Modulo (remainder) division	7/3=1	7/3=2 with a remainder of 1, so 7Mod3=1

Table 5.2

Relational Operators in Access

Operator	Description	Example
=	Equal	Pages=100
<>	Not Equal	Pages<>101
<	Less Than	Pages<200
>	Greater Than	Pages>50
<=	Less Than or Equal to	Pages<=1000
>=	Greater Than or Equal to	Pages>=100

Table 5.3

String Operators in Access

Operator	Description	Example
&	Concatenation	("Eric" & "and" & "Deborah") returns "Eric and Deborah"
Like	Similar to	Like "comm" returns "**comm**unity," "tele**comm**unications," and so on.

Table 5.4

Logical (Boolean) Operators in Access

Operator	Description	Example	Notes
And	Logical And	A And B	Both A and B are true.
Or	Logical Or	A Or B	Either A or B (or both) is true.
Xor	Exclusive Or	A Xor B	Either A or B (but not both) is true.
Not	Negates the affected expression.	Not (A Or B)	Neither A nor B is true.

Table 5.5

Miscellaneous Operators in Access

Operator	Description	Example
Between...and	Between two values (inclusive)	Books.Publisher Between "Peachpit" and "Wiley"
In (list)	A value occurs in an enumerated list.	In ("Peachpit", "O'Reilly", "Wiley")
Is Null	The field or calculation returns a null value (not zero).	Is Null (Books.ISBN)

Querying with Wildcards

Wildcards are characters that represent one or more characters in an expression. For instance, to query an Authors table to find names beginning with "B," just set your criteria to B*. The asterisk tells Access to find every record where the value in the LastName field begins with the letter "B" and is followed by any other character.

The three wildcard characters you'll use most often are the asterisk (*), which matches any number of characters ("Bl*" returns Blank, Block, and Bly, but not Barnum); the question mark (?), which matches any single character ("Bl?ck" returns Black and Block, but not Blosovick); and the pound sign (#), which returns any numerical character ("199#" finds 1999 and 1998, but not 1989).

To query with wildcards:

1. Open (or create) the query in which you want to use wildcards.

2. Click the criteria cell in which you want the expression with wildcards to appear, and type the expression (**Figure 5.17**).

✔ Tip

- If you want to search your records for characters Access recognizes as wildcards, surround the character in square brackets ([]). For example, if you wanted to find records containing an asterisk, your criteria would read "[*]".

Figure 5.17 A query using this wildcard in the criteria will return all Publisher names beginning with "W."

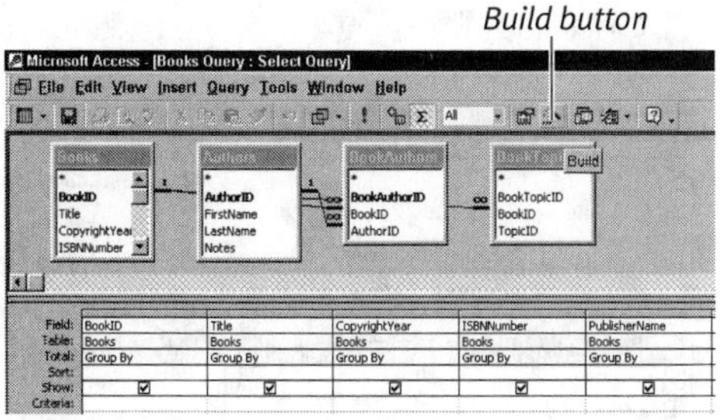

Build button

Figure 5.18 Clicking the Build button lets you create a custom criteria.

Using the Expression Builder

Remembering all of your table and field names can be difficult. If you must also remember the comparison and arithmetic operators you can use in your criteria the challenge becomes Everest-like. Rather than requiring you to work with a blank criteria line in the query grid, Access uses a handy tool called the Expression Builder that creates criteria and other expressions. The Expression Builder gives you a larger working area than the query design grid, has a list of every table and field in your database, and contains a list of all the operators you can use. Several of the more common operators are located on the Expression Builder's main interface.

In Access, an *expression* is a series of field names, operators, and values used to find or calculate values. The criteria "[Sales.Subtotal] > 1500" is an expression, as is "[Sales.Subtotal] * .07".

To use the Expression Builder:

1. In Design view, open the query into which you want to insert an expression.

2. Click the Criteria cell in which you want the criteria to appear and click the Build button (**Figure 5.18**).

   The Expression Builder appears. Note that you can enter the most common comparison and arithmetic operators into your expressions with the buttons on the main screen.

3. Click the operator you want to use in your expression, click Paste, and type the value to which you want to compare the values in the table. Click OK when you're done.

   (continued on next page)

We decided to look for every book in our database that was published in a year other than 1996. The criteria for that is "<>1996", so we clicked the <> button, clicked Paste, and typed 1996 into the Expression Builder window (**Figure 5.19**).

The expression appears in the criteria cell.

✔ Tip

■ To see a list of all the operators you can use in your expressions, click the Operators folder in the lower-left corner of the Expression Builder. The Expression Builder has folders for the tables, queries, forms, and reports in your database, as well as the functions, constants, operators, and common expressions you can include in your queries.

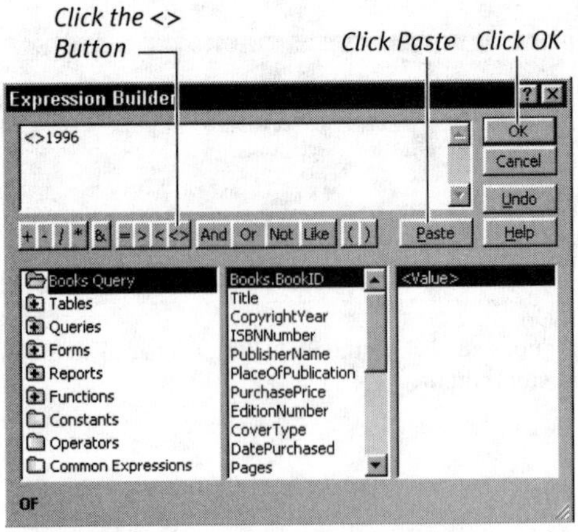

Figure 5.19 The Expression Builder is a versatile and easy-to-use tool.

USING THE EXPRESSION BUILDER

Figure 5.20 Click the Build toolbar button to launch the Expression Builder.

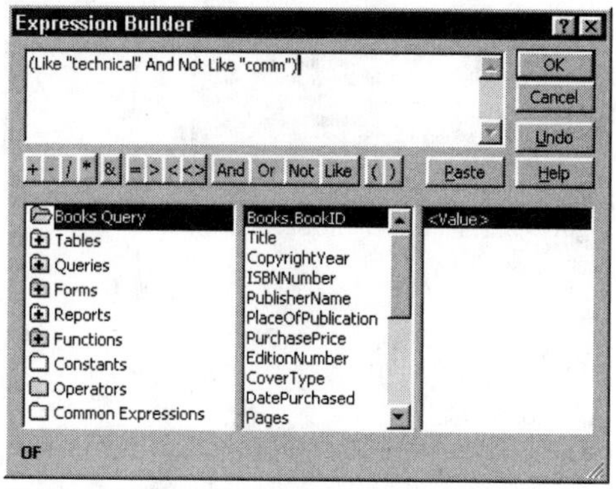

Figure 5.21 Create the first half of your criteria...

Create an Advanced Criteria with the Expression Builder

Although the Expression Builder is easy to use, it can take you a little time to understand how it works. We'll demonstrate how to create a a more complex criteria.

First, decide *exactly* which records you want your query to find for a particular field. Once you've defined your goal, you can start building your query.

In this example, we'll construct a criteria that finds every book in our library with the word "technical" in the title, but without words beginning with "comm" unless they co-occur with the word "international." In other words, we want to find a book titled *International Technical Communities*, but not one called *Technical Communicating*.

To create an advanced criteria with the Expression Builder:

1. Create a query in Design view and click the Criteria cell of the column representing the field for which you want to set your criteria.

   For this example, the field is Title.

2. Click the Build button to launch the Expression Builder (**Figure 5.20**).

3. Create the first part of your expression (**Figure 5.21**).

   In this example, we created the following expression fragment:

   `(Like "technical" And Not Like "comm")`

   There's a lot going on in that statement, so we'll break it down some more. The first term, `Like "technical"`, tells Access to look for titles that contain the word

   (continued on next page)

"technical." The Like comparison operator tells Access that the word should occur anywhere in the title (not just at the beginning).

The second half of the fragment, And Not Like "comm"), adds a second condition to the statement using the And operator that tells Access to ignore titles with words like "communication" and "communicating." The Not operator is very handy, but you do need to make sure that you're negating the proper part of the expression.

If we ran this half of the query by itself we would find every title that contains the word "technical" and *doesn't* contain words like "communication" or "communicating." Now that we have the first part of the criteria working, we can build the second half.

4. Create the second part of your criteria in the Expression Builder (**Figure 5.22**).

We typed (Like "technical" And Like "comm" And Like "international").

In this part of the criteria we will find the titles with "communication" and "communicating" in the same title as the words "technical" and "international." Because we want all three terms to occur, we used the And operator in the fragment.

Now that we have both halves of our expression, all we need to do is link them so Access returns titles that meet either half of the expression.

Choosing an operator can be tricky when you translate from English to Access. We want to find every title in which "technical" doesn't occur with "communication," "communicate," and so on *and* titles in which the words "technical," "communicate," and so on, and "international" *do* occur together.

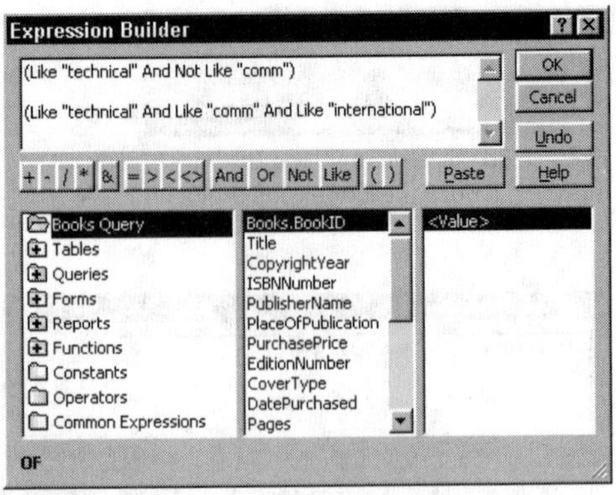

Figure 5.22 ...and then the second half...

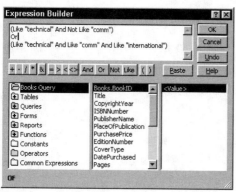

Figure 5.23 ...and link the halves with the proper operator (in this case, "Or").

Figure 5.24 Click the Run button to see your query's results.

Run button

The tricky part is that the English "and" sometimes translates to the logical Or. Because we want titles that meet either half of our criteria, we link the halves with the Or operator (**Figure 5.23**). Using And would require the title to meet both halves of the criteria, and thus return no values. Why? Because the first half of the criteria asks for titles in which "technical" and "*comm*" *don't* occur together, while the second half looks for titles in which they *do*.

We added the asterisk wildcard around "comm" so we won't find titles with words like "telecommunication," which "comm" won't exclude (it doesn't start with "comm") but "*comm*" will (the string "comm" appears somewhere in the title).

Our finished criteria looks like this:

```
(Like "technical" And Not Like
"comm") Or (Like "technical" And
Like "comm" And Like "interna-
tional")
```

5. Click OK to close the Expression Builder.

6. Click the Run button to see your query's results (**Figure 5.24**).

   In this instance, our query returned 11 out of 53 titles in our Books table.

✔ Tip

- Build your criteria one element at a time and test each element. Once you've created a criteria that finds some of the records you want, you can work on modifying it.

Introducing SQL

SQL, or Structured Query Language, is a standardized way of forming databases and writing queries to get information from those databases. You'll encounter SQL if you work with Access Projects, which lets you create an Access-like interface for a database on an SQL server (see Chapter 15).

Take the following query as an example:

```
SELECT DISTINCTROW Topics.Topic,
Books.Title, Books.URL
```

```
FROM Topics INNER JOIN (Books INNER
JOIN BookTopics ON Books.BookID =
BookTopics.BookID) ON Topics.TopicID =
BookTopics.TopicID;
```

The first element of the statement is the SELECT command, which tells Access the fields you want to pull out of your tables. In this case, we want to retrieve values from the Topics table's Topic field, and the Title and URL fields from the Books table. The DISTINCTROW command tells the database to insert a carriage return after each set of values the query returns.

The second element identifies which records to look in. This FROM statement has Access join (or combine) records from the Books and BookTopics tables where the records have the same value in the BookID field.

```
(Books INNER JOIN BookTopics ON
Books.BookID = BookTopics.BookID)
```

After Access obtains those records, it combines them with records from the Topics table where the value in the two table's TopicsID fields match.

```
ON Topics.TopicID = BookTopics.TopicID;
```

The semicolon at the end of the statement indicates that no more commands will follow.

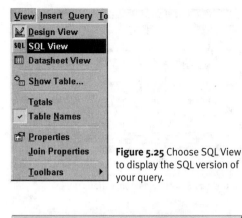

Figure 5.25 Choose SQL View to display the SQL version of your query.

Figure 5.26 You can copy or modify the SQL statements behind your query while in SQL view.

Querying with SQL

SQL is a flexible and powerful language that lets you specify precisely which records and fields you want to use in your query. Actually, you're working in SQL whenever you create a query! Access automatically translates your queries to SQL. To see the SQL source behind a query, simply open your query and choose View > SQL View.

This view shows you what actions Access has to take when it creates and runs your query. Because SQL is a very common feature of databases, viewing Access queries can help you understand SQL queries generated for other databases.

To query with SQL:

1. Create a query, or open an existing query, in Design view.

2. Choose View > SQL View (**Figure 5.25**).

3. Copy the text in the window (**Figure 5.26**), click wherever you want to insert it (such as in a Visual Basic code module or a Properties box) and type Ctrl-V to paste it.

✔ Tip

■ You can edit the SQL behind a query by opening the query in SQL view and editing the source directly. We recommend this option only if you are confident in your abilities!

QUERYING WITH SQL

Creating Crosstab Queries

Crosstab queries are like spreadsheets in that they both summarize data based on three values: a row value, a column value, and data that represents the intersection of a row and column. If, for example, you want to search the books in your library to see how many pages a certain author had written for certain publishers, you can use a Crosstab query.

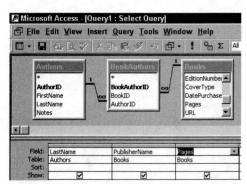

Figure 5.27 Select fields from various tables.

To create a Crosstab query:

1. Create a new select query in Design View.

    For this example we added the Authors, Book Authors, and Books tables to the query design screen. From there, we selected the LastName field from the Authors table and the PublisherName and Pages fields from the Books table (**Figure 5.27**).

2. Choose Query > Crosstab Query (**Figure 5.28**).

    When you select Crosstab Query from the Query menu, a Crosstab row appears in the design grid.

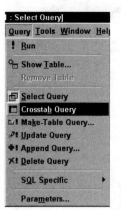

Figure 5.28 The Crosstab Query menu item.

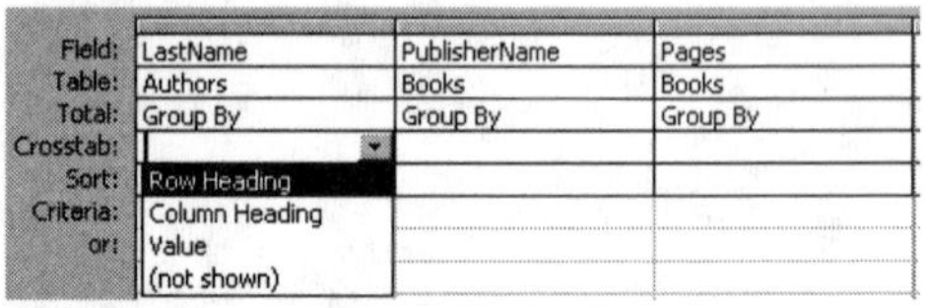

3. Click the Crosstab cell under the field you want to use as your row heading. Click the drop-down menu button that appears and choose Row Heading (**Figure 5.29**).

4. Do the same for the field that contains your column headings, but choose Column Heading from the drop-down menu. We used the PublisherName field (**Figure 5.30**).

Figure 5.29 Choose your row heading...

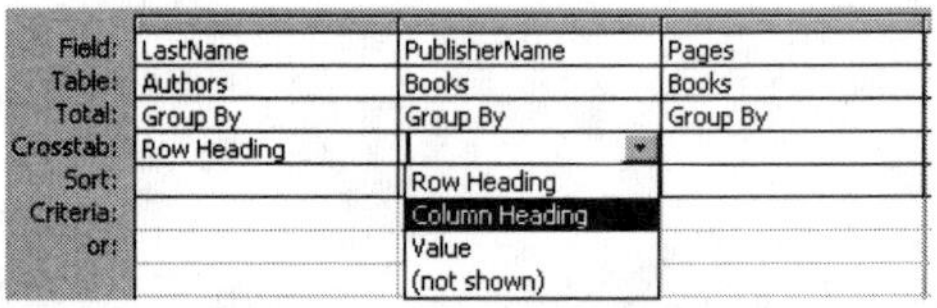

5. Click the Crosstab cell under the field that contains the data for the body of the query, click the drop-down menu button that appears, and choose Value from the menu (**Figure 5.31**).

Figure 5.30 ...and your column heading...

6. You're not quite done with the field that will be providing your values. Click in the Total cell, click the drop-down menu

Field:	LastName	PublisherName	Pages
Table:	Authors	Books	Books
Total:	Group By	Group By	Group By
Crosstab:	Row Heading	Column Heading	
Sort:			Row Heading
Criteria:			Column Heading
or:			Value
			(not shown)

Figure 5.31 ...the source of your Values...

Field:	LastName	PublisherName	Pages
Table:	Authors	Books	Books
Total:	Group By	Group By	Group By
Crosstab:	Row Heading	Column Heading	Group By
Sort:			Sum
Criteria:			Avg
or:			Min
			Max
			Count
			StDev
			Var

Figure 5.32 ...and how you want to summarize your data.

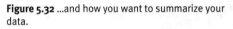

Field:	LastName	PublisherName	Pages
Table:	Authors	Books	Books
Total:	Group By	Group By	Sum
Crosstab:	Row Heading	Column Heading	Value
Sort:			

Figure 5.33 Click the Run button and you'll be off and running.

button that appears, and choose Sum (**Figure 5.32**).

The options in the Total drop-down menu represent the different types of summaries Access can perform on the data in the Value column.

7. Your Crosstab query will calculate the pages each author has written for each publisher. Click the Run button to run it (**Figure 5.33**).

✔ Tips

■ If the data doesn't appear in your Crosstab query, the tables in the design window may not be related; you'll need to build a special table to create a relationship between the tables in your query. See Chapter 8 for instructions on creating relationships.

■ There is a Crosstab Query Wizard, but it limits you to working with values found in one table or query. Use it if you want, but unless all your data's in one place it's actually less work to create a Select query and change it to a Crosstab query in Design view.

CREATING CROSSTAB QUERIES

Calculating in Queries

Not only can you use Crosstab queries to summarize the data in your tables, but you can perform calculations on your data (such as finding sums, averages, and standard deviations) and display the output in your query results. For this example, we'll create a calculation to estimate the length of the first drafts of the books in our library.

To perform calculations in queries:

1. Create a query in Design view and add the tables and fields you want to use.

   For this example we added the Authors, BookAuthors, and Books tables to the query design screen. From there, we selected the LastName field from the Authors table and the PublisherName and Pages fields from the Books table.

2. Click the next open Field cell and type the expression you want to use to calculate the value for the field (**Figure 5.34**).

   We entered a simple expression to estimate the pages in the first draft of a book, but yours can be as complex as you like. If you want to use the Expression Builder, click the Build button (**Figure 5.35**).

3. Click the Run button to set your query in motion (**Figure 5.36**).

✔ Tip

■ You can name the field that displays your calculation's results by typing "FieldName: " at the beginning of the calculation. For example, you can type "DraftLength: ." Make sure you follow the colon with a space so that Access doesn't confuse the name you give the calculated field with the name of an existing field.

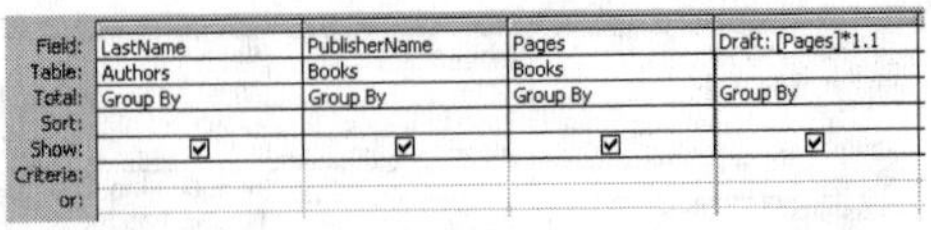

Field:	LastName	PublisherName	Pages	Draft: [Pages]*1.1
Table:	Authors	Books	Books	
Total:	Group By	Group By	Group By	Group By
Sort:				
Show:	☑	☑	☑	☑
Criteria:				
or:				

Figure 5.34 Type the calculation you want to perform in the next open Field cell.

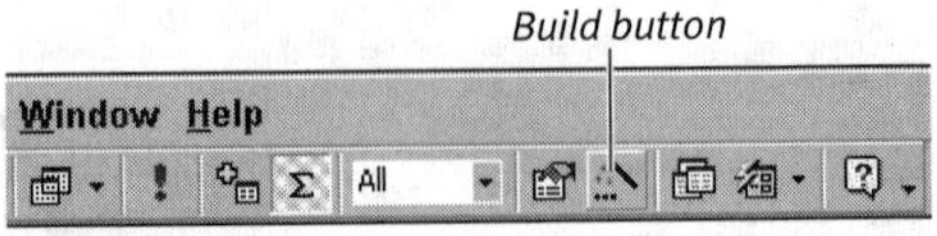

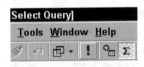

Figure 5.35 Build your new expression using the Expression Builder.

Figure 5.36 You're off and running again!

Field:	LastName
Table:	Authors
Total:	Group By
Sort:	
Show:	☑

Figure 5.37 A simple yet powerful checkbox.

Specifying Fields to Appear in Results

By now you've probably come up with a solid query that presents your data just the way you want. The problem is that you've invited all of these fields to help you with your data, but you don't necessarily want them all to show up in the results. For instance, if you use a field in a calculation but don't want the field the calculation's based on to appear in the query's results, you can hide that field

To specify which fields appear in the results:

◆ Click the checkbox in the Show cell under the field you want to show or hide. If the box is checked, the field appears in the results. If the box is cleared, it doesn't appear (**Figure 5.37**).

✔ Tip

■ When you close a query with hidden fields, Access automatically moves those fields to the right edge of the design grid.

CALCULATING IN QUERIES

89

WORKING WITH REPORTS

Manipulating data through tables or forms is pretty straightforward, although if you're viewing data only Datasheet view can display more than one record at a time. So, for more sophisticated data views, Access allows you to create reports.

You can use reports to present the contents of your tables and queries, perform calculations on the contents of your database objects, and even print address labels.

One way to think of forms and reports is as the input and output channels of table data. With forms you can enter data through an easily understood interface, while reports present that information in an easy-to-read format. You'll usually work with reports when you need to print out information that you obtain through queries.

Look at Reports

Reports are objects that present table contents or query results in an easily assimilated format. We'll show you a report in Design view (**Figure 6.1**) to give you a look at how reports are put together.

1 Menu bar

The menu bar appears at the top of the Access window and makes all of the program's commands available to you.

2 Page header

The page header contains information and graphics that appear at the top of every page in your report. This section is a good place to put headers for the fields used in your report.

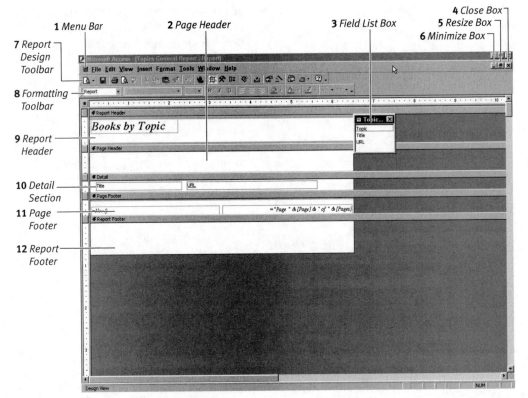

Figure 6.1 A report, in Design view.

3 Field list box

The field list box displays the fields you've chosen to work with in your report.

4 Report close box

The report close box closes the report you're working on without shutting down Access.

5 Report resize box

The report resize box expands your report to fill the entire Access window or shrinks it to its last unexpanded size.

6 Report minimize box

The report minimize box collapses the report you're working on to a bar within the main database window.

7 Report design toolbar

The report design toolbar presents buttons for many basic commands like saving, sorting, and printing your report's contents.

8 Formatting (Form/Report) toolbar

The Formatting (Form/Report) toolbar presents buttons that allow you to change the font, color, line width, and other aspects of items in your report.

9 Report header

The report header contains information and graphics that appear at the top of the first page of your report. You could put the title of your report in this section, for instance.

10 Detail section

The detail section contains the data from the table or query used to create your report.

11 Page footer

The page footer contains information and graphics that appear at the bottom of every page in your report.

12 Report footer

The report footer contains information and graphics that appear at the bottom of the last page in the report.

Viewing Reports

You use reports to generate a nicely formatted summary of information within the database. A report is divided into five sections: *detail, page headers, page footers, report headers,* and *report footers.*

Records from the table or query underlying the report are displayed in the report's detail section. Most of the design choices you'll make change how the detail section presents your data.

Page headers and footers are placed at the top and bottom of each page of your report, respectively. Page headers are great places to put column titles and other explanatory notes that you want to appear on each page of your report (such as page numbers).

Report headers and footers are like page headers and footers, but they only occur at the very top of the first page and at the bottom of the last page in your report.

To view reports:

1. Open the database you want to use. Make sure that the database window is visible.

2. Click Reports at the left side of the database window (**Figure 6.2**).

3. Select a report and click Preview at the top of the Database window to open and view the report (**Figure 6.3**).

   You can page through your report using the Navigation Bar at the bottom left of the report window.

✔ Tip

■ You can find out basic information about your reports such as when they were created and modified last, by clicking the report's name in the main database window, and then clicking the Properties toolbar button. You can do the same for other objects in your database as well.

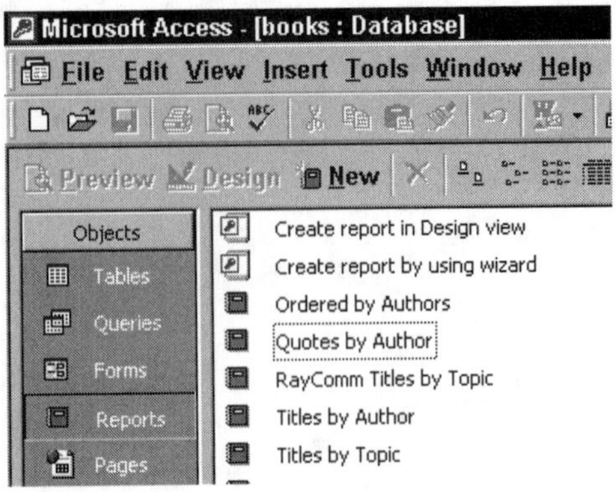

Figure 6.2 Open a report by selecting one from the list provided.

Figure 6.3 Move from page to page in your report using the Navigation Bar.

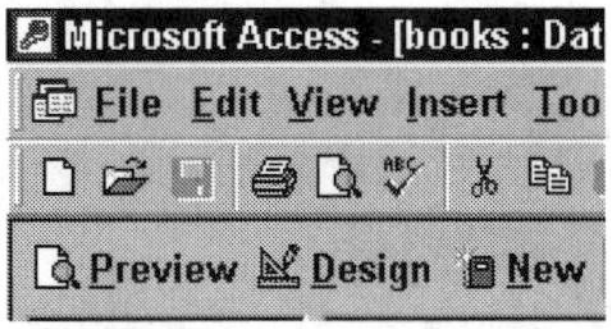

Figure 6.4 Open your report in Design view.

Modifying Existing Reports

You can assign fields, grouping levels, and formatting elements to your report from scratch, or while you're stepping through the Report Wizard. You can change your report's design at any time using the techniques in this chapter and those in Chapter 4.

To modify an existing report:

1. Select the report you want to open.

2. Click the Design toolbar button (**Figure 6.4**).

   Your report appears in Design view. You can relocate, redefine, and remove any item you wish using the skills you learned in Chapter 4.

✔ Tip

■ If you want to see how your report will look when it's printed, choose File > Print Preview. If you prefer using toolbars, just click the Print Preview button on the report toolbar.

Understanding Report Types

Access lets you create three types of reports, each with its own strengths:

◆ **Columnar reports** display a single record on a page, making them ideal for detailed reports on items in a collection, such as CDs or books.

◆ **Tabular reports** are like datasheets in that they are row-oriented, with the fields of the table or query behind the report represented as a column on the page. Each row contains the full contents of one record.

◆ **Justified reports** combine the Columnar report's emphasis on highlighting individual records and the Tabular report's emphasis on saving space by packing the table or query's fields into as small a space as possible. Unlike a Tabular report, which gives each field a uniform width, a Justified report uses the width defined in the table or query's definition to determine each field's width.

Creating New Reports with a Wizard

The mass-market science magazines from the 1950s and 1960s offered a lot of predictions about what gadgets would be invented by the year 2000 to make your life easier. We still haven't received the robot maid we ordered in 1965, but we did discover a handy wizard that makes creating Access reports a snap.

To create a new report with a wizard:

1. Click the Reports icon in the Objects pane of the main database window and double-click Create report by using wizard.

2. In the first wizard window, click the Tables/Queries drop-down menu and choose the table or query you want to base your report on (**Figure 6.5**).

   You can choose fields from more than one table or query.

3. Click the first field you want to add to your report and click the > button (**Figure 6.6**). Click Next when you're done.

4. Click the name of a field you want to group your report by and click the > button to establish it as a group criteria. Click Next when you're ready to continue (**Figure 6.7**).

   Grouping a report by the contents of a field arranges your records according to the values in that field. For instance, if you grouped a report on books by the year they were published, all of the books from the earliest year would appear first, followed by the books from the next earliest year, and so forth.

5. Select which (if any) fields you want to sort your report's contents by (**Figure 6.8**). Use the drop-down menus to select

Figure 6.5 Choose a table or query for your report.

Figure 6.6 Click the Add button to include fields in your report.

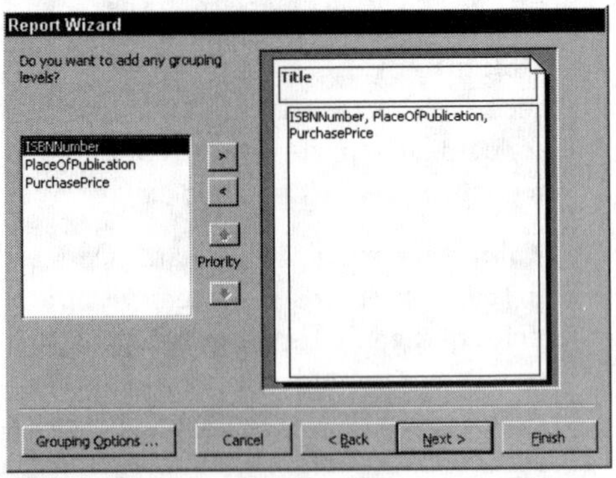

Figure 6.7 Use this Add button to tell Access which fields you want it to use to group records in your report.

Figure 6.8 Specify which fields Access should use to sort your report's contents.

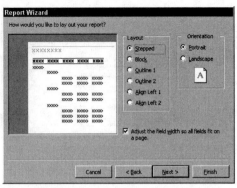

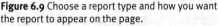

Figure 6.9 Choose a report type and how you want the report to appear on the page.

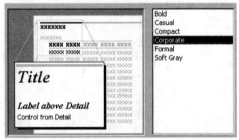

Figure 6.10 Click the name of the AutoFormat you want to assign your report.

Creating an AutoReport

Using a wizard to create a report is easy, but it takes a little bit of time. If you'd rather create a simple report in a few seconds, you can create an AutoReport.

1. From the list in the main database window, select the table you want to draw data from for your report.

2. Click the drop-down menu button attached to the New Object toolbar button and choose AutoReport from the menu that appears.

Your AutoReport appears in Print Preview mode. The layout, color, and font of the report depends on the AutoFormat you chose when you created it, and the fonts you have installed on your system.

the field(s) you want to sort on. Click Next when you're done.

The order in which you enter the fields in this screen determines their priority in sorting the report's contents.

6. Click the option button next to the type of report you want to create (**Figure 6.9**). Choose portrait (short side up) or landscape (long side up) mode. Click Next to continue.

See the "Understanding Report Types" sidebar in the preceding section for a quick rundown of the types of reports you can create.

7. Select a style for your report by clicking a style name in the right-hand pane (**Figure 6.10**). Click Next to continue.

A preview of the style you selected appears in the left-hand pane. You'll learn how to reformat your reports later in this chapter.

8. Last screen! Type a name for your report in the space provided and click Finish.

If you'd rather modify your report than look at its contents, click the Modify the report's design option button.

✔ Tips

■ You can change the priority of a grouping field by clicking the field's name in the right-hand pane of the window and clicking the up or down arrow buttons.

■ If you want to sort the contents of a field in descending order (for example, more recent publication dates first) rather than ascending, click the button to the right of the field name (**Figure 6.8**). A field sorted in ascending order is represented by a 🔳 button, one in descending order by a 🔳 button.

Formatting Reports with AutoFormats

If you created a report with the Report Wizard then you had a chance to select an AutoFormat for the finished product. If you created your report from scratch and want to assign a pre-fab format to it, or if you want to change the AutoFormat you chose when you created your report in the wizard, you can select an AutoReport from the list available in the wizard.

To format a report using an AutoFormat:

1. In Design view, open the report you want to reformat.

2. Choose Format > AutoFormat.

3. Fom the list of available AutoFormats (**Figure 6.11**), select the AutoFormat you want to use and click OK.

   A preview of the AutoFormat appears in the left-hand pane of the window.

✔ Tips

- You can choose which elements of the AutoFormat you want to apply by clicking Options and selecting or deselecting the checkboxes next to the Font, Border, and Color elements (**Figure 6.12**).

- To create your own AutoFormat, first create a style for your report, then open the AutoFormat window, click the Customize button, and click the Create a new Auto-Format option button (**Figure 6.13**).

Figure 6.11 Assign an AutoFormat to your report from the AutoFormat list.

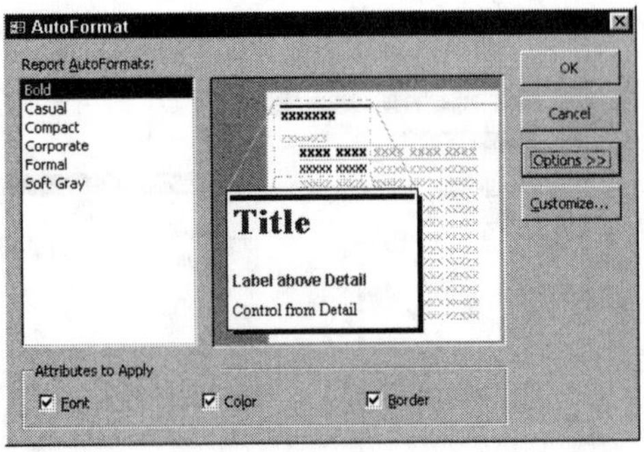

Figure 6.12 You can choose which pieces of an AutoFormat to apply to your report...

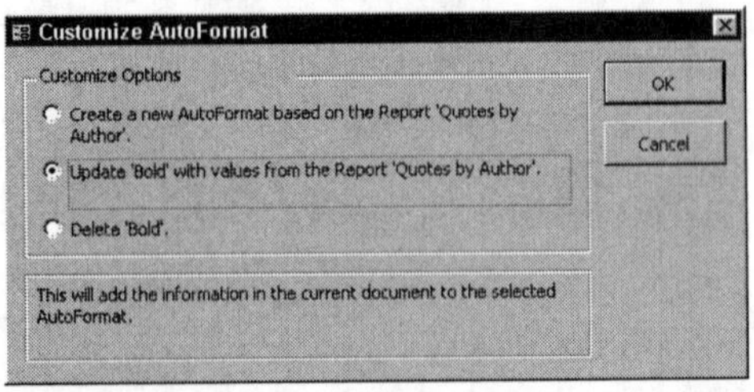

Figure 6.13 ...or you can create your own AutoFormat based on the design of your current report.

Figure 6.14 Click the Design button to make your report amenable to change.

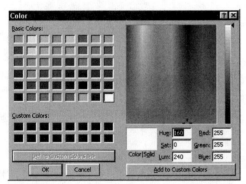

Figure 6.15 Use the drop-down menu on the toolbar that corresponds to the aspect of your report element you'd like to change.

Figure 6.16 Select your color (and its brightness) from the spectrum.

Formatting Reports in Design View

You can use AutoFormats to add some life to your reports, but if you don't care for any of the prefabricated designs and want to design your own, you can modify the appearance of every element on your report. You can change the color of any element (the report's background, fore/font color of an object, line/border color, back/fill color, and so on); the font and size of text; or the alignment of the text (centered, left-justified, or right-justified) among other options.

To format reports in Design view:

1. Select a report.

2. Click the Design button (**Figure 6.14**) to open your report in Design view.

3. Click the report element you want to reformat and click the Formatting (Form/Report) toolbar button that modifies the element you chose (**Figure 6.15**).

✔ Tip

■ If you want to assign a custom color, right-click the element, choose Properties from the pop-up menu that appears, click the property you want to change (for example, Back Color) and click the Build button. In the dialog box that appears, click Define Custom Colors and choose the color you want from the spectrum. Click OK when you're done (**Figure 6.16**).

Fine-Tuning Your Reports

After you've created your report, you may wish you'd included a certain field and left another one out. You don't need to create a completely new report to make these changes–you can dive right into Design view, remove the fields you don't want, and add the ones you do.

To fine-tune your reports:

1. In Design view, open the report you want to modify.

2. To add a field, click the Field List button on the Report Design toolbar (**Figure 6.17**). A list of all of the fields in the table or query you used to create your report appears.

3. Click the name of the field you want to add. When you've finished adding fields, click the Close button at the top right of the Field List box.

✔ Tips

■ To remove a field, simply click it (but *don't* click the label to the left of the field itself) and press Delete (**Figure 6.18**).

■ If you'd like to rename a field, click the label and type a new value in the box. The field is still tied to the same element of the underlying table or query.

■ You can drag a control or field from one place to another by moving the mouse pointer over the control, pressing and holding down the left mouse button, and dragging the control to its new location.

■ You can add more than one instance of a field to your report if you'd like. For instance, if you have a report that lists the fields in an order, you can put the OrderID next to each item so that users can refer to the order quickly, regardless of where they are in the report.

Figure 6.17 Display the list of fields you can add to your report by clicking the Field List button.

Topic Header

| Topic | Topic |

Figure 6.18 To remove a field from your report, click the text area that displays a field's contents—not the label—and press Delete.

Figure 6.19 Create a new report to contain your mailing labels.

New Report

This wizard creates a report formatted for printing on labels.

Design View
Report Wizard
AutoReport: Columnar
AutoReport: Tabular
Chart Wizard
Label Wizard

Choose the table or query where the object's data comes from: Contacts

OK   Cancel

Figure 6.20 Choose the Label Wizard from the list of wizards.

Label Wizard

This wizard creates standard labels or custom labels.

What label size would you like?

Product number:	Dimensions:	Number across:
5095	2 1/2" x 3 3/8"	2
5096	2 3/4" x 2 3/4"	3
5097	1 1/2" x 4"	2
5160	1" x 2 5/8"	3
5161	1" x 4"	2

Unit of Measure
● English   ○ Metric

Label Type
● Sheet feed   ○ Continuous

Filter by manufacturer: Avery

Customize...

Cancel   < Back   Next >   Finish

Figure 6.21 Pick the brand of labels you're using.

Making Mailing Labels

One of the more popular reasons for keeping a database is to maintain a list of names and mailing addresses so you can send out notices, invitations, and common holiday letters. We can't help you overcome the guilt of writing one-size-fits-all holiday cards, but we can tell you how to use Access to create the labels for the envelopes.

For information about performing mail merges (using table contents to flesh out form letters in Microsoft Word) see Chapter 12.

To create mailing labels:

1. Select the table from which you want to get the names and addresses for your mailing labels.

2. Click the New Object drop-down menu and choose Report (**Figure 6.19**).

3. Click Label Wizard and click OK (**Figure 6.20**).

   The table selected appears in the box at the bottom of the window.

4. Select the specific brand and model of the labels you're using. The list is quite extensive (**Figure 6.21**).

(continued on next page)

MAKING MAILING LABELS

5. Use the drop-down menu buttons to select the font, size, style, and color of the type to appear on your labels (**Figure 6.22**). Click Next when you're done.

Clicking the Build button next to Color launches the Color dialog box. You can choose one of the colors from the color palette or click the Define Custom Colors button to see a complete spectrum.

6. Click the first field you want to add and click the > button (**Figure 6.23**). Add the fields and spacing you want and click Next when the label appears exactly the way you want it to when it's printed.

7. Click the first field you'd like Access to sort your records by and click the > button (**Figure 6.24**). Click Next when you're done.

You can add as many fields as you'd like. Access sorts on the fields in the order that you entered them. The field at the top of the sorting priority list is at the top of the field list in the Sort by pane.

8. Type a name for your report in the space provided and click Finish.

✔ Tips

■ If you'd like to open the Labels Report in Design view, select the Modify the Label Design option.

■ You'll need to add the punctuation and spacing you want to include on your labels. For instance, add FirstName, type a space, and add LastName. After LastName type Enter, add the street address, and type Enter again. Enter the city (followed by a comma and a space), state or province (followed by a space), and postal code.

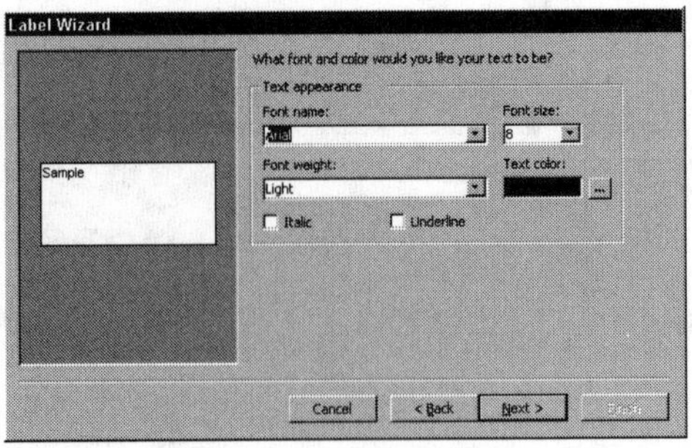

Figure 6.22 Choose a font for your labels.

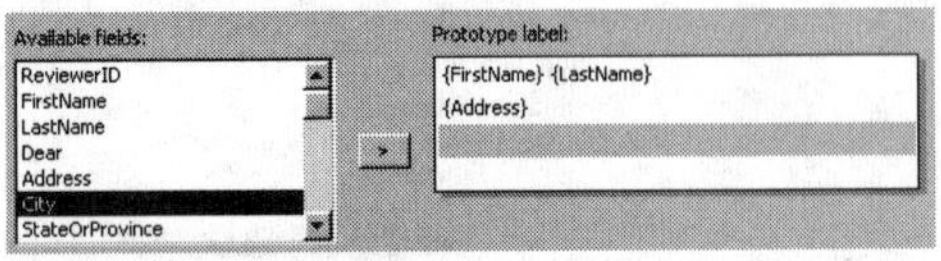

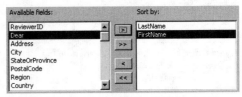

Figure 6.23 Add fields to the sample label on the screen. Don't forget to add spaces and punctuation!

Figure 6.24 Assign a sort field (or fields) to set the order in which you want to print your labels.

Figure 6.25 Click the Print toolbar button to print your entire report.

Printing a Report

Once you've designed your report, you should print a copy. Not only does printing a hard copy of your report give you a snapshot of your data at the time the report is printed, but it's also handy to have a hard copy around. If you see items that should be modified, you can refer to your hard copy while you make changes.

To print a report:

1. Display the reports in your database and double-click the report you want to print. The report appears in Print Preview mode.

2. Choose File > Print and fill in the boxes telling Access which range of pages to print, which printer to use, and so forth.

✔ Tip

■ If you want to print an entire report, you can click the Print button on the toolbar (**Figure 6.25**).

Saving a Report as a Word Document

One nice thing about Access is that it's part of the Microsoft Office 2000 family of programs. You can export your tables to spreadsheets and save your reports as Microsoft Word documents. Once in Word you can do things with your documents that would be tougher if they were still in Access, such as include all or part of a report in another Word document.

To save a report as a Word document:

1. Open your report in Print Preview mode.

2. Click the Office Links drop-down menu button and choose Publish It With MS Word (**Figure 6.26**).

   Access saves a copy of your document as a Word file.

✔ Tip

■ You can also export your file to Excel by clicking the Office Links drop-down menu button and choosing Analyze It with MS Excel.

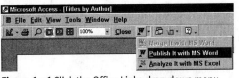

Figure 6.26 Click the Office Links drop-down menu button to save your report as an Office object.

FINDING, FILTERING, AND SORTING

If a table has only a handful of records, it's easy to scroll through it and find the information you need. But if you're the impatient type, or if your table has too many records to scroll through, you can search for records that fit any criteria you care to define.

You can also *filter* and *sort* your data. Though filtering and sorting are similar, they have one important difference: where *sorting* a table arranges the table's records according to the criteria you set, *filtering* finds records that match a set of criteria, and hides any remaining records in the table. You can sort your filter's results as well, so don't think filtering and sorting are mutually exclusive.

Choosing Filters or Queries

On the surface, *filters* and *queries* (see Chapters 4 and 10 for information on queries) seem similar, but they are actually quite different. A filter *temporarily* modifies the contents of a table; you can turn a filter on and off by clicking a button or selecting a menu item. By contrast, a query is a separate object in your database and can't be "turned off," only modified and run to update its contents.

You should use Find to locate instances of a certain value within a table. Scrolling through large tables can be time-consuming, but going from record to record does let you see the type of record your value appears in. You might run a query to narrow the number of records, and then use Find to examine the results.

You should also run a query if you want to:

◆ See the contents of fields from more than one table.

◆ Hide fields used to select records for your results. (For instance, if you want your query results to list every company to whom you've sold over $10,000 of merchandise in the past year but you don't need to see the exact amount of sales, you could use a field titled OrderTotal in the query but not that field's contents in the results.)

◆ Calculate values based on the contents of fields in your results (See Chapter 4).

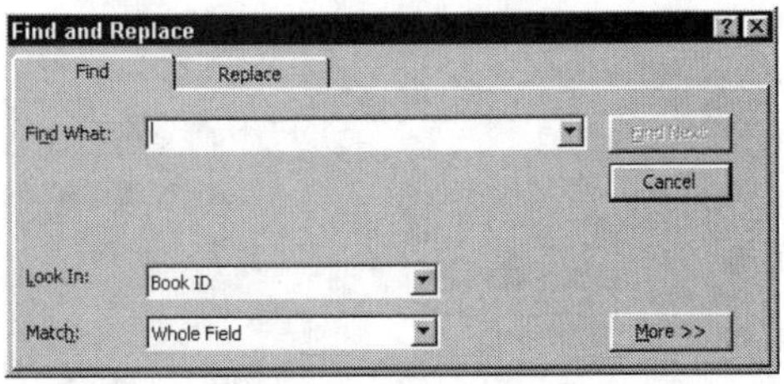

Figure 7.1 Use the Find and Replace dialog box to search for values in your tables and query results

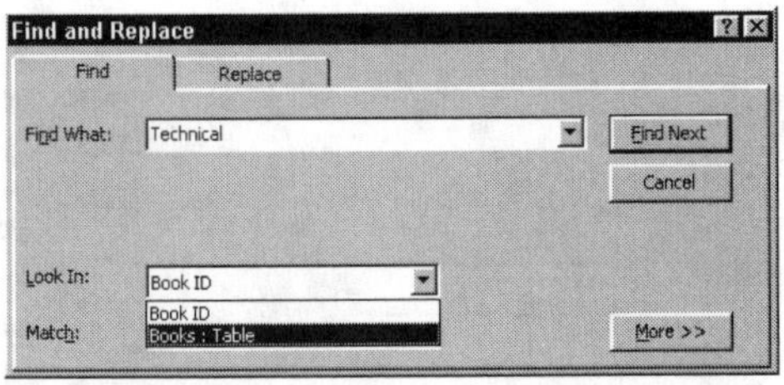

Figure 7.2 Search for a value by selecting a field from the Look In drop-down menu.

Finding Records

Some databases contain so much information that it becomes impossible to locate specific records, or even related sets of records. Follow the directions in this task to locate your data needles without getting "pricked."

Access can search for values that match the case of the term you entered. For example, a search for "Mark" with the Match Case checkbox selected limits searches to the first name "Mark," not every single appearance of "mark" used as a noun or verb. You can also require the value you're searching for to occur anywhere in the field (the default choice), to occur at the beginning of a field, or to be the entire value in a field.

To find records:

1. In Datasheet view, open the table or run a query that contains the record(s) you want to find.

2. Select Edit > Find.

   The Find and Replace dialog box appears (**Figure 7.1**).

3. Type a value or term you want to find in the Find What text box.

4. Click the Look In drop-down menu and search for a value by selecting a field (**Figure 7.2**). Click Find Next.

   Access highlights the first instance of the value it finds. Click Find Next again to move to the next example, or click Cancel to close the Find and Replace dialog box. Access warns you when it can't find any more instances of the value.

FINDING RECORDS

To match the case of your value:

1. Open the Find and Replace dialog box and type the value or term you want to search for in the Find What text box.

2. Click More (**Figure 7.3**).

   An additional set of options appears at the bottom of the dialog box.

3. Click the Match Case checkbox to search for a case-sensitive value. Click Find Next (**Figure 7.4**).

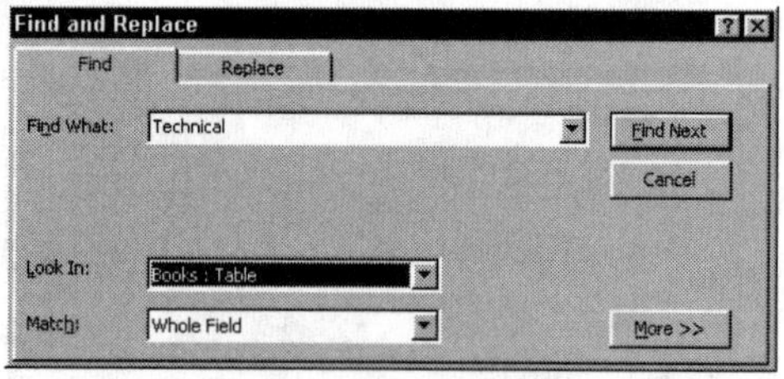

✔ Tips

■ Access saves all of your previous search terms. To find a value you previously searched for, click the drop-down menu in the Find What text box, and select a value from the list.

■ You don't always have to match the entire value in a field. If you click the Match drop-down menu, you can search Access based on the Whole Field, Any Part of the Field, or the Start of the Field. For instance, click Start of Field and type mas in the Find What text box to return "Masters," "Mason," and "Maslich."

■ You can have Access search for records that come before or after the current record in the database by clicking More, and choosing Up or Down from the Search drop-down menu that appears.

Figure 7.3 Click the More button to give you more options in the Find and Replace dialog box.

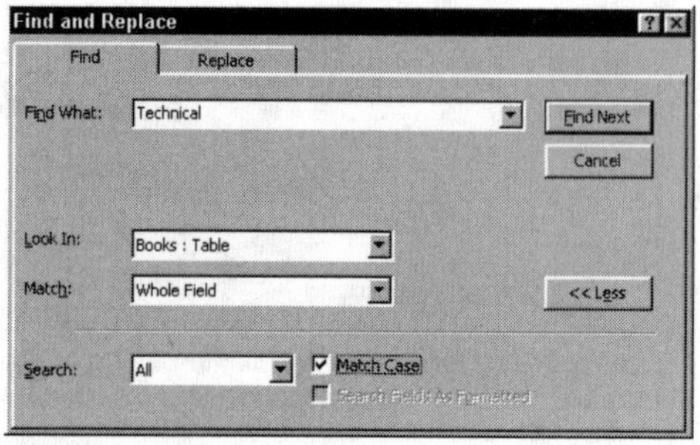

Figure 7.4 Selecting the Match Case checkbox requires a term that exactly matches your search term's capitalization and spelling.

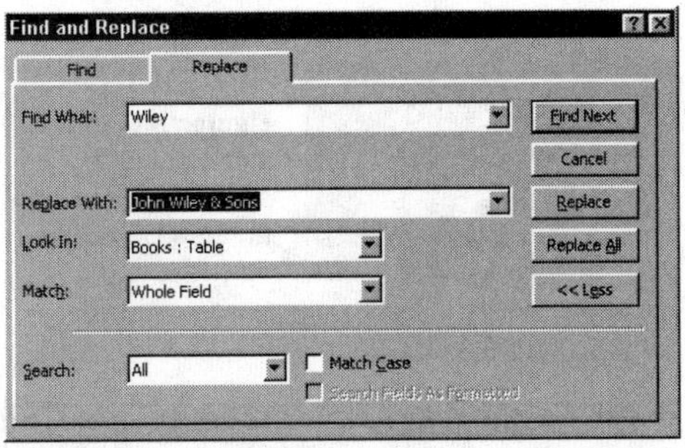

Figure 7.5 Click the Find Next button to locate the next instance of your search term in the table.

Figure 7.6 Click Replace to insert your new value in place of the old one.

Finding and Replacing Data

Have you ever found out that you've been mispronouncing one of your favorite words for years? Or that you've consistently misspelled something in your database? Access can easily replace misspelled words (or any other value that needs changing) with the correct version.

Finding and replacing data is a handy way to update ZIP codes, area codes, and business names that have changed. The Find feature quickly locates each individual record that contains a particular value. Of course, you can also write a query to find those records, but using Find is often the quicker way to go.

To find and replace data:

1. Open the table containing the data you want to find and replace.

2. Select Edit > Find. The Find and Replace dialog box appears.

3. Click the Replace tab.

4. Type a value in the Find What text box, and then type the value you want to replace it with in the Replace With text box.

5. Click Find Next (**Figure 7.5**).

6. Click Replace to replace the value in the field with the value in the Replace With text box (**Figure 7.6**).

✔ Tip

■ You can tell Access to limit its replacements to instances of the Find value above or below the active record. Click More to expand the dialog box options, click the drop-down menu in the Search text area, and then select Above or Below. Choose All to have Access search the entire field or table regardless of where you began the search.

Finding Duplicates

Duplicate records in a database can be a hindrance. Sending a form business letter to the same client more than once costs you extra postage and makes you look silly. With Access, you can find duplicate values in your tables and eliminate duplicate records of the same entity (like two records referring to the same client but with a slight difference, such as records that abbreviate or spell out "Suite" in an address). You can also verify when similar records represent distinct entries in your table.

To find duplicate records:

1. Click the New Object drop-down menu and select Query. (**Figure 7.7**).

2. Select Find Duplicates Query Wizard and click OK (**Figure 7.8**).

3. On the first wizard screen, select the name of the table or query in which you want to search for duplicate values. Click Next (**Figure 7.9**).

4. In the Available fields pane, select a field that might contain duplicate information and click the > button to add it to the Duplicate-value fields pane. Click Next (**Figure 7.10**).

   You can click the >> button to add all of the fields, or select a field and click the < button to remove it from the Duplicate-value fields pane.You can remove all of the fields by clicking the << button.

5. Add any other fields you want to display in your query's results, and then click Next.

6. Type a name for your query in the space provided. Click Finish.

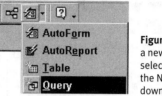

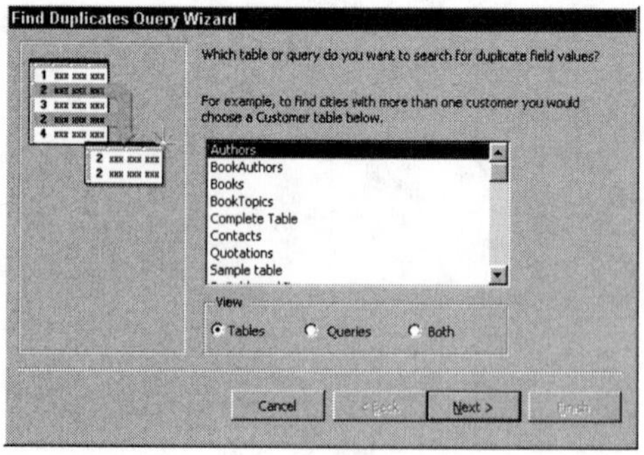

Figure 7.7 Create a new query by selecting Query from the New Object drop-down menu.

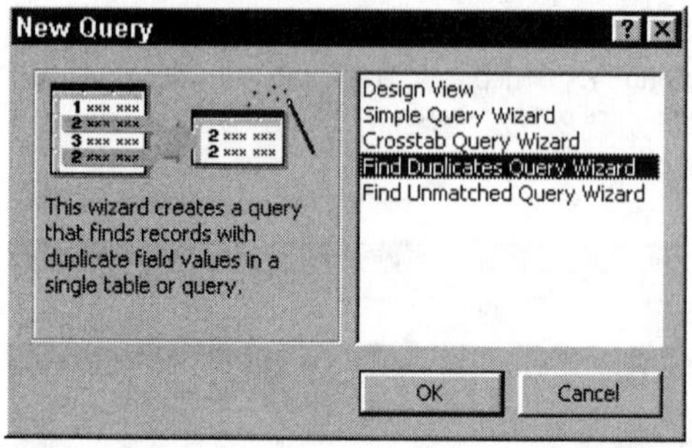

Figure 7.8 Select Find Duplicates from the menu.

Figure 7.9 Click the table in which you want to look for duplicate values.

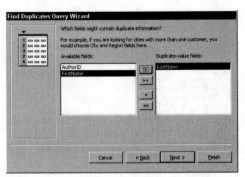

Figure 7.10 Select the field (or fields) that might contain duplicate values.

✔ Tips

- If you want to change your query's design rather than display its results, click the Modify the Design option button in the last screen of the wizard.

- To save time when creating your duplicate query, look for duplicates in fields that won't vary (a person's last name will always be entered the same way, as opposed to a street address, which might be entered as Avenue or Ave.) and visually compare the records. For instance, searching for "Jones" in the LastName field could show records for "Mike Jones" and "Michael Jones."

Finding Unmatched Records

Sometimes you need to know if records in one table have no matching records in a related table. If you're running a business, for instance, it's handy to see which of your sales leads has generated business. It's also important, if not more so, to know which of those leads hasn't produced any business so you can call on those potential clients again. Here's how to create a query to do just that.

To find unmatched records:

1. Click the New Object drop-down menu and select Query.

2. Select Find Unmatched Query Wizard and click OK (**Figure 7.11**).

3. On the first wizard screen, select the table or query that contains the records you want to appear in the search results, and then click Next (**Figure 7.12**).

   That is, select the table with records that may not have corresponding records in another table. For this example, we'll use our Contacts table.

4. Select the table or query to compare the first table to and then click Next (**Figure 7.13**).

   In our example, we want to see how many of our friends are non-authors, so we select Authors.

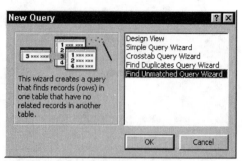

Figure 7.11 Select the Find Unmatched Query Wizard from the New Query dialog box.

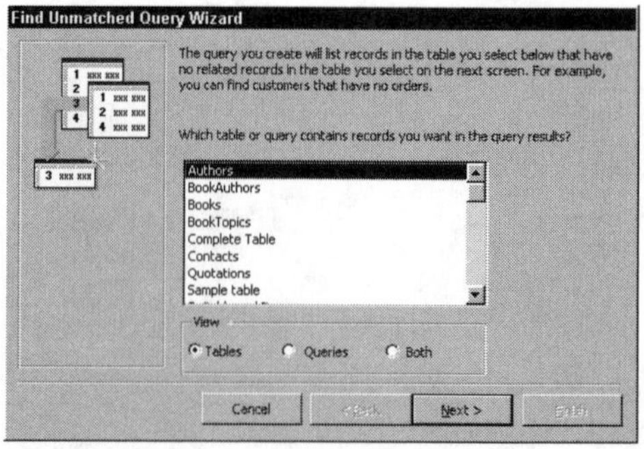

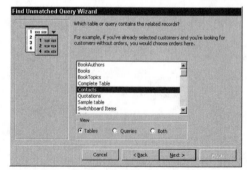

Figure 7.12 Select the table containing the values you want to check for matches...

Figure 7.13 ...and select the table containing the values you want to match with.

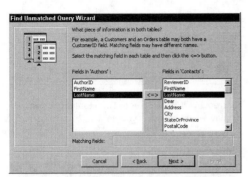

Figure 7.14 Select the fields that might contain matching values, and then click the <=> button.

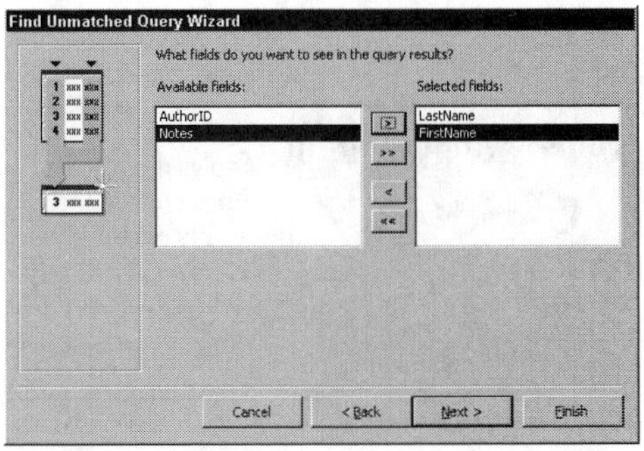

Figure 7.15 Add the fields that you want to appear in your results.

5. Select the related fields in the two tables and click the <=> button (**Figure 7.14**).

   In this case the field we want is called LastName in both tables.

   Click Next.

6. Select a field name in the left pane and click the > button to add it to your query results. Click Next (**Figure 7.15**).

7. Type a name for your query in the text box at the top of the checkered flag screen and click Finish.

   Just in case you're interested, our query turned up 41 (out of 62) of our contacts that aren't authors.

✔ Tip

- Unmatched records on the "one" side of a one-to-many relationship aren't usually a problem—a customer may not have placed an order yet or you may not have received a response to a survey from the individual in question. Unmatched records on the "many" side of the relationship, on the other hand, require investigation. If you received an order from a customer who isn't in your client database, for example, you should make sure you get contact information from the client to enter into your customer contact table.

FINDING UNMATCHED RECORDS

Filtering with Forms

Access makes it easy to search for data in your tables and determine if certain values repeat in a table or appear in a related table. Another handy skill is filtering, or *limiting* the data Access displays from a table. Filtering by form is a simple way to do just that.

When you filter a table or query by form, you can enter values for one, some, or all of the fields in your table or query. You can also use *wildcards* (discussed in Chapter 4) to expand the number of records caught in your filter.

Filtering by form is a handy way to find records in a large database when you know more than one value in the record but can't seem to locate it. By limiting the number of records shown in your table, you can use Filter by form to find records (or sets of records) more easily.

To filter with forms:

1. In Datasheet view, open the table that you want to filter.

2. Click the Filter By Forms toolbar button (**Figure 7.16**).

   A simple form representing the fields in your table appears.

3. Type (or select from a drop-down menu) the values you want Access to use when it filters your table (**Figure 7.17**).

   In this example, we typed **A*** into the LastName field to find every author with a last name that begins with "A."

4. Click the Apply Filter toolbar button. (**Figure 7.18**).

   Access displays the filtered table. Click the Apply Filter button to remove (or reapply) the filter.

Filter by Form button

Figure 7.16 Click the Filter by Form toolbar button to display a form based on your table.

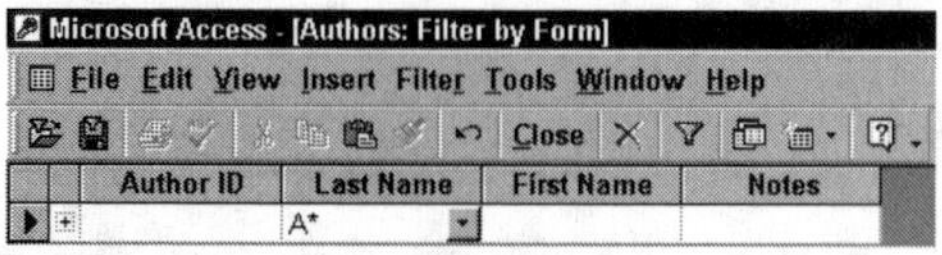

Figure 7.17 Use the form based on your table to enter values to filter your table or query.

Figure 7.18 Click the Apply Filter toolbar button to see the results of your filter.

✔ Tips

- To save your filter as a query, click the Save As Query toolbar button while you're viewing the filter.

- To apply a query as a filter, click the Load from Query toolbar button, select the query you want to load, and then click OK.

Filtering by Selection

Filtering by selection allows you to select the values that you want to appear in the filtered version of your table. For example, if you want to see all of the books by authors with a particular first name, you should filter your table by selection. Selecting the name Peter from your table and filtering by selection returns books by authors with the first name of Peter.

To filter by selection:

1. In Datasheet view, open the table that you want to filter.

2. Click the cell containing the value you want to use as your filter criteria (**Figure 7.19**).

   This step is the "selection" part of the Filter by Selection operation. In this example, we want to see every book by authors with the first name of Peter, so we click a cell in the FirstName field containing the value Peter.

3. Click the Filter by Selection toolbar button. (**Figure 7.20**).

   The filtered version of your table appears displaying books by authors with the first name of Peter (**Figure 7.21**).

✔ Tip

- To filter by selection with more than one field, position the mouse pointer over the first field, press and hold down the left mouse button, and drag the pointer over the rest of the cells that contain the values you want to filter by. In our example, if we selected Peter from the FirstName field and Morville from the LastName field, the filtered table would display two records. Cells must be next to each other in the same record for this feature to work.

	18	Siegel	David	
	19	Horton	William	
	20	Rosenfeld	Louis	
▶	21	Morville	Peter	

Figure 7.19 Click the cell with the value you want to use as your filter criteria.

Figure 7.20 Click the Filter by Selection toolbar button to display only those records with the value you want to search for.

Filter by Selection button

Microsoft Access - [Authors : Table]

File Edit View Insert Format Records Tools Window H

Author ID	First Name	Last Name	Notes
▶ ⊞ 21	Peter	Morville	
⊞ 23	Peter	Kent	
⊞ 41	Peter	Morville	
* (AutoNumber)			

Figure 7.21 The table after the filter is appied.

FILTERING BY SELECTION

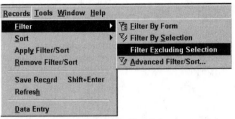

Figure 7.22 Select Filter Excluding Selection to show every record in your table or query that doesn't contain the value (or values) you selected.

		7	Henry	Korman	
		27	James	Mason	
		51	MS	Microsoft Corp.	
		58	Nancy	Mulvany	C.
		45	Jakob	Nielsen	
		60	Donald	Norman	
		5	Walter	Oliu	

Figure 7.23 After the filter is applied, your table doesn't show records for books by authors with the last name of Morville.

Filtering by Exclusion

Filtering by exclusion is the opposite of filtering by selection (see the previous section). Rather than displaying records containing the value or values you selected, filtering by exclusion hides records with the values you've chosen.

For example, you might want to filter a table or query by exclusion if one client placed the majority of orders for a particular sales period. By excluding that client's orders from the active view of your table, you can see what other customers in that territory are ordering, how often they are ordering, and (by applying and removing the filter) compare their orders to those of the high-volume client.

To filter by exclusion:

1. In Datasheet view, open the table that you want to filter.

2. Click the cell or cells containing the values you want to use as your filtering criteria.

   For this example we choose to exclude books by authors with the last name of Morville.

3. Select Records > Filter > Filter Excluding Selection (**Figure 7.22**).

   Your table will appear in filtered form excluding books written by authors with the last name of Morville (**Figure 7.23**).

✔ Tip

■ To switch between filtered and unfiltered views of your table, click the Apply Filter toolbar button.

Sorting Query Results

Rather than present your query results in the order that they occur in the component tables and queries, you can establish a *sort order* for the query's results based on the values in one or more fields of your results. For instance, you could create a query to find author names and sort the results of that query alphabetically by last name. You can establish different sort orders for different fields.

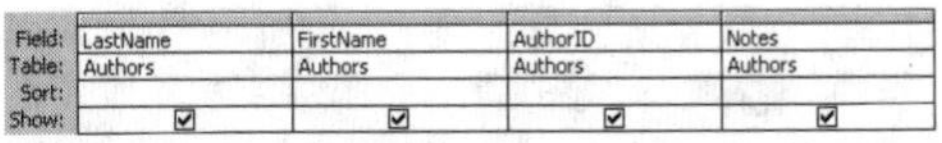

Figure 7.24 Access sorts the results of your query based on the fields' left-to-right order in the query design grid.

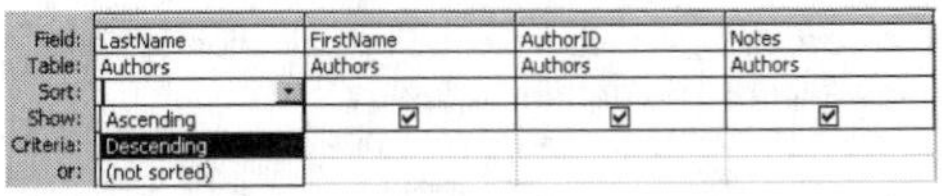

Figure 7.25 Select the sort method you want to apply to each field in your results.

To sort query results:

1. Open (or create) your query in Design view.

2. Arrange the fields in your query so the first field to sort by is the farthest to the left, the second field is next farthest to the left, and so forth (**Figure 7.24**).

   If you want Access to sort your query results based on the values in two fields, those two fields don't need to be the first and second fields in the query, but the fields must be in the proper left-to-right order in the query design grid.

3. Click the Sort cell of a field you want to sort your results by, and then click the drop-down menu that appears. Select the sort method you want to employ for that field (**Figure 7.25**).

   You can sort your results according to the selected field's values in ascending or descending order.

4. Choose the sort method to use for your other fields and click the Run button to see your results.

✔ Tips

■ To remove a query result field from your sort criteria, choose "(not sorted)" from the drop-down menu accessed via that field's Sort cell.

■ You can use different sort patterns on different fields to produce the results you want. For instance, if you wrote a query to return the names of the authors of books in your library, you could sort the LastName and FirstName fields in ascending order (starting with "A") and the CopyrightYear field in descending order. Under that scheme, if an author wrote more than one book you would see the author's most recent works first.

Sorting Table Records

When you enter records into a table, Access usually stores them in the order you entered them. If you created the table using a wizard, or if you created the table from scratch and included an AutoNumber field to keep track of your entries, the implied sort order (sorted by the order entered) is embodied in an AutoNumber field.

The default chronological sort order may not be the best choice if you would rather view your records in another order, such as alphabetically or by the date of a client's last purchase. Access makes it easy to change the sort order of records you enter into your tables.

To sort table records:

1. Click anywhere in the column that contains your sort criteria.

2. Click either the Sort Ascending (**Figure 7.26**) or the Sort Descending (**Figure 7.27**) toolbar button.

✔ Tip

■ To sort your table by more than one field, click the column selector of the first field you want to sort by, drag the mouse over the column selectors of the additional fields to sort the records by, and click either the Sort Ascending or Sort Descending button. The records must be adjacent in your table's Datasheet.

Figure 7.26 Sort your table in ascending order...

Figure 7.27 ...or descending order with one mouse click.

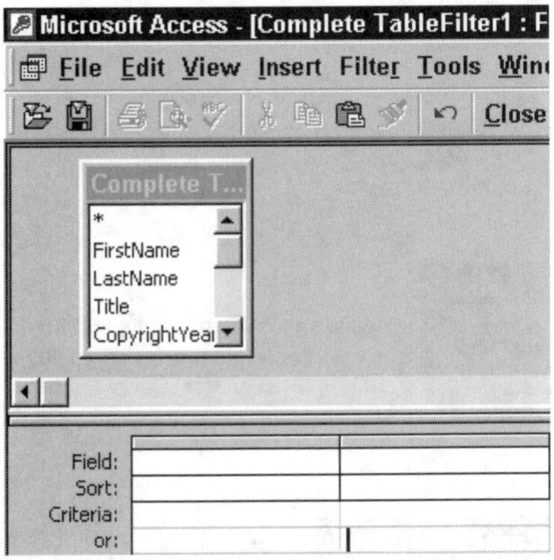

Creating an Advanced Filter or Sort

You can create more advanced filters and sorts using a tool very much like the query design grid you encountered in Chapter 5. Once you've created a sort or filter you like, you can keep it close at hand by saving it as a query.

You might want to create an advanced filter or sort when there are multiple factors to consider in picking and ordering records in your table or query. For instance, you might want to see only the books published after 1996, ordered by the author's last name, first name, and book titles.

To create an advanced filter or sort:

1. In Datasheet view, open the table or query to which you want to apply your advanced filter or sort.

2. Select Records > Filter > Advanced Filter/Sort.

   The design grid appears with a list box containing all of the fields in your table or query (**Figure 7.28**).

3. Click the drop-down menu in the first Field cell and select the field that you want to include in your sort or filter (**Figure 7.29**).

4. Click the Sort cell of the field you're adding, click the drop-down menu button that appears, and select the sort order you want to apply to that field (**Figure 7.30**).

   Click the Criteria cell of the field you're adding and type the criteria Access will use to select which records to show when your filter or sort is applied (**Figure 7.31**).

(continued on next page)

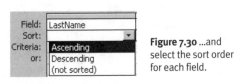

Figure 7.28 The design grid with a list box containing all the fields in your table or query.

Figure 7.29 Add the fields you want to use in your filter or sort...

Figure 7.30 ...and select the sort order for each field.

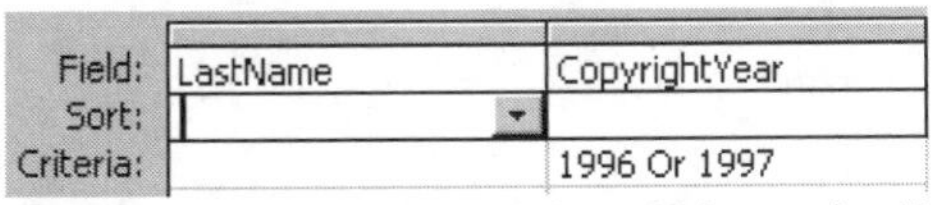

Figure 7.31 Enter a criteria to define which records will appear in your results.

5. Save your filter or sort as a query by clicking the Save as Query toolbar button (**Figure 7.32**).

6. Click the Apply Filter toolbar button to see your filter or sort's results.

✔ Tips

■ To add fields to your sort or filter, click the next open Field cell, click the drop-down menu button that appears, and then select the field you want to add.

■ To load an existing filter into your Advanced Filter/Sort design grid, click the Load from Query toolbar button (**Figure 7.33**), select the name of the filter you want to load, and click OK.

■ You can clear the query grid and start over by clicking the Clear Grid toolbar button (**Figure 7.34**).

Figure 7.32 Save your work by clicking the Save as Query toolbar button.

Figure 7.33 You can load an existing filter or query into the design grid by clicking the Load from Query toolbar button.

Figure 7.34 The Clear Grid toolbar button clears your grid so you can start fresh.

MANAGING RELATIONSHIPS

Relationships, or links between your tables, help Access manage your databases more efficiently. Relationships are the backbone of the *entity-relationship model*, which is in turn the essence of a *relational database*.

An entity is represented by a table, with each record in it representing an *instance* of the entity described by that table. A Customers table—the entity—with fields for name, address, and company name, describes "customers" in general, while each record—the instance—describes a specific customer.

Relational databases allow you to create a scheme that recognizes the interaction of entities. In the simplest case, you can establish relationships to link tables logically. For instance, in a relational database with tables that list customers and customer orders, you can define a connection between those tables based on a common field (in this case, probably a customer's identification number).

Relationships mean you don't have to store the same data repeatedly. If you have a table of customers and a table of orders related by a CustomerID field, you can find (and combine) records in both tables using a query. In unrelated tables, you either need to combine the records by hand or store the contact information with the record for each order.

Establishing Relationships

Access makes it easy for you to view and create relationships between the tables in your database with a tool called the *Relationship Builder*. The Relationship Builder shows the tables in your database as well as the relationships between those tables.

You can view all of the relationships in your database, or just those relationships involving a limited number of tables.

To establish a relationship between two tables:

1. Open the database that contains the tables you want to relate and choose Tools > Relationships.

   The Relationship Builder appears (**Figure 8.1**).

   Move the mouse pointer over the field on the "one" side of the relationship and click and drag it to the related field in the other table. The mouse pointer changes into a representation of the field you selected as you drag it across the window (**Figure 8.2**).

   When you release the left mouse button, the Edit Relationships dialog box appears (**Figure 8.3**).

2. Click Create to establish the relationship.

   The relationship is represented as a line between the two tables (**Figure 8.4**). You can relate each table to any number of other tables with which it has a field in common.

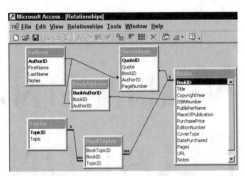

Figure 8.1 Create and work with relationships in your database using the Relationship Builder.

Figure 8.2 The mouse pointer changes when you drag the field across the window.

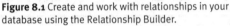

Figure 8.3 The Edit Relationships dialog box lets you define and create a relationship...

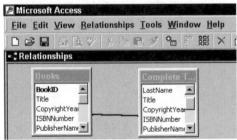

Figure 8.4 . ...which appears as a line between the related fields.

✔ Tip

- To create a relationship in the Edit Relationships dialog box, select an empty cell in the left (Table/Query) column and click the drop-down menu in the cell. From the list that appears, choose the primary table and field for the origin of your relationship, and click Create. Repeat the process to select the foreign table and field in the corresponding cell in the right (Related Table/Query) column.

ESTABLISHING RELATIONSHIPS

To add tables to the Relationship Builder:

1. Open the Relationship Builder and click the Show Table toolbar button (**Figure 8.5**).

   The Show Table dialog box appears with a list of the tables in your database.

2. Select the name of the table you want to show in the Relationship Builder and click Add (**Figure 8.6**).

   The table you select will appear in the Relationship Builder.

3. Click Close when you're done adding tables.

To delete a relationship:

1. Click the line that represents the relationship (**Figure 8.7**).

   The line is highlighted.

2. Press Delete.

   Access displays a dialog box asking if you're sure you want to delete the relationship. Click OK.

Show Table button

Figure 8.5 Click the Show Table toolbar button to list the tables in your database.

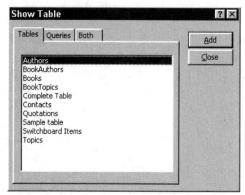

Figure 8.6 Add tables to the relationship window by clicking the table's name, and then clicking Add.

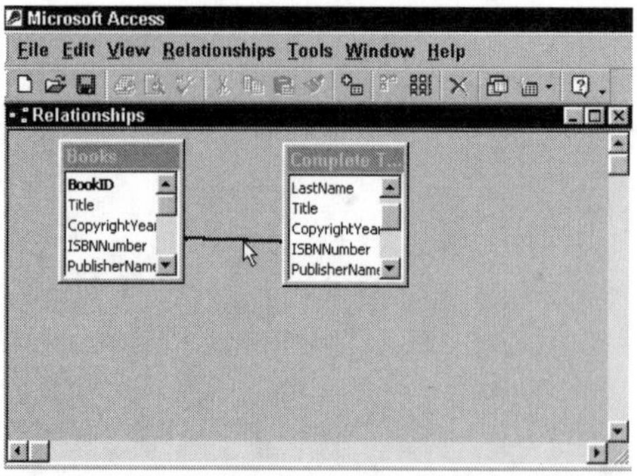

Figure 8.7 Click the relationship you want to delete and press the Delete key to get rid of it.

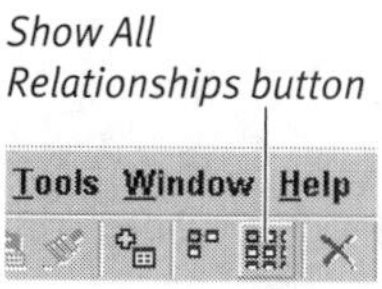

Show All Relationships button

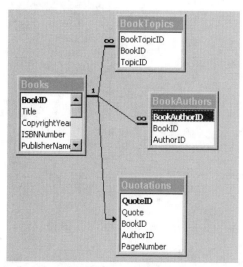

Figure 8.8 The Show All Relationships button displays every relationship in your database.

Figure 8.9 Clicking the Show Direct Relationships toolbar button displays the relationships of the table you've selected.

✔ Tips

- If your tables have the same multiple-field primary key (see Chapter 9), you should relate each field used in the key to its counterpart in the other table.

- You can show all of the relationships in your database by clicking the Show All Relationships toolbar button (**Figure 8.8**). To show the relationships associated with just one table in the Relationship Builder, click the title bar of the table's box and click the Show Direct Relationships toolbar button (**Figure 8.9**).

- You can remove a table from the Relationship Builder by right-clicking the table's title bar and choosing Hide Table from the pop-up menu that appears.

- You can print the contents of the Relationship Builder (as it appears on the screen) by choosing File > Print Relationships. This is a new (and quite welcome) feature of Access 2000.

ESTABLISHING RELATIONSHIPS

Enforcing Referential Integrity

Referential integrity is a system Access uses to ensure that the data in your database remains consistent. Enforcing referential integrity protects you from accidentally deleting data tied to records in a related table, or from entering records in the *foreign* (or non-primary) table that aren't related to records in the primary table.

The *primary* table is the table on the "one" side of a one-to-many relationship. For instance, in a relationship between an Employees table and a Sales table that tracked sales by each employee, the Employees table would be the primary table.

Enforcing referential integrity also prevents you from deleting or changing a primary key value of records in a primary table that have related records in a foreign table.

You can enforce referential integrity between two tables with a common field if they meet the following three conditions:

◆ The matching field in the primary table must have unique values in each record or must be a *primary key*.

◆ The related fields must have the same data type.

◆ Both tables must be in the same database.

To enforce referential integrity, simply double-click the line representing the relationship you want to enforce; this brings up the Edit Relationships dialog box (**Figure 8.3**). Click the Enforce Referential Integrity checkbox.

If you want to delete or update information in a table on the "one" side of a one-to-many relationship, you can do so by having Access *cascade* changes from your table to related tables. Select Cascade Update Related Fields to have Access search related fields whenever a primary key value in the primary table is changed and change all occurrences of the old value to the new value you just entered. It's quite a bit like performing a find-and-replace, covered in Chapter 7.

Cascade Delete Related Records is similar. When you delete a record in the primary table, Access deletes every related record in the foreign table.

Because both operations can drastically change the makeup of your database, Access displays a dialog box to confirm that you want to Cascade Update or Cascade Delete in your tables.

Enforcing referential integrity in your database helps keep your data consistent, but that consistency comes with a price: performance. Because Access checks to make sure each addition or deletion doesn't violate referential integrity, the process can take some time in large databases. You need to weigh the benefits of enforcing referential integrity with the loss of performance. If your system runs too slowly, you can always choose not to enforce referential integrity.

Changing Relationships

Once you've created a relationship between two tables, you can modify the relationship. For instance, if you accidentally create a relationship between two unrelated fields, you can open the relationship and assign a new field to either end of the relationship.

Access doesn't warn you if you create a relationship between fields of different types, so you should take care to ensure that you've created the exact relationship you want.

To change relationships:

1. Open the Relationship Builder, click the Show Tables button, add the tables involved in the relationship, and click the line representing the relationship you want to change (**Figure 8.10**).

2. Choose Relationships > Edit Relationship.

    The Edit Relationships dialog box appears, with the primary table and field in the left column and the foreign table and field in the right column.

3. Click the cell in the Related Table/Query drop-down list that contains the name of the field you want to change and the drop-down menu appears (**Figure 8.11**).

4. Choose the name of the proper field from the menu.

    The field name will appear in the cell.

5. Click OK.

    The Edit Relationships dialog box will disappear, revealing the changed relationship (**Figure 8.12**).

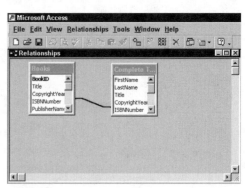

Figure 8.10 Click the relationship you want to change...

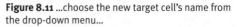

Figure 8.11 ...choose the new target cell's name from the drop-down menu...

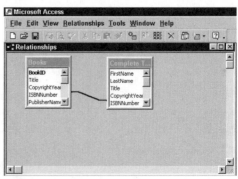

Figure 8.12 ...and your relationship will change for the better.

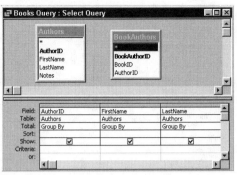

Figure 8.13 In Design view, open the query in which you want to join tables.

Joining Tables in a Query

When you create a query with related tables, Access assumes you want to show records in which a field common to both tables contains the same value. (You can also show parts of records, depending on the fields you choose to show in your query results.) For instance, if you have a table listing book authors, each with his or her own AuthorID value, and you used the AuthorID value in another table (such as a bibliography), you can have Access query the tables and return the records that contain the same AuthorID values in both tables.

On the surface, a relationship and a *join* seem like the same thing. In a limited sense, they are—both terms imply two tables have a common field. The difference is in how that commonality takes shape in the database. When you establish a relationship between two tables, you create a logical link between the tables via the field they have in common. A join, on the other hand, represents an actual combination of the two tables. That combination (usually created by a query) manifests as a *dynaset* containing the records you've joined together, but the join can easily produce a permanent table if initiated by a Make Table query.

To join tables in a query:

1. In Design view, open (or create) the query containing the tables you want to join (**Figure 8.13**).

   Displaying a query in Design view shows the tables above the query design grid, with lines representing the existing relationships between the tables, if any.

2. Click the primary field for your relationship and drag it to the related field in the other table.

(continued on next page)

A line appears between the related fields (**Figure 8.14**).

3. Click File > Save.

To change a join type:

1. Open the query in Design view and double-click the line that represents the join you want to change.

The Join Properties dialog box appears (**Figure 8.15**).

2. Click the appropriate option for the join type you want to assign to the join you selected.

The first option is an inner join, the second and third are outer joins.

3. Click OK after you've selected an option.

✔ Tips

■ You can modify other joins by choosing the appropriate table name (and field in that table) from the left column's drop-down menus. The field joined to the field you chose in the left column will appear in the right column.

■ To create a join in the Join Properties dialog box, click New and choose the tables (and fields) that you want in your new join.

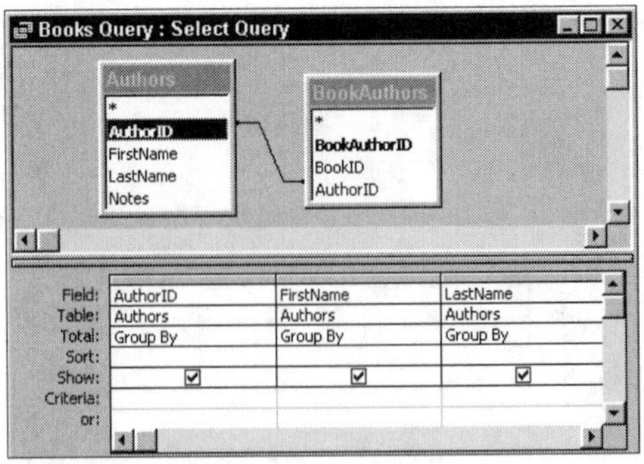

Figure 8.14 A line representing the join appears in the Query design screen.

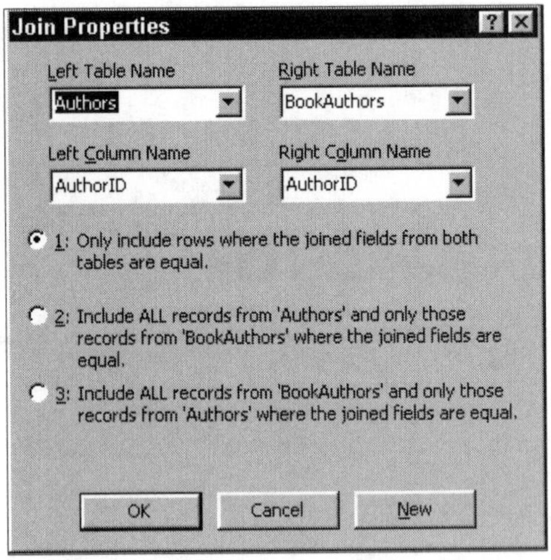

Figure 8.15 The Join Properties dialog box.

Types of Joins.

When you show only those records with the same value in the common field, you create an *inner join*, the most common type of join. For instance, if you create a query using two tables that include a CustomerID field (such as one table with customer orders and another with each customer's billing address), Access performs an inner join on the two tables based on the values in the CustomerID fields.

An *outer join* lists all of the records in the source table, but lists only those records in the joined table with common values in the shared field. An example of an outer join is finding the books authored by members of a Contacts table. If you assign each contact a ContactID and an AuthorID (assuming your contact has written a book), you can use an outer join to show every member of your Contacts table and what books they've written, if any.

The *self-join* is used when records in one table are related to other records in the same table, for example, in a table of Employees that lists each employee's supervisor. Because every supervisor is also an employee, you need to relate the Employees table to itself by adding the Employees table to the Relationship Builder window twice. (The second instance of the Employees table will appear as Employees_1.) You can then relate the SupervisorID field from an employee's record in the original Employees table to the EmployeeID field in the supervisor's record in Employees_1.

A final type of join is the *Cartesian join*, which matches every record in one table with every record in another table without regard to common values. The results of Cartesian joins are rarely useful.

ADDITIONAL TABLE CAPABILITIES

In Chapter 3 you learned how to create tables using a wizard, work with table data, and change your table's appearance in Datasheet view to make entering data easier. Those are all basic Access skills that you need in order to get started. Now it's time to go a bit further under the hood.

In this chapter you'll learn how to copy and move fields, set your table's primary key, and facilitate data entry with lookup fields. We'll also show you how to create hyperlinks and to link to or embed objects from other programs.

Copying, Moving, and Renaming Fields

Once you've added all of the fields you'll need in your table, you can change their order, copy and paste them into other tables, or give them new names to better reflect their contents or to resolve a naming conflict with other fields in the table.

Changing your fields' top-to-bottom order in the table design grid changes the left-to-right field order in datasheets based on the table. Access takes the first (top) field and places it in the first (left-most) column of the datasheet, puts the second field in the next column to the right, and so on. The field order in the table design grid also changes the arrangement of fields in wizard-generated forms based on the table; the exact arrangement depends on the type of form you create.

To copy a field:

1. Open your table in Design view and click anywhere in the field that you want to copy.

2. Select Edit > Copy.

3. Click anywhere in the first open row and select Edit > Paste.

   The field you copied appears in the design grid (**Figure 9.1**).

To move a field:

1. Click the row selector of the field you want to move.

   The row is highlighted (**Figure 9.2**).

2. With the mouse pointer still over the row selector you just clicked, hold down the left mouse button and drag the row to the desired position in the table (**Figure 9.3**).

   The row appears in its new position when you release the mouse button (**Figure 9.4**).

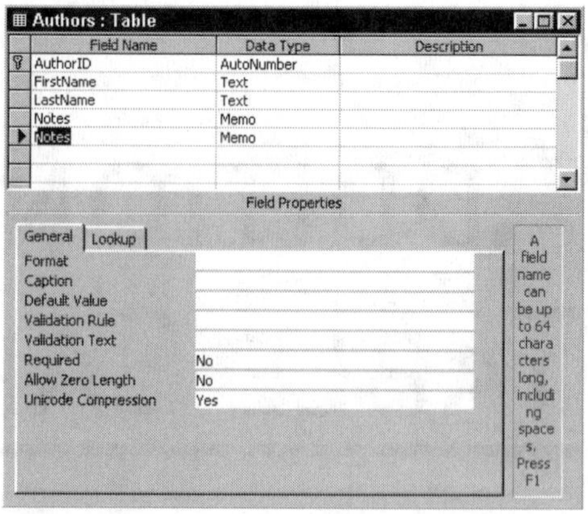

Figure 9.1 You can paste your copied field elsewhere in your table (a good way to create two similar fields with half the work).

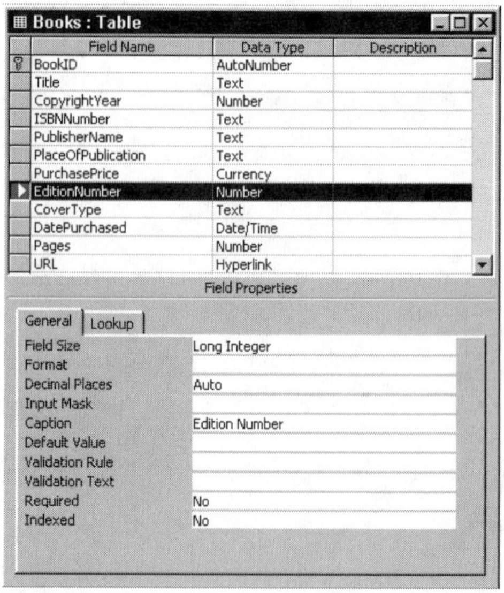

Figure 9.2 The arrow in the row selector indicates which row is active.

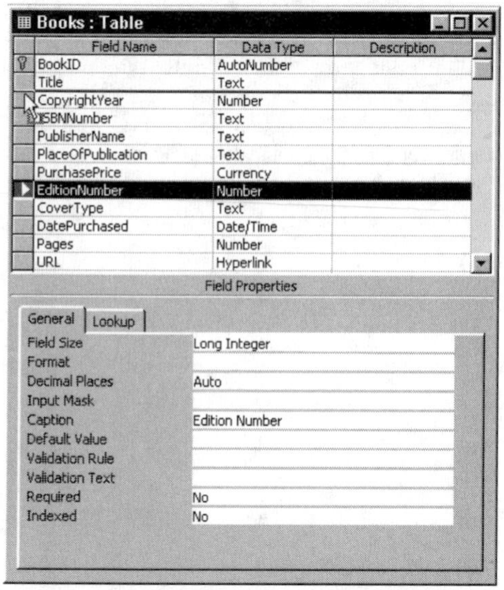

Figure 9.3 The insertion point for the field you're moving appears as a gray line in the table design grid.

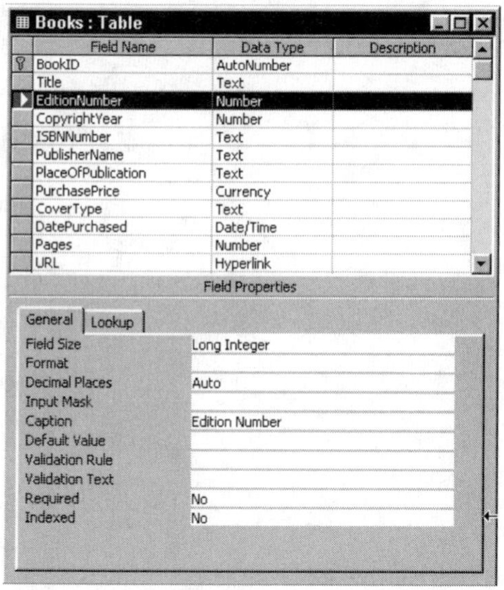

Figure 9.4 Your move is complete when you release the left mouse button.

To rename a field:

1. Double-click the Field Name cell containing the field name you want to change. Access highlights the contents of the cell.

2. Type the new field name in the cell.

3. Select File > Save to save the new field name.

✔ Tips

- To copy a field to another table, select the field, select Edit > Copy to copy it, close the table, open the destination table, click in the first open row, and select Edit > Paste.

- You can have two fields with the same name in your table while you're making changes, but you can't save your table until every field has a distinct name.

Setting Primary Key Fields

Tables often contain one or more fields whose values differentiate individual records in the table from the other records. These fields are called *key fields* or, more precisely, *primary key fields*.

Primary key fields always contain unique values in each record; that is, the same value can't occur twice in a primary key field in a table. Keys are an integral part of relational databases—by ensuring that each record refers to a unique entity, keys allow you to create relationships between tables. Car license plates are a perfect example of a primary key field value; no two cars (in the same state, at least) will have the same license plate numbers. For more information on relationships, see Chapter 8.

To make a field a primary key field:

1. In Design view, open the table to which you want to assign a primary key field.

2. Click anywhere in the row that contains the field you want to make the primary key.

3. Click the Primary Key toolbar button. (**Figure 9.5**).

   A key icon appears on the row selector of the field you selected.

4. Select File > Save to save your primary key field.

Primary key button

Figure 9.5 Click the Primary Key toolbar button to set the field you've selected as the table's primary key.

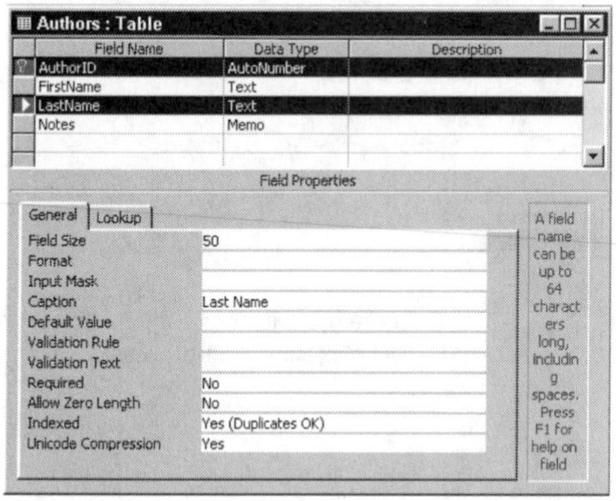

Figure 9.6 You can create a multifield primary key for your table based on more than one field.

Multiple-field (multifield) primary keys are used when a single field doesn't contain enough information to clearly distinguish that record from every other record in the table. For instance, a customer's order can have a distinct OrderID field value, but to make each line item unique , you must combine the OrderID and ProductID fields into a multifield primary key.

To make a multiple-field primary key:

1. In Design view, open the table to which you want to assign a multiple-field primary key.

2. Hold down the Ctrl key and click the row selectors of the fields you want to include in the table's primary key (**Figure 9.6**).

3. Click the Primary Key toolbar button.

   A key icon appears in the row selectors of the fields used in your multifield primary key.

4. Select File > Save.

✔ Tip

- The fields you include in a multiple-field primary key need not be next to each other in your table.

Using Lookup Fields

Data entry can be a time-consuming and error-prone process. If the value to be entered into a field is limited to one or two different choices, such as one of three different states in an address field, you can save time and reduce typing errors by allowing your users to enter data using a *lookup field*.

Lookup fields are also valuable because they link fields to data from a table. You can create a lookup field that includes single fields or entire records, so you can display as much information as you want through your lookup field. Lookup fields come in three varieties: the text box, the list box, and the combo box. A text box is the standard way to enter data into a table—the user just clicks the text area of the box, enters the value, then presses Enter or Tab (**Figure 9.7**). A list box, by contrast, allows users to select values from a pre-existing list (**Figure 9.8**). Combo boxes combine the best features of text boxes and list boxes. Users can enter their own values or select a value from a list you define (**Figure 9.9**).

The instructions presented in this task apply to all three types of lookup fields. You can choose the type of lookup field you want by setting the object's Display Control property to the appropriate type (as you learned to do in Chapter 4).

To use lookup fields:

1. Open your table in Design view and add the field you want to turn into a lookup field to the table design grid.

   or

   Set the data type of the field to become a lookup field to "Lookup Field" as you learned to do in Chapter 3.

Last Name: [   ]

Figure 9.7 A text box, for entering data manually.

Figure 9.8 A list box, which lets a user pick from a list of values.

Figure 9.9 A combo box, which lets users pick a value from a list or enter their own.

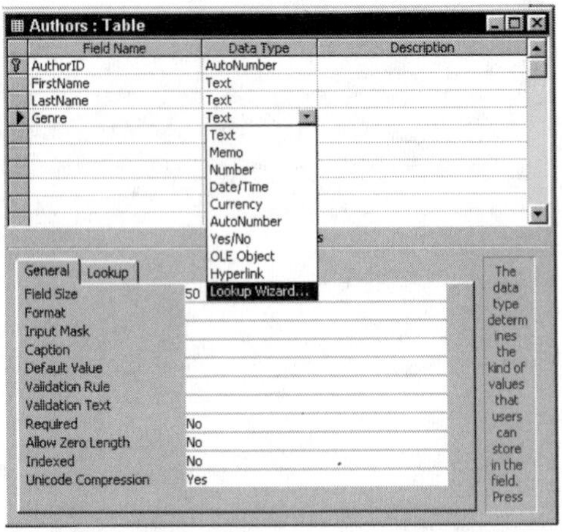

Figure 9.10 Select Lookup Wizard from the data type drop-down menu to launch the Lookup Wizard.

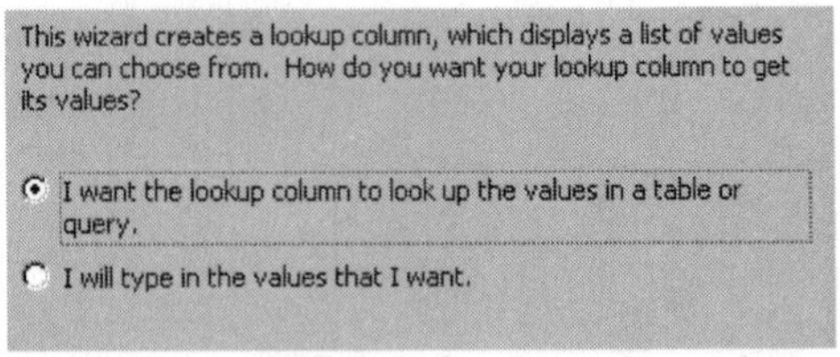

This wizard creates a lookup column, which displays a list of values you can choose from. How do you want your lookup column to get its values?

○ I want the lookup column to look up the values in a table or query.

○ I will type in the values that I want.

Figure 9.11 Select the option button indicating you want Access to draw values for your lookup field from an existing table or query...

USING LOOKUP FIELDS

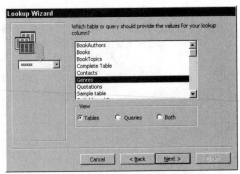

Figure 9.12 ...direct Access to the table or query...

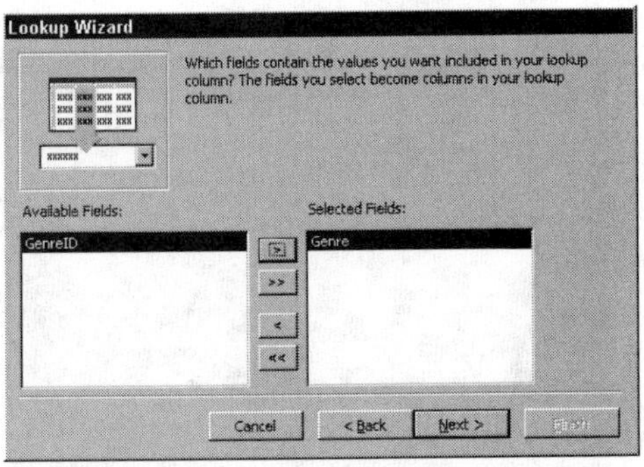

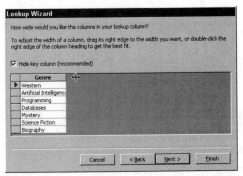

Figure 9.13 ...and then select the field (or fields) from the table or query.

Figure 9.14 You can resize the lookup field to display the entire contents of the field.

2. Click the Data Type cell of the field you want to become a lookup field, click the drop-down menu that appears and select Lookup Wizard. (**Figure 9.10**). The Lookup Wizard launches.

3. Click the "I want the lookup column to look up the values in a table or query." option button and click Next (**Figure 9.11**).

4. Select the table or query that you want to draw values from and click Next (**Figure 9.12**).

   You can draw values from your tables, queries, or both by clicking the corresponding option button in this wizard screen.

5. In the Available Fields pane, select the field containing the values you want available in your lookup field and click the > button to add it to the Selected Fields pane. Click Next (**Figure 9.13**).

6. Click the right edge of the column and drag it until the field is the desired width. Click Next (**Figure 9.14**).

   The field width chosen here will be the width of the lookup field in Datasheet view.

7. Type a label for your lookup column and click Finish.

8. Select File > Save to save your changes.

To enter your own values when you create a lookup field:

1. Open your table in Design view and add the field you want to turn into a lookup field to the table design grid.

   or

   Set the data type of the field you want to make a lookup field to "Lookup Field."

   The Lookup Wizard launches.

2. Select the "I will type in the values that I want." option button and click Next. (**Figure 9.15**)

   The next screen of the Lookup Wizard appears. (**Figure 9.16**).

3. Type the number of columns you want in your lookup field in the Number of columns text area.

4. Click in the cell in the middle pane of the wizard screen, type the first value in your list, and press Enter.

   As you type, a new row appears automatically. Press Enter (or Tab) to move the insertion point to the first cell of the next row. (**Figure 9.17**)

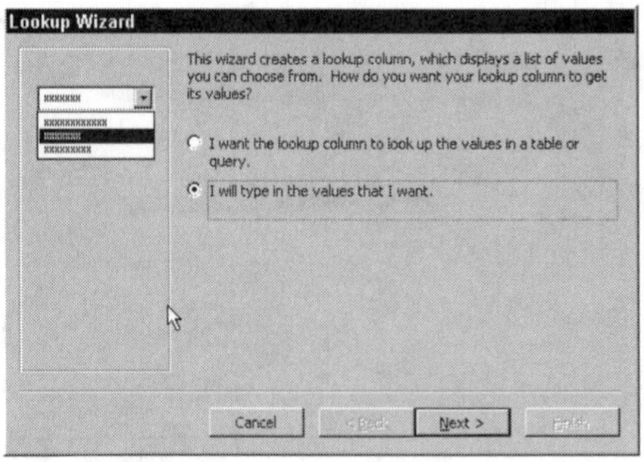

Figure 9.15 Select the option button that lets you enter your own values for the lookup field.

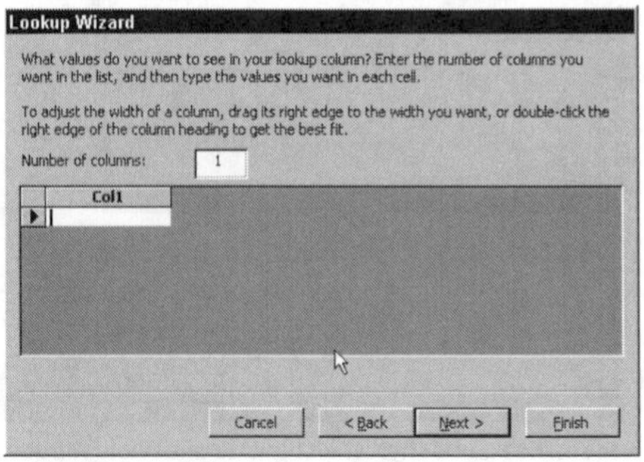

Figure 9.16 Use this screen to set the number of columns and enter the values for your lookup field.

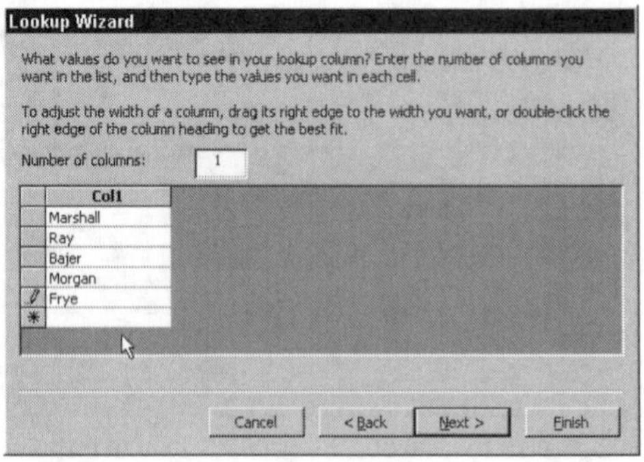

Figure 9.17 A new row of cells appears, just in case you need it.

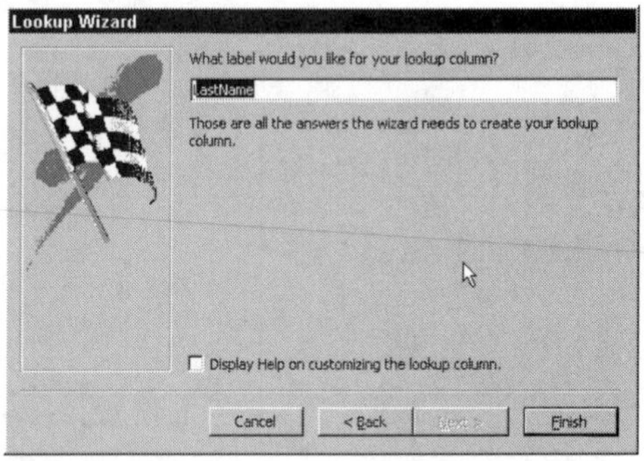

Figure 9.18 The final Lookup Wizard screen–enter a name for your lookup field and click Finish.

5. Click Next when you're done adding values.

   The final screen of the Lookup Wizard appears. (**Figure 9.18**)

6. Type a name for your field in the space provided and click Finish to create your lookup field.

✔ Tip

■ You can transform an existing text or number field into a lookup field by opening the table containing the field in Design view and changing the field's data type to Lookup Wizard.

Checking Spelling

Spelling errors in a personal document are one thing, but data you make available to the public must be spelled correctly so your visitors' viewing isn't interrupted by mistakes. The Access spellcheck dialog box will be familiar to most Windows users, but one difference is the Ignore Field button, which tells Access to ignore all of the values in the current field. The field to be ignored is identified on the button, so if the cursor is in the Notes field, the button reads "Ignore Notes Field." Another feature is AutoCorrect, which replaces the word in the Not In Dictionary text area with the corresponding value in the AutoCorrect list (see Chapter 4).

USING LOOKUP FIELDS

Using Hyperlinks

Access 2000, like the other programs in the Office 2000 suite, places a great deal of emphasis on using the Internet and intranets to disseminate your information. *Hyperlinks*, or connections from objects in your database to other database objects or documents accessible via a network, let you expand your database's capabilities beyond your local system. You can add hyperlinks to forms, reports, and data access pages.

The most obvious use for a hyperlink in a database is to guide the user to a Web page. For instance, if you list your library's contents in a table and want to give users access to the publisher's Web site, you might include a hyperlink in the book's record.

You can also use hyperlinks to help users jump from one object in your database to another. For example, if your users want to open a form from within another form, you could create a macro to open the other form and tie the macro to a control, but it's quicker to create a hyperlink to the other form. Rather than running the macro, opening the new form, and closing the macro, Access identifies the object referred to by the hyperlink and opens it.

You can also create a hyperlink that generates an email message to the address specified in the link. This function is the equivalent of the HTML mailto command.

To create a hyperlink to an existing file or Web page:

1. In Design view, open the database object to which you want to add a hyperlink.

2. Choose Insert > Hyperlink
   In the Insert Hyperlink dialog box, click the Existing File or Web Page button in

Type the file or Web   Type your hyperlink
page to link to here   text here.

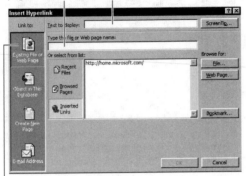

Pick the object to link to here.

Figure 9.19 You can pick the file or Web page you want to link to using the Insert Hyperlink dialog box.

the left-hand pane of the window (**Figure 9.19**).

3. Type the text to appear as your hyperlink in the Text to Display text area.

   This text forms the body of the hyperlink and usually appears underlined and in a different color than the surrounding text. The default color for Access hyperlink text is blue.

4. Type the name of the file you want to set as your hyperlink target in the "Type the file or Web page name" text area

   or

5. Click the Recent Files, Browsed Pages, or Inserted Links icon in the center pane of the dialog box and select the item you to which want to link from the list that appears.

6. Click OK.

   The hyperlink appears in your form.

✔ Tip

■ You can browse for a file or Web page that doesn't appear in the list by clicking either the File or Web Page button in the Browse For pane of the Insert Hyperlink dialog box.

USING HYPERLINKS

To create a hyperlink to another object in your database:

1. In Design view, open the form, report, or data access page into which you want to insert a hyperlink.

2. Choose Insert > Hyperlink.

3. In the Link to pane of the Insert Hyperlink dialog box (**Figure 9.20**), select Object in This Database.

   A list of object types appears in the "Select an object in this database" pane.

Figure 9.20 Double-click the object type you want to display.

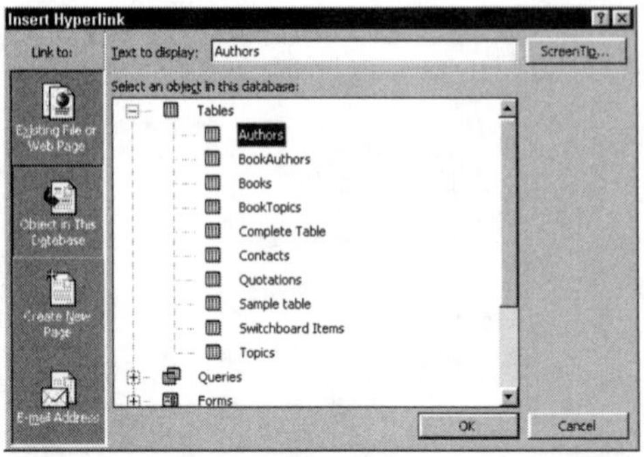

4. Double-click the object type you want to make the target of your hyperlink.

   We double-clicked Tables (**Figure 9.21**). A list of the tables in our database appears in the center pane of the window.

5. Click the object you want to link to and click OK.

   Set the text of the hyperlink by typing the text in the Text to Display text area at the top of the dialog box.

To create a hyperlink that lets a user send e-mail to a specific address:

1. In Design view, open the form, report, or data access page to which you want to add your hyperlink.

2. In the Insert Hyperlink dialog box, click the E-mail address button in the leftmost pane of the window.

3. Type the e-mail address you want to receive the message in the E-mail address text area (**Figure 9.22**).

4. Type a subject for the message in the Subject text area, then click OK.

Figure 9.21 Link to an object by clicking its name and clicking OK.

Figure 9.22 Type the e-mail address and a subject for the message in the dialog box.

✔ Tip

- To find the target file or Web page, click the File or Web Page button and navigate through your directories or the Web.

Using Object Linking and Embedding

Although Access can create rudimentary graphics for your forms, reports, and pages, it has none of the power and flexibility of the dedicated graphics programs. It gets around its limitations, however, with Object Linking and Embedding (OLE). OLE-compliant applications can share data by *linking* to another object or *embedding* an object from one program in another program.

Linking, as used in this chapter, is different than the linking discussed in Chapter 12. That refers to linking external tables and compatible files (like spreadsheets) to a database in the form of tables. Here you'll learn how to display the data in an external file inside a control on a form or report.

Linking to another object is useful if the object is large or if it will be used in more than a few places. For instance, if you want to include an OLE-compliant spreadsheet on every page of a report, you should definitely link to (not embed) it. Rather than store the spreadsheet data in the database itself, Access draws the data from the other application, thereby saving disk space and automatically updating the Access object whenever the original spreadsheet changes.

You should embed an object in an Access form, report, or data access page if you only use the object once, or if the object was not created in OLE-compliant program.

You can also create an OLE object from within Access by launching the OLE-compliant program and creating the object while Access runs in the background.

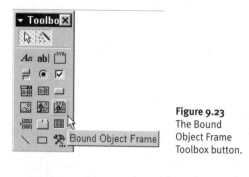

Figure 9.23
The Bound Object Frame Toolbox button.

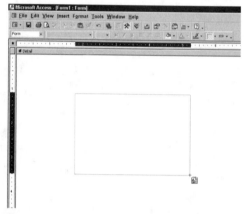

Figure 9.24 Create a home for your OLE data with a Bound Object Frame.

Microsoft Excel - NewTopics

File Edit View Insert Format To

	A	B
1	TopicID	Topic
2	17	Travel
3	18	Political Science
4	19	Internet
5	20	Electronic Commerce
6	74	Databases

A1 = TopicID

Figure 9.25 Pick the information you want to include in your frame.

Paste Special

Source: Sheet1!R1C1:R6C2

As:

Microsoft Excel Worksheet
Text

○ Paste
◉ Paste Link

☐ Display as Icon

Result

Inserts a picture of the Clipboard contents into your document. Paste Link creates a link to the source file so that changes to the source file will be reflected in your document.

OK
Cancel

Figure 9.26 The Paste Special dialog box appears with a list of available information you can paste into your frame.

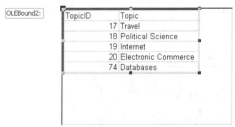

OLEBound2:

TopicID	Topic
17	Travel
18	Political Science
19	Internet
20	Electronic Commerce
74	Databases

Figure 9.27 Your information appears in the frame.

To link to an OLE-compliant object:

1. In Design view, open the database object you want to link to the OLE-compliant object.

2. Open the Toolbox and click the Bound Object Frame button (**Figure 9.23**).

3. Draw a frame for the object (**Figure 9.24**).

   The frame appears in your form or report.

4. Open the program containing the information you want to link to your Access object, select the information you want to link, and choose Edit > Copy.

   We used an Excel spreadsheet as the data source for our link (**Figure 9.25**).

5. Move to Access and select the frame you created earlier.

6. Choose Edit > Paste Special.

   In the Paste Special dialog box (**Figure 9.26**), select Paste Link and choose the type of data to link to.

7. Click OK to display your information in the control frame (**Figure 9.27**).

USING OBJECT LINKING AND EMBEDDING

To embed an object in your database:

1. In Design view, open the database object in which you want to embed the OLE-compliant object.

2. Choose Insert > Object.

   The Insert Object dialog box appears (**Figure 9.28**).

3. Select the Create New option button, select the program with which you want to create your new object, and click OK.

   or

   Select the Create from File option button, navigate to the directory containing the file, select the file, click OK to return to the Insert Object dialog box, and click OK.

   The object will appear in your form.

4. If necessary, create (or edit) the object using the source program (**Figure 9.29**).

   In this case, we used Paintbrush (a paint program included with Windows) to create our object.

5. Choose File > Save to save your work, then choose File > Exit to return to Access.

   The object appears in your form (**Figure 9.30**).

✔ Tips

- To modify a linked or embedded object using its source program, double-click it while in Design view.

- You can display an embedded object as an icon by selecting the Display as Icon check box in the Insert Object window. To display the object, double-click the icon.

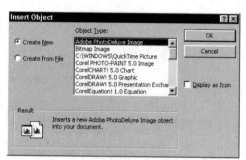
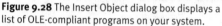

Figure 9.28 The Insert Object dialog box displays a list of OLE-compliant programs on your system.

Figure 9.29 Work with or create the object you want to embed in your database.

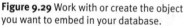

Figure 9.30 The object appears in your database.

USING SPECIALIZED QUERIES

In Chapter 5, you learned how to select records from your tables (and other queries) to answer questions about your data. This chapter shows you how to create more specialized queries that can answer specific questions about the contents of your database.

Updating Records

Access makes it easy to manage databases of all sizes, but updating information by hand is time-consuming at best in small databases, and impossible in any data collection of substantial size. Updating your records without using a query becomes even trickier if you don't want to replace every instance of a value. If, for instance, you only wanted to change certain instances of "Smith" in a LastName field because one out of the fifteen Smiths in your table had changed their name, you would need to find each record manually and decide whether to make the replacement or not.

Using an update query to automatically find and replace the correct values is much simpler. For instance, if a publisher changed its name, you could use an update query to change every occurrence of the name in the PublisherName field.

To update records in a database:

1. In Design view, create a query to find the records with the values you want to replace.

   In this example, we're searching for the publisher name "Wilkey," which the company changed, so we type "Wilkey" in the Criteria cell.

2. Choose Query > Update Query.

3. Type the replacement value in the Update To cell (**Figure 10.1**) of the field that contains the values you're replacing.

   We want to replace the previous value with "Wiley."

4. Click the Run button to run your query.

5. A dialog box appears asking you to confirm the update. Click Yes to update your values.

Figure 10.1 Type the replacement value for your query in the Update To row.

✔ Tips

- After you run an update query you can't undo the changes automatically. If you want to return the values you changed to their original values, you'll need to locate the records that contain the values and run another update query. Make sure your new query doesn't capture too many records!

- If you query returns too many records, look for a pattern you can use to exclude those extra records. For more information on building criteria to find records, see Chapter 5.

Finding High and Low Values

As you learned in Chapter 7, you can sort your records in ascending or descending order based on the contents of one or more fields, but you can't easily limit your results to the top (or bottom) five, ten, or twenty values in a field using a standard filter or sort.

For instance, you might want to see the ten most recently published books you own, or find your ten least active customers so you can entice them to place more orders. Fortunately, Access allows you to display any number of high or low values in your tables.

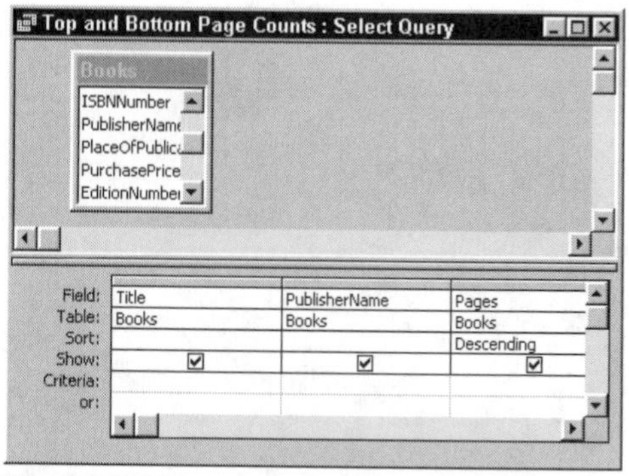

To find high and low values in a field:

1. Create a query to find the records you want to work with.

2. Open the query in Design view (**Figure 10.2**).

3. Click the Sort cell of the field in which you want to find the top or bottom values, and choose Descending from the drop-down menu to find the top few records (**Figure 10.3**).

   or

   Click Ascending to select the lowest values in the table.

4. In the Top Values combo box, click the drop-down menu (**Figure 10.4**) and choose the number of records (or percentage of all records) that you want to appear in your results.

✔ Tip

■ You can enter the exact number (or percentage) of records you want to see in your query's results by typing that number in the Top Values combo box.

Figure 10.2 Open your query in Design view.

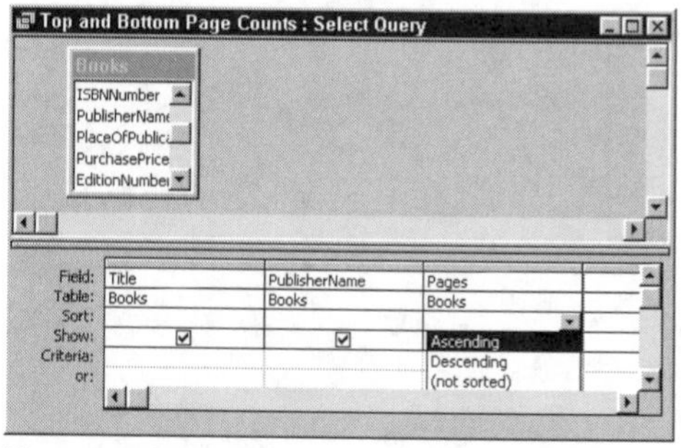

Figure 10.3 Sort your query's results in ascending order to see the lowest values in the table and in descending order to see the highest values.

Figure 10.4 Choose (or type) the number of values you want to appear in your results.

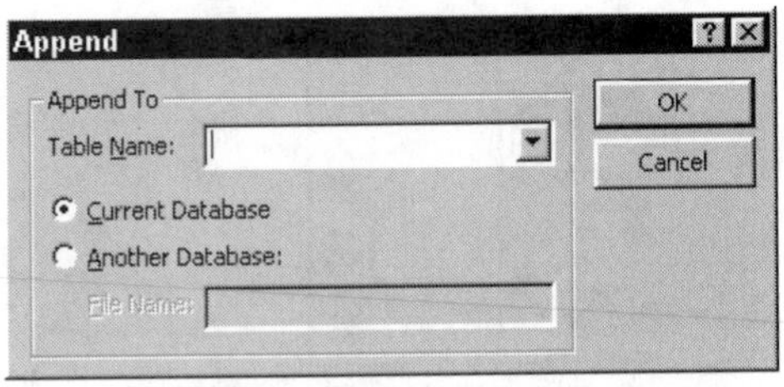

Figure 10.5 In the Append dialog box, type the name of the table you want to add records to...

Figure 10.6 ...or click the drop-down menu button to select the table from a list.

Copying Data to a Table

Like most Windows-based programs, Access has cut-and-paste functions to move records from one table to another. You can also write a query to automatically add records from one table to another table.

For example, you may want to append records from one table to another if you purchased a number of new books for your library while on a trip. You can enter records for those new books in a new table using an Append query. The new table must have the same structure as the table you're appending the records to.

To append records to a table:

1. Create a query to find the records that you want to append to another table.

2. Choose Query > Append Query.

3. In the Append dialog box (**Figure 10.5**), type the name of the table to which you want to append records in the Table Name text box. Click OK.

   or

   Click the drop-down menu button and select the name of the table from the list that appears (**Figure 10.6**), and then click OK.

4. Click the Run button to run your query.

✔ Tip

■ You can append records to a table in another database by selecting the Another Database option in the Append dialog box. From the drop-down menu, select the database and then the table to which you want to append records.

Querying to Delete Records from Tables

Data entry isn't an exact science. It's possible to enter records into the wrong table or enter incorrect data, both of which could compromise your database's usefulness. You can delete records from a table using a Delete query.

To delete records from tables with a Delete query:

1. Create a Select query to find the records you want to delete and then open the query in Design view.

    Choose Query > Delete Query to bring the Delete row into the query design grid (**Figure 10.7**).

2. Switch from Design view to Datasheet view to ensure that your query finds only those records that you want to delete.

3. Click Run.

    A dialog box confirms that you want to delete the records found by your query.

✔ Tip

■ You can *cascade delete* (delete records in other tables that are related to the records you're deleting in the current table) by enforcing *referential integrity* between the tables. For more information, see "Enforcing Referential Integrity" on page 128.

Figure 10.7 The Delete row indicates that your query is a Delete query.

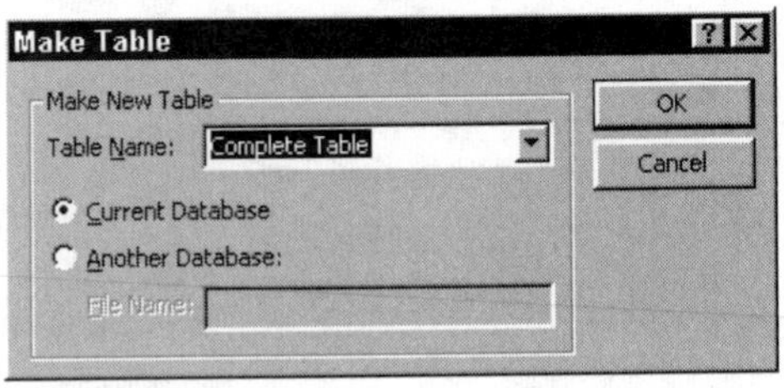

Figure 10.8 Type a name for your new table in the Make Table dialog box.

Creating a Table from Query Results

Query results usually take the form of *dynasets*, or dynamic collections of data that change whenever you run your query. You can work with dynasets the same way you work with table data, but there are times you'll want to write your query results to a table.

For instance, if you create a query for your traveling sales representative that finds customers who haven't placed an order in three months, you probably want to make a table out of the results. By writing the query's output to a table, you can fix the records and allow the sales rep to carry only that table on a laptop, instead of the entire database.

To create a Make Table query:

1. Create a select query to locate the records that you want to write to your new table.

2. In Design view, open the query you created.

3. Choose Query > Make Table Query.

4. When the Make Table dialog box appears (**Figure 10.8**), type the name of your new table in the Table Name text box and click OK.

5. Click Run.

   Your new table appears in the main database window.

✔ Tip

■ You can create a table in another database by selecting the Another Database option in the Make Table dialog box. From the drop-down menu, select the database to which you want to add your new table. You can then type the name of the table you want to create and click Run.

WORKING WITH PIVOT TABLES

This chapter introduces you to one of the most powerful and flexible tools in your Access arsenal: the *pivot table*. Pivot tables aren't native to Access—they're actually Microsoft Excel objects available to those with both Access and Excel installed on their system.

You can think of pivot tables as an extension of the crosstab query, discussed in Chapter 5. Like crosstab queries, pivot tables present data in a spreadsheet, with each cell in the body of the table at the intersection of a column and row. Datasheets present data in the same manner, but don't give you the same capabilities (such as formulas) that spreadsheets give you. Pivot tables go beyond simple crosstab queries by allowing you to change how the table displays your data in much the same way you can change the priority order of grouping fields for reports (see Chapter 6).

Perhaps the most important aspect of pivot tables is the time they save. Rather than creating a separate query or form to display your data differently, you can modify your pivot table to arrange your data in the most effective way. Every unique arrangement of the fields in your pivot table tells a story.

Creating Pivot Tables

Create a pivot table whenever you want to display your data to emphasize different aspects of the information. In the Sales Analysis pivot table for the Northwind sample database, for example (**Figure 11.1**), you can emphasize the year (and quarter) sales took place, the employee who made the sales, the country the goods were shipped to, and any combination of the values you can imagine.

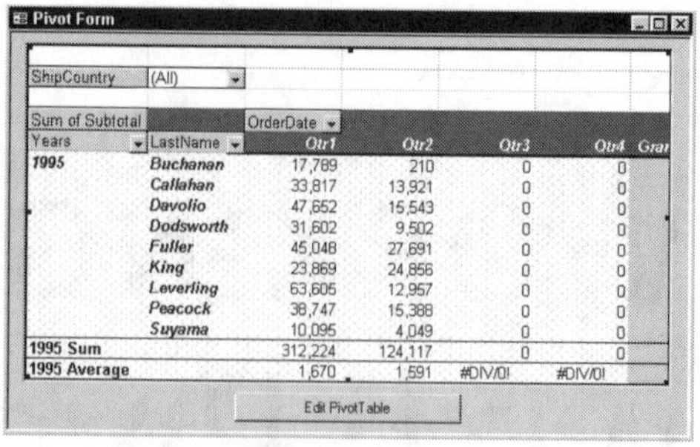

While pivot tables seem quite complex at first glance, they're actually very easy to create using the Pivot Table Wizard. You add the fields to the table, choose their positions in the table, and arrange the fields to establish an initial grouping order.

Grouping a pivot table by the contents of a field arranges your data according to the values in that field. For instance, if you created a pivot table tracking sales data, you could group the data by Employee Name, Year, and Quarter.

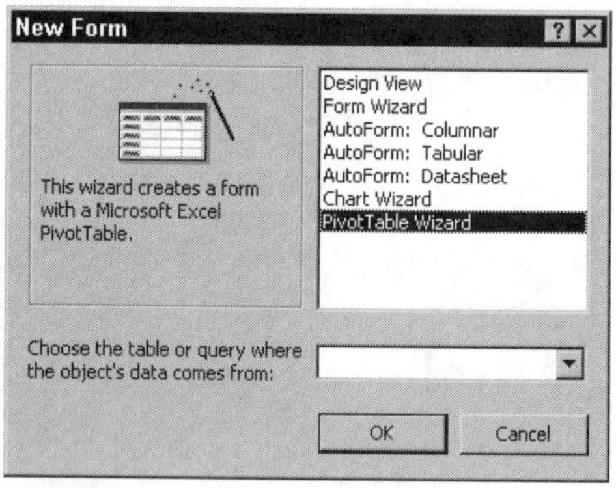

To create a pivot table:

1. Click the New Object drop-down menu in the main database window and choose Form.

   The New Form dialog box appears.

2. Select Pivot Table Wizard from the list and click OK (**Figure 11.2**).

   The first Pivot Table Wizard screen explains what a pivot table is and how to edit it once you've created it. Click Next to continue.

3. Click the Tables/Queries drop-down menu to display the first table or query from which you want to draw fields for your pivot table (**Figure 11.3**).

   You can use fields from more than one table or query in your pivot table. In this

Figure 11.1 This pivot table analyzes the sales of the Northwind company.

Figure 11.2 Launch the Pivot Table Wizard to get started.

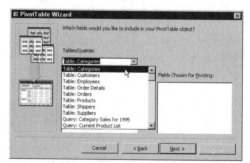

Figure 11.3 Select the first table or query you want to add fields from.

Figure 11.4 Add fields to your pivot table using the familiar wizard interface.

Figure 11.5 Click Layout to place fields in your pivot table.

example, we're interested in seeing our customers' orders by product and product category. To generate that information, we will use the Company Name field from the Customers table, Category Name from the Categories table, Product Name from the Products table, and Extended Price (total price per item after discount) from the Order Details Extended query. All of these tables and queries are in the standard edition of the Northwind sample database.

4. Add fields to your pivot table by selecting the field you want to add from the list in the Available Fields pane and clicking the > button (**Figure 11.4**).

5. Repeat steps 3 and 4 until all of the fields you want to include in your pivot table are listed in the Fields Chosen for Pivoting pane. Click Next to continue.

   Excel launches and displays the first screen of its Pivot Table Wizard (**Figure 11.5**).

6. Click Layout.

   The layout composition screen appears. The layout area has four sections: Data, Row, Column, and Page. The Row area contains the fields that will provide data for the rows of the pivot table, the Column area contains the fields that will provide data for the columns, and the Data area contains the numerical values that will fill in the body of the pivot table.

   The Page area is different from the other areas. Fields in the Page area don't affect the grouping of data in the table, but you can use them to filter the data in the body of the table. You'll learn how to filter a pivot table later in this chapter.

7. Drag the name of the field containing the data for your pivot table to the Data area (**Figure 11.6**).

(continued on next page)

CREATING PIVOT TABLES

In this example, we're using the Extended Price field for our data. Our goal is to display the total amount spent by each customer on specific products (and categories of products).

8. Drag the field containing the data for the rows to the Row area (**Figure 11.7**).

   We chose Company Name.

9. Drag the field containing the data for the columns to the Column area (**Figure 11.8**).

   We chose Product Name.

10. Drag the field that will reside in the Page area to the Page area (**Figure 11.9**).

    We moved the Categories field to the Page area.

11. Click OK.

    Excel's Pivot Table Wizard screen reappears.

12. Click Finish to create your pivot table.

    Your pivot table appears (**Figure 11.10**).

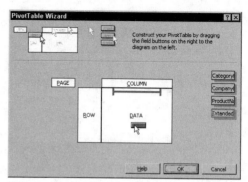

Figure 11.6 Drag the field that you want to supply your data to the Data area...

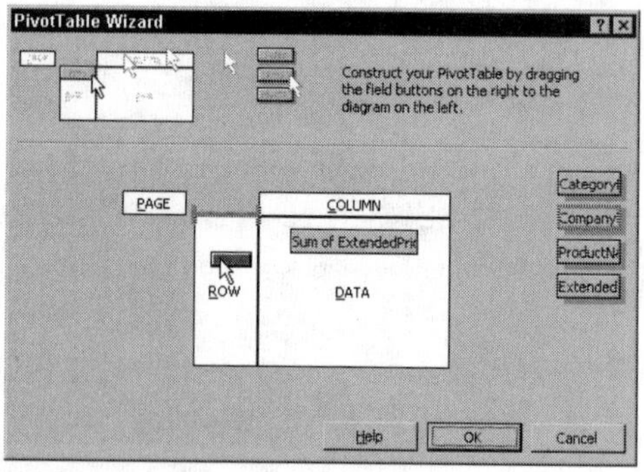

Figure 11.7 ...and then drag the field for your row headings to the Row area...

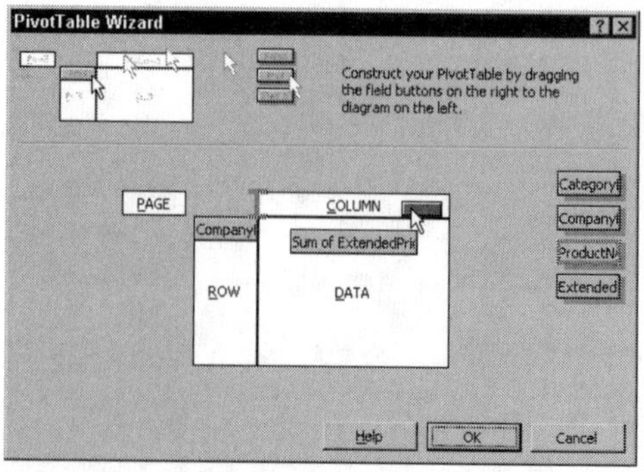

Figure 11.8 ...followed by the field for the column headings to the Column area...

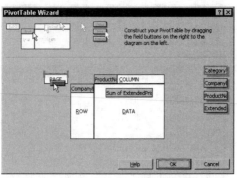

Figure 11.9 ...and the fields for the Page area to the Page box.

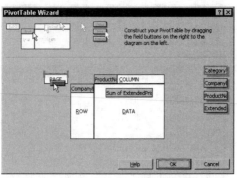

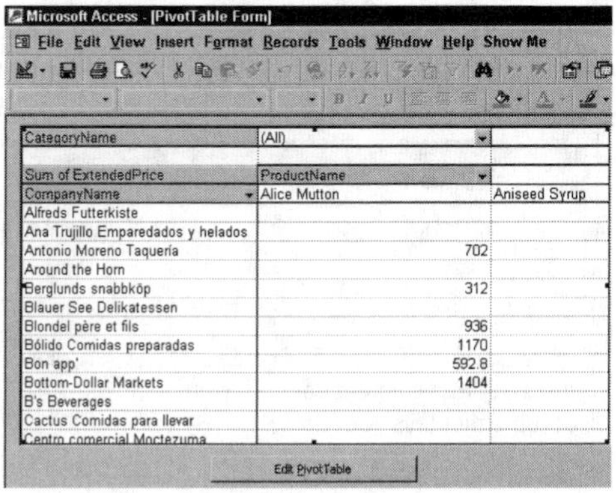

Figure 11.10 Your pivot table as it appears after you've finished.

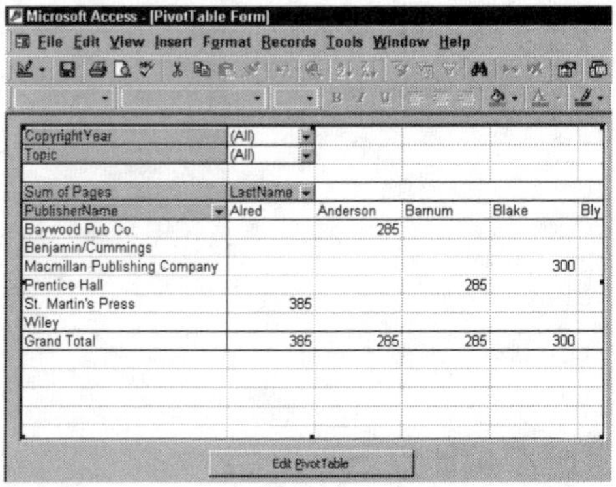

Figure 11.11 You can open your pivot table for editing and relaunch the Pivot Table Wizard from within Excel.

Relaunching the Pivot Table Wizard

Each different arrangement of your fields brings up a unique calculation of data. You can rearrange the fields in your pivot table while in Excel, but the process can take a while if your computer is slow or if Excel needs to calculate a substantial amount of data every time you pivot your table. Relaunching the Pivot Table Wizard lets you move your fields without forcing Excel to recalculate your table after every move.

To relaunch the Pivot Table Wizard:

1. Open the form containing your pivot table in Access and click Edit Pivot Table (**Figure 11.11**).

    Your pivot table appears as an Excel file.

2. Choose Data > PivotTable and PivotChart Report.

    The Pivot Table Wizard appears. Click Layout to rearrange the fields in your pivot table.

✔ Tip

■ If you get an error saying "Trouble Obtaining Data" you may need to create a relationship between the tables you want to use in your pivot table. Make sure all of the tables used in your pivot table are related. For more information on creating relationships between tables, see Chapter 8.

Pivoting a Pivot Table

The key to working with pivot tables is knowing how to change the way the table groups your data so it displays your data the way you want it to. These changes are called *pivots*.

To pivot a pivot table:

1. Display the forms in your database and double-click the form containing the pivot table you want to work with.

   In this example, we're using the Sales Analysis form from the Northwind sample database.

2. Click the Edit Pivot Table button at the bottom of the window.

   Excel launches and opens your pivot table as an Excel document (**Figure 11.12**).

   The Sales Analysis pivot table draws on five fields to provide its data and groupings: LastName (of the employee that made the sale), Years, Subtotal (of a specific order), OrderDate, and ShipCountry (the destination country for the order). In **Figure 11.12,** the Subtotal field provides the data for the body of the table, the Years field groups the values in the rows, and the LastName and OrderDate fields (in Quarters), group the values in the columns. The ShipCountry field's header resides in the Page area.

3. Click the LastName field header and drag it to the left of the Years field header (**Figure 11.13**).

   The pivot table appears with the data rows grouped by LastName, then by Years (**Figure 11.14**). The table now displays yearly sales data for each employee.

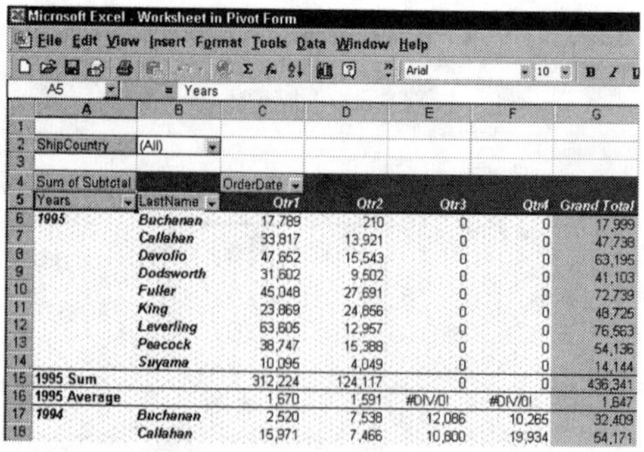

Figure 11.12 Arrange the fields to display your data effectively.

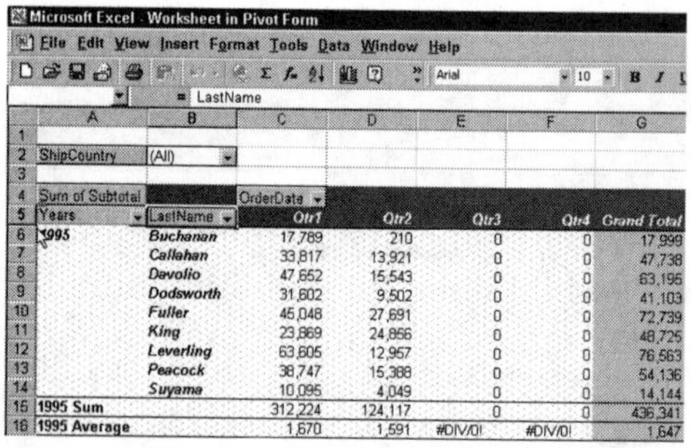

Figure 11.13 Move a field name to change how the pivot table displays your data.

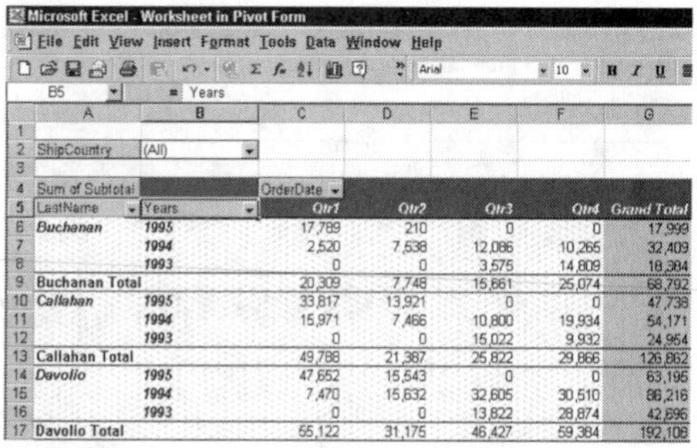

LastName	Years	Qtr1	Qtr2	Qtr3	Qtr4	Grand Total
Buchanan	1995	17,789	210	0	0	17,999
	1994	2,520	7,538	12,086	10,265	32,409
	1993	0	0	3,575	14,809	18,384
Buchanan Total		20,309	7,748	15,661	25,074	68,792
Callahan	1995	33,817	13,921	0	0	47,738
	1994	15,971	7,466	10,800	19,934	54,171
	1993	0	0	15,022	9,932	24,954
Callahan Total		49,788	21,387	25,822	29,866	126,862
Davolio	1995	47,652	15,543	0	0	63,195
	1994	7,470	15,632	32,605	30,510	86,216
	1993	0	0	13,822	28,874	42,696
Davolio Total		55,122	31,175	46,427	59,384	192,108

Figure 11.14 Your table, changed to reflect the pivot.

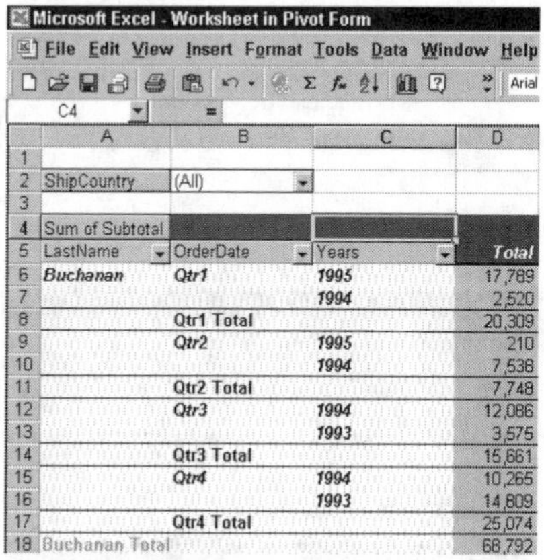

LastName	OrderDate	Years	Total
Buchanan	Qtr1	1995	17,789
		1994	2,520
	Qtr1 Total		20,309
	Qtr2	1995	210
		1994	7,538
	Qtr2 Total		7,748
	Qtr3	1994	12,086
		1993	3,575
	Qtr3 Total		15,661
	Qtr4	1994	10,265
		1993	14,809
	Qtr4 Total		25,074
Buchanan Total			68,792

Figure 11.15 This arrangement focuses on quarterly sales.

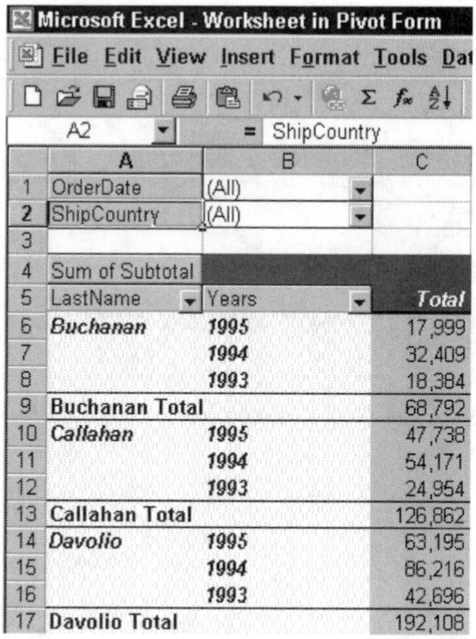

LastName	Years	Total
Buchanan	1995	17,999
	1994	32,409
	1993	18,384
Buchanan Total		68,792
Callahan	1995	47,738
	1994	54,171
	1993	24,954
Callahan Total		126,862
Davolio	1995	63,195
	1994	86,216
	1993	42,696
Davolio Total		192,108

Figure 11.16 This arrangement focuses on yearly sales.

4. Drag the OrderDate field header between the LastName and Years field headers.

   The data rows are now grouped by LastName, then OrderDate, and then Years (**Figure 11.15**). This arrangement emphasizes which quarter of the year the sales took place.

5. Drag the OrderDate field header to the right of the ShipCountry field header in the Page area.

   The pivot table appears with the data rows grouped by LastName and Years (**Figure 11.16**). This arrangement emphasizes yearly sales without considering quarterly fluctuations.

6. Drag the ShipCountry field header from the Page area to the right of the Years field header.

(continued on next page)

The pivot table appears with the ShipCountry fields in the Rows area (**Figure 11.17**).

7. Drag the ShipCountry field header onto the Total header (**Figure 11.18**).

When you drag a field header onto the Total header, the values in the field you moved (in this case, the ShipCountry field) modify how data is displayed in the pivot table's body (**Figure 11.19**).

✔ Tips

- You can undo a pivot by choosing Edit > Undo Pivot. You can undo as many pivots as you like.

- You can drag a field header from the Page area to the Row or Column heading to change how the pivot table displays your data. Likewise, you can drag a field header from the Row or Column headings area to the Page area to remove it from the grouping order.

- Pivot tables are wonderfully flexible, but it can be difficult to re-create the look you want if you're using more than a few fields. Note the arrangement of field headers that gives you the results you're looking for.

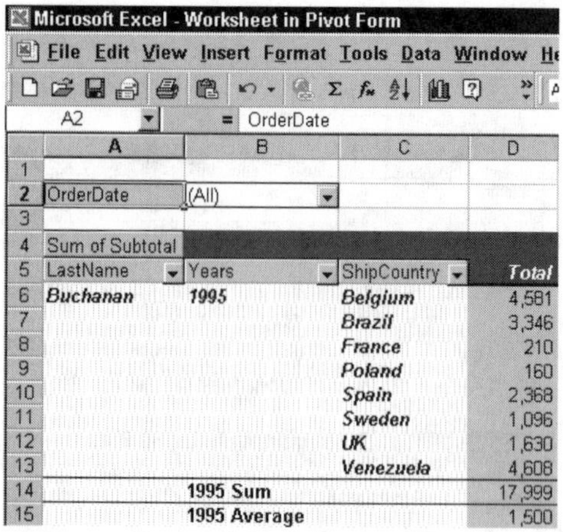

Figure 11.17 This arrangement breaks out sales by country.

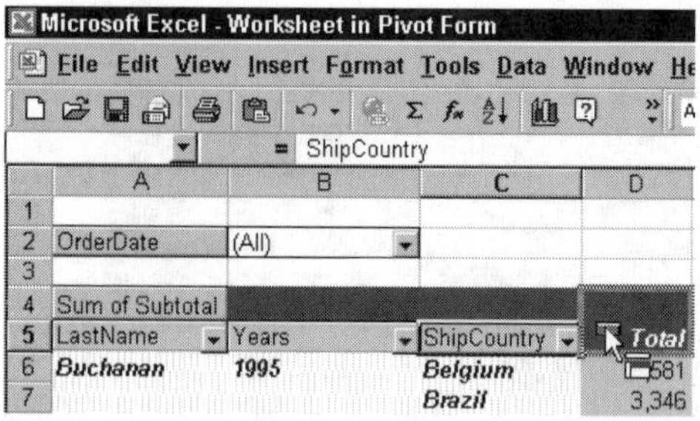

Figure 11.18 Move the Ship Country field header over the Total header...

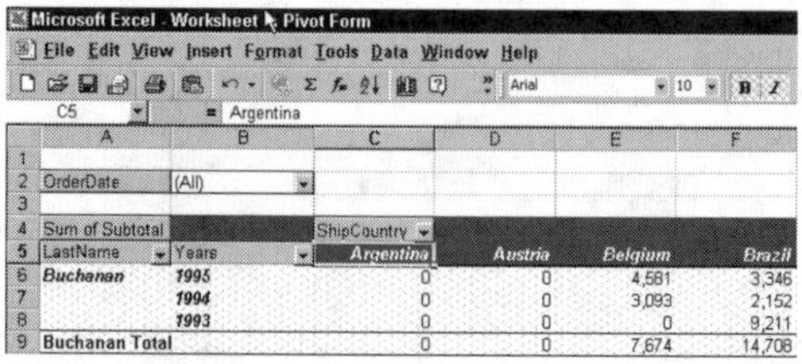

Figure 11.19 ...to display the countries to which sales were made.

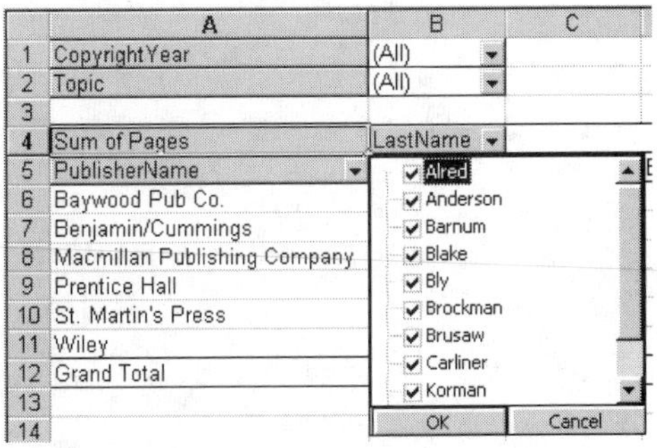

Figure 11.20 Click the drop-down menu on a field's header to display a list of the values in that field.

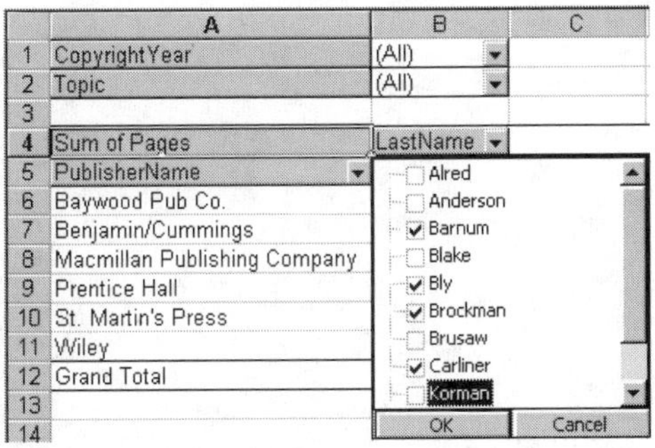

Figure 11.21 Every selected value is displayed in your pivot table; to hide information, clear its checkbox.

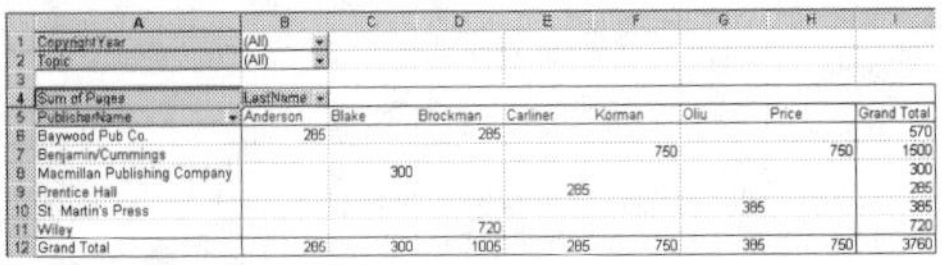

Figure 11.22 Click OK to present your pivot table in filtered form.

Filtering a Pivot Table

You can exert even more control over the display in your pivot table by choosing which of a field's values to display. For instance, you can choose to display only books published during a particular calendar year, you can look at sales from a particular quarter over several years, or you can just view sales from specific sales reps.

To filter a pivot table:

1. Open the pivot table you want to filter and click the Edit Pivot Table button at the bottom of the window.

2. Click the drop-down menu on the field header to display the values in that field.

    By default, they are all selected to be displayed in your results (**Figure 11.20**).

3. Clear the checkbox next to the values you don't want displayed in your results (**Figure 11.21**).

4. Click OK.

    Excel redraws your pivot table using only the values you selected in the drop-down menu (**Figure 11.22**).

✔ Tips

- You can undo a filter by choosing Edit > Undo Pivot from Excel's main menu bar.

- To close a drop-down menu without changing which values will be displayed, click the Cancel button at the bottom of each menu.

- You can use the fields in the Page area of your pivot table to filter your data as well. Select the values you want to display, click OK at the bottom of the list, and Excel will filter your table automatically.

IMPORTING

AND EXPORTING DATA

Access is a powerful program, but it's not the only database program available. Fortunately, you can *import* data from tables produced by other database programs, *link* tables in your Access databases to tables from other programs, and even include tables from other databases (and spreadsheet programs like Excel and Lotus 1-2-3) in your queries.

Data exchange in Access isn't a one-way street. You can *export* your Access tables to Paradox, dBASE, and other compatible database and spreadsheet programs. You can also export your table data to Microsoft Word for use in mass mailings or other documents.

Importing Data into Access

Access lets you work with tables created by other database programs in several ways. The simplest way to use table data from another database is to *import* the table into your Access database, which you can do with tables from a number of other popular database and spreadsheet programs.

Import tables from other programs when you want to use the table data and don't need to have any updates, additions, or deletions appear in the original copy of the table; in other words, if you don't need to have your copy of the table linked to the original. For instance, if you purchase a number of books for your library and record the book information in a file on a floppy disk, you can import that data to your main database and consolidate your records.

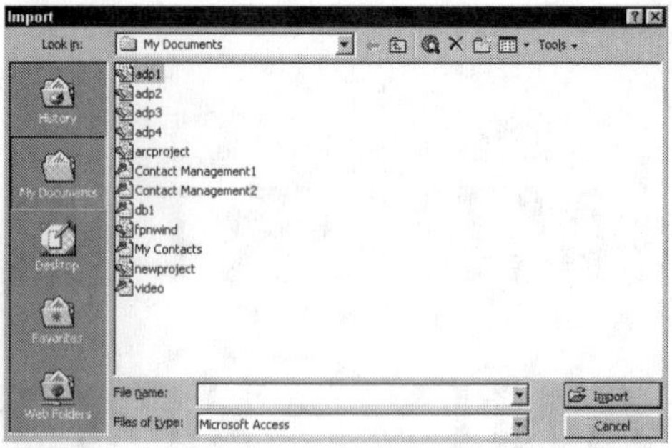

To import data into Access:

This task assumes that the data you want to import into Access is already on your computer or local network.

1. Open the database into which you want to import data and choose File > Get External Data > Import.

2. In the the Import window (**Figure 12.1**), click the Files of type drop-down menu and select the program used to create the table you want to import (**Figure 12.2**).

Figure 12.1 Open the Import window...

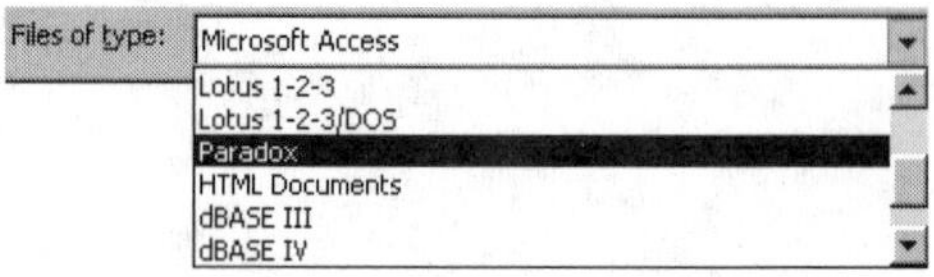

Figure 12.2 ...and select the type of file you want to import.

Figure 12.3 Click the file's icon to import it to your database.

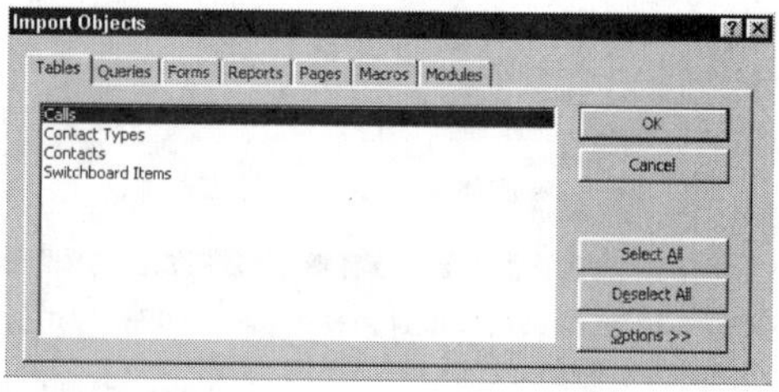

Figure 12.4 Click the table you want to import and click OK to import it.

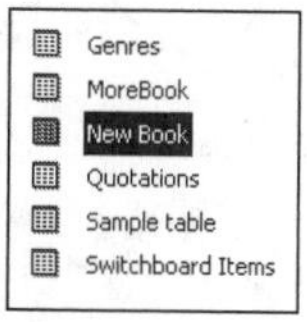

Figure 12.5 Your new table appears in your database with the rest of the tables.

3. Navigate to the directory containing the table you want to import, click the table's icon, and click Import (**Figure 12.3**). When you've finished importing tables, go to step 5.

or

Navigate to the directory containing the database with the table you want to import, click the database's icon, and click Import.

4. From the list of tables that appears, select the table you want to import and click OK (**Figure 12.4**).

For this example, we chose the New Books table.

5. Click Close.

The imported table appears in the list of tables in your database (**Figure 12.5**).

✔ Tips

■ You can use Access to translate a table to another format by importing the table into an Access database and exporting it to a table in the desired format. For example, you can import a text file into Access and then export the file to dBASE, Paradox, or any other format supported by Access.

■ You can, of course, import tables from other Access databases into the database you're using, as well.

IMPORTING DATA INTO ACCESS

Linking to Data

Importing tables into your Access databases creates an independent copy of the table you imported. Because the imported table exists independently of the original, any changes you make in one version of the table won't be reflected in the other.

If you want the changes made in either version of the table to be reflected in the other, you should *link* the table from the other program to your database instead of importing it. Linking a table to your database creates a logical pathway between the original table and the copy. When Access detects modifications in either version of the table, it changes both tables so they are identical.

You should link a table to your database whenever you need to work with the table in more than one database but want the tables to contain identical data. For instance, if you and another sales representative maintain Contacts tables in separate databases, you could link your tables together and keep both of them up to date.

To link a table:

1. Open the database you want to link to an external table and choose File > Get External Data > Link Tables.

2. In the Link window (**Figure 12.6**), click the Files of type drop-down menu and choose the program used to create the table that you want to link to (**Figure 12.7**).

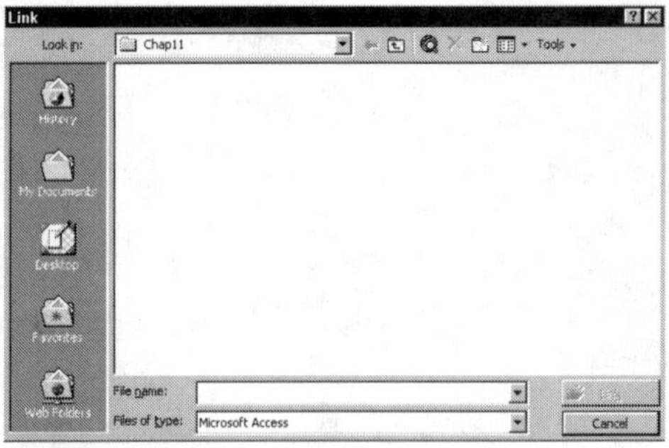

Figure 12.6 Find the file you want to link to your database using the Link navigation window.

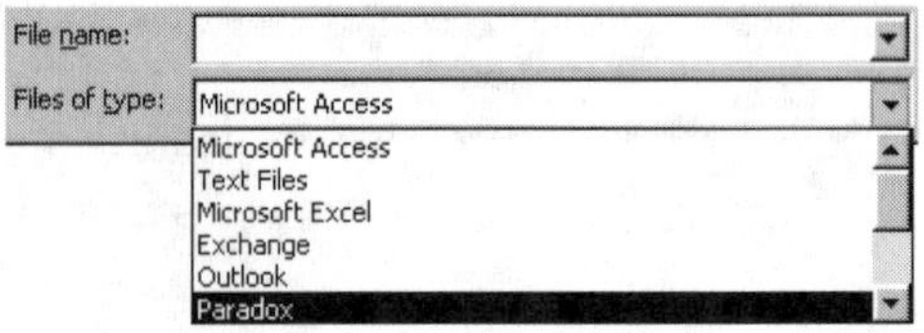

Figure 12.7 Choose which types of files to display in the Link window.

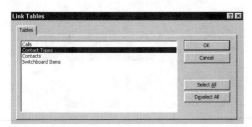

Figure 12.8 Select the table in the database to which you want to link.

3. Navigate to the directory containing the table you want to link to, click the table name, and then click Link. Access links the table to your database.

   or

   Navigate to the directory containing the database with the table you want to link to, click the database name, and then click Link. A list of tables in the selected database appears (**Figure 12.8**).

3. Click the table you want to link to your database and click OK.

   Access displays a dialog box verifying the link was created.

4. Click Close.

✔ Tips

- The icon displayed beside the name of a table indicates whether the table has been linked or imported from another database. Imported table icons indicate the table's source program. Linked table icons show the source program and an arrow.

- You can use linked tables in queries the same way you use tables created in your database.

- You can link Excel spreadsheets to your database. Access treats the linked spreadsheet like a linked table–any changes you make to the linked file in Access are reflected in the Excel spreadsheet, and vice versa.

LINKING TO DATA

Importing Data from Excel

In addition to working with data from other database programs, Access lets you import data from Excel, Lotus 1-2-3, and other spreadsheet packages.

Spreadsheets are like tables, though spreadsheet cells often contain formulas to calculate values based on other cells in the spreadsheet. Access doesn't import Excel formulas with the spreadsheet data, only the output of the formulas. While you can't calculate values within a table, you can create a query to *reproduce* the formula from the original Excel document (as you learned in Chapter 5).

To import an Excel file:

1. Open the main database window and choose File > Get External Data > Import.

2. Navigate to the directory containing the Excel file you want to import, click the name of the file, and click Import.

3. In the first window of the Import Spreadsheet Wizard (**Figure 12.9**), you can choose to see either aWorksheet or a specific range of cells.

   The data in the sheet appears in the Sample Data pane (**Figure 12.10**). Click Next to continue.

4. Select the checkbox at the top of the screen if you want Access to use the values in the first row of the spreadsheet as the field names for your new table (**Figure 12.11**).

   If you don't use the values in the first row of the spreadsheet as the field names for your new table, Access automatically assigns the name "F1" to the first field, "F2" to the second, and so forth. Click Next to continue.

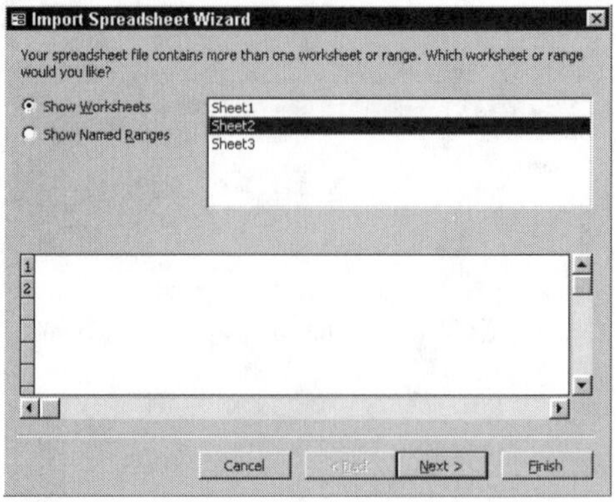

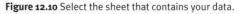

Figure 12.9 The Import Spreadsheet Wizard makes incorporating spreadsheet data a snap.

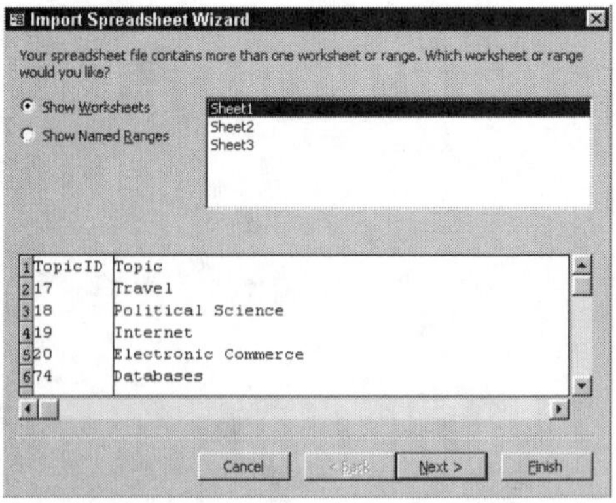

Figure 12.10 Select the sheet that contains your data.

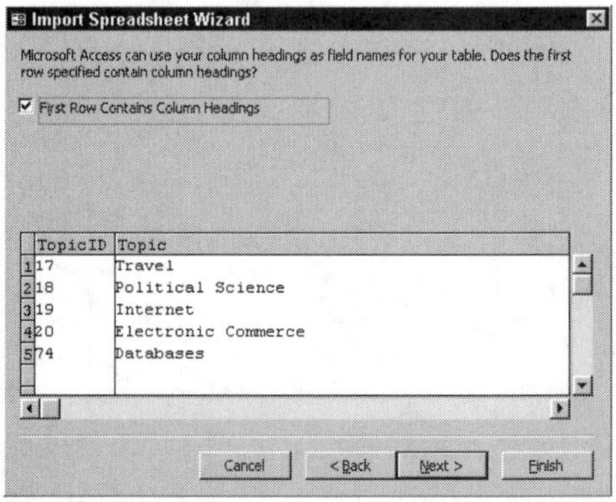

Figure 12.11 Let Access know if the first row of the spreadsheet contains field names.

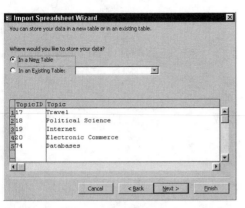

Figure 12.12 Click In a New Table to create a separate repository for your information.

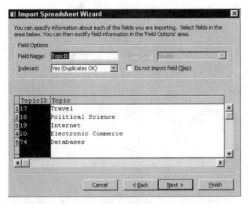

Figure 12.13 Set each field's Field Options.

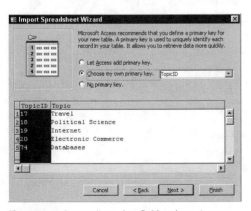

Figure 12.14 Set a primary key field, or have Access do it for you.

5. Select the In a New Table option to have Access create a new table based on your spreadsheet data. Click Next (**Figure 12.12**).

A representation of your spreadsheet appears in the middle of the wizard screen.

6. Select a field, modify its name as necessary, or use the Indexed drop-down menu to have Access index the field's values. Click Next when you're done (**Figure 12.13**).

7. Access offers three options for choosing a primary key (**Figure 12.14**).

◆ Click the Let Access add primary key option button to have Access choose a key.

◆ Select the field you want to be the primary key field for your new table and click the Choose my own primary key option button.

◆ Click the No primary key option button to create your table without a key.

Select an option and click Next.

8. Type the name of your new table in the Import to Table text box and click Finish.

To append Excel data to an existing table:

1. Display the main database window and choose File > Get External Data > Import.

2. Navigate to the directory containing the Excel file you want to import, click the name of the file, and click Import.

3. In the first window of the Import Spreadsheet Wizard (**Figure 12.15**), click the option button that corresponds to the Excel sheet that contains your data. (The default selection, Sheet 1, will almost always contain the data you want.)

   The data in the sheet appears in the Sample Data pane. Click Next to continue.

4. Select the checkbox at the top of the screen if the first row of the spreadsheet contains the field names for your table. If so, the field names must match the field names in the table you're appending data to. Click Next.

5. Select the In an Existing Table option, enter the name of the table you're appending to in the text box, and then click Next (**Figure 12.16**).

   You can also click the drop-down menu button at the edge of the In an Existing Table text box and choose a target table from the list that appears.

6. Click Finish.

   Access displays a dialog box indicating that the import was successful.

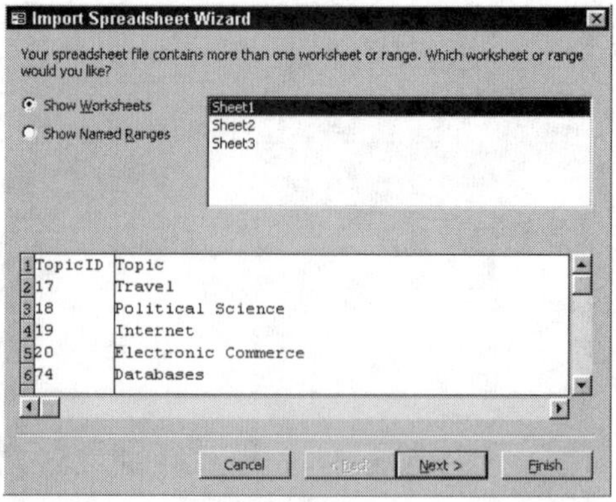

Figure 12.15 The Import Spreadsheet Wizard makes it easy to bring Excel and other spreadsheet data into Access.

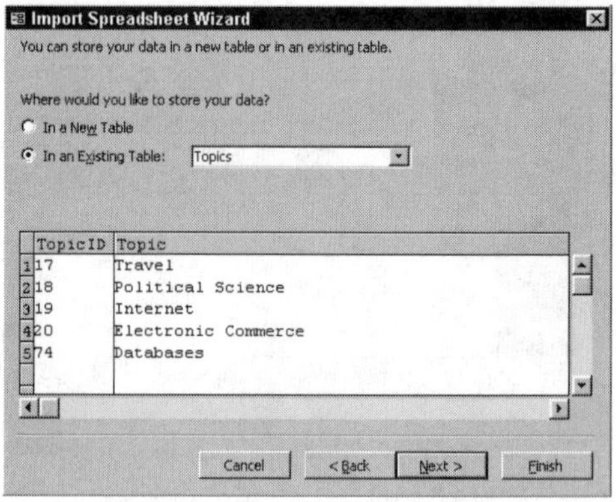

Figure 12.16 Choose In an Existing Table to append your spreadsheet data to an existing table.

✔ Tips

- You can import spreadsheets from programs other than Excel and Lotus 1-2-3, though you will need to save the file in either Excel or Lotus format before attempting the import.

- Access makes its best guess as to the best data type for each field it imports, but you should open your new table in Design view and make sure the data type assignments are correct. (For information on data types, see Chapter 3 and Appendix B).

APPEND EXCEL DATA TO EXISTING TABLES

Creating a Mail Merge with Word

As you learned in Chapter 6, Access can create mailing labels based on the records in a table.

What Access can't do very easily by itself is use those records to create a mailing based on your contact file. When combined with Microsoft Word, however, Access is the perfect tool for creating mass mailings quickly and easily. Access *shares* its data with Word...it doesn't export it. It's more like a link so that Word can use the data from an Access table or query.

Mail merges, the technical term for combining a series of records from one file with a static document, help businesses and organizations stay in contact with their suppliers and customers. You can use Word's mail merge capabilities to generate mailings for press releases, invitations, and even the dreaded holiday form letter.

To create a mail merge:

1. Launch Microsoft Word and choose Tools > Mail Merge.

2. When the Mail Merge Helper appears (**Figure 12.17**), click Create and choose the type of merge you want to perform from the list that appears (**Figure 12.18**).

   For this example, we chose Form Letters. A dialog box appears (**Figure 12.19**).

3. Click New Main Document, and the Mail Merge Helper reappears.

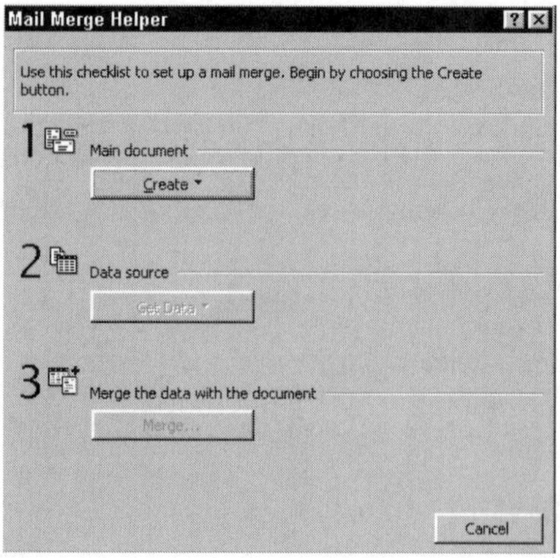

Figure 12.17 The Mail Merge Helper keeps you from making mincemeat of your mail merge.

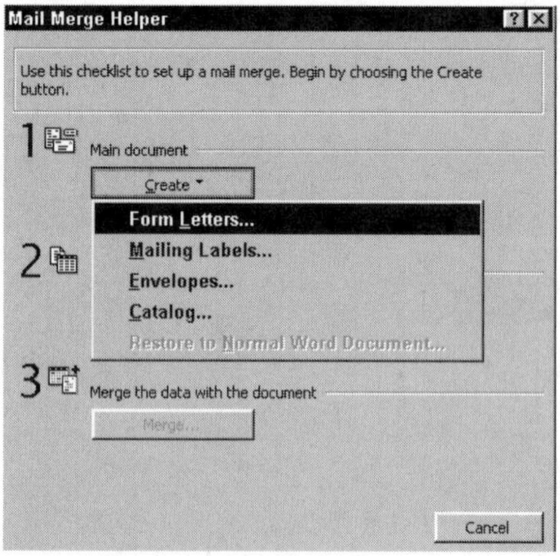

Figure 12.18 Choose how you want to merge your database and Word document.

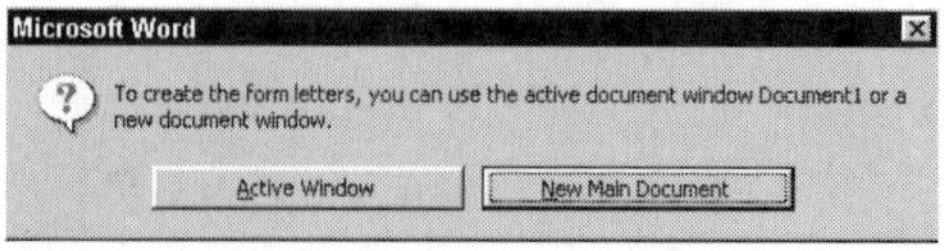

Figure 12.19 Click New Main Document to start with a blank slate.

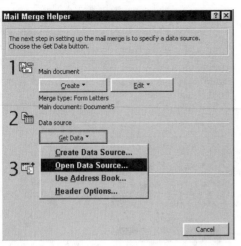

Figure 12.20 Navigate to the database containing the table for your mail merge...

Files of type: All Word Documents
- All Word Documents
- Word Documents
- Web Pages
- Rich Text Format
- Text Files
- MS Access Databases

File name:

Figure 12.21 ...let Word know you're looking for an Access database...

Microsoft Access

Tables | Queries

Tables in books:
- Authors
- BookAuthors
- Books
- BookTopics
- Complete Table
- Contacts
- Quotations
- Sample table

OK | Cancel | View SQL...

Figure 12.22 ...and select the table in the Access dialog box.

4. Click Get Data and choose Open Data Source from the menu (**Figure 12.20**). The Open Data Source navigation window appears (**Figure 12.21**).

5. Click the Files of type drop-down menu and choose MS Access Databases from the menu .

6. Navigate to the directory containing the database you want to draw your data from, click the name of the database, and then click Open.

7. In the Microsoft Access dialog box (**Figure 12.22**), click the name of the table containing the records you want to merge into the Word documents and click OK.

Word displays a dialog box indicating that it found no merge fields in your document (that is, there's no place for Access to put your records yet.).

(continued on next page)

8. Click Edit Main Document (**Figure 12.23**).

9. When the Mail Merge toolbar appears, type your form letter's body text.

10. Click Insert Merge Field on the Mail Merge toolbar and choose the first field you want to add to your documents (**Figure 12.24**).

    Continue adding fields to your document. You will need to type in all punctuation and spacing.

11. Save your document by choosing File > Save and click the Merge toolbar button (**Figure 12.25**).

12. The Merge dialog box appears (**Figure 12.26**). Click Merge.

    Access merges your database records and the base Word document into a new Word file, which appears when the merge is completed.

13. Choose File > Save to save your new Word document.

✔ Tips

- You can click the OfficeLinks toolbar button to perform a mail merge, publish your table as a Word document, or analyze it using Excel.

- You can't undo a mail merge by choosing Edit > Undo, but you can discard the results by closing the resulting file without saving it. Your base document will still remain open for editing.

- To print the results of your mail merge automatically, click the Merge to Printer toolbar button.

Figure 12.23 Click Edit Main Document to make your Word file presentable.

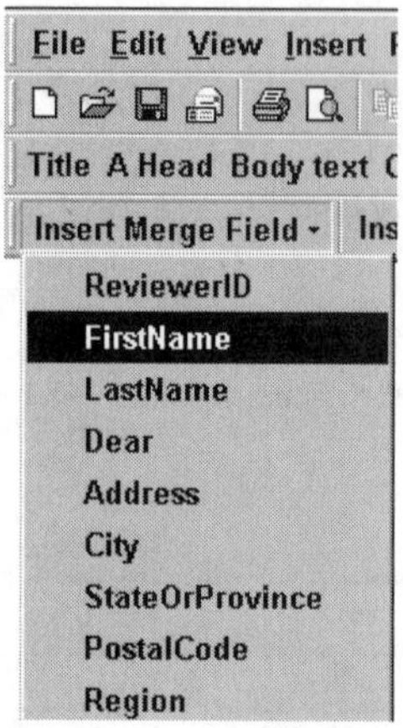

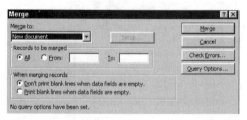

Figure 12.24 Add fields to your document using the Insert Merge Field drop-down menu.

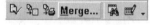

Figure 12.25 Click the Merge toolbar button to open the dialog box...

Figure 12.26 ...from which you can run your mail merge.

```
109,"(The) Elements of Technical
Writing",1995,"20130856","Macmillan Publishing
Company",,,,"General",,150,"Buy at Amazon!#http://Buy at
Amazon!#",,|
110,"Handbook of Technical Writing",1997,"312166907","St. Martin's
Press",,,,"General",,385,"http://www.amazon.com/exec/obidos/ISBN=0
312166907/raycomminca/#http://www.amazon.com/exec/obidos/ISBN=0312
166907/raycomminca/#",,
```

Figure 12.27 A text file with comma delimiters.

```
109       (The) Elements of Technical Writing
1995  20130856                          Macmillan Publishing
Company
General                             150    Buy at Amazon!#http://Buy
at Amazon!#
110       Handbook of Technical Writing
1997  312166907                          St. Martin's Press
General                             385
http://www.amazon.com/exec/obidos/ISBN=0312166907/raycomminca/#http://www.amazon
.com/exec/obidos/ISBN=0312166907/raycomminca/#
```

Figure 12.28 A text file with fixed-width fields.

Exporting Data from Access to Another Database

Access gives you lots of ways to import data from other sources, but data exchange works both ways. You can use data from databases like Paradox and dBASE and spreadsheets like Excel and Lotus 1-2-3, and you can export your data to those formats as well.

You can export your Access data as a *delimited* or a *fixed width* text file. Delimited text files are files where values in fields are separated by a particular character, like a comma or semicolon (**Figure 12.27**). Fixed width text files don't separate field values with special characters. Instead, they allot a specific number of characters to each field and wherever necessary, add extra spaces to the value to make the character count come out right (**Figure 12.28**). In a fixed width table with three fields of 30, 20, and 20 spaces each, the value in the first field always starts in the first space, the second field's value always starts in the 31st space, and the final field's value always starts in the 51st space (the first space following the first and second fields).

You can export data to most of the newer PC-based database packages without specifying field sizes, so usually you won't have to worry about fixed field widths. Exporting your data with fixed field sizes is quite useful if you want to create a uniform (and uniformly legible) presentation of your data for use in a text document or an old clunky database program.

EXPORTING DATA TO ANOTHER DATABASE

To export data from Access to another database:

1. Display the tables in your database, click the table you want to export, and choose File > Export.

   The Export navigation window appears (**Figure 12.29**).

2. Navigate to the directory in which you want to save the exported table.

3. Type a name for the file in the File Name text box.

4. Click the Save as type drop-down menu and choose the file format you want to assign to your exported table.

5. Click Save.

   Access exports your table to a file with the name and format you choose; however, the transfer doesn't preserve the table's formatting.

To export data from Access to a delimited text file:

1. Display the tables in your database, click the table you want to export, and choose File > Export.

   The Export navigation window appears.

2. Navigate to the directory in which you want to save the exported table.

3. Type a name for the file in the File Name text box.

4. Click the Save as type drop-down menu and choose Text Files (**Figure 12.30**).

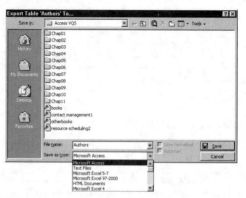

Figure 12.29 Choose a home for your file using the Export navigation window.

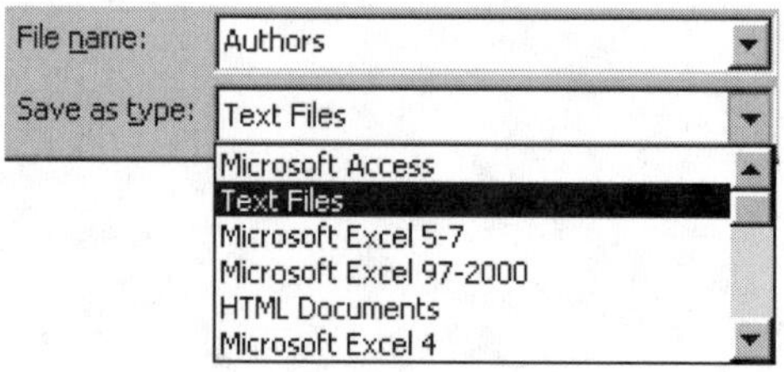

Figure 12.30 Choose Text File from the Save as type menu.

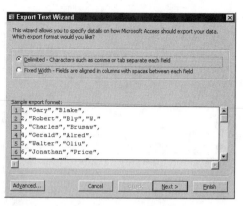

Figure 12.31 Move through the Export Text Wizard to save your table as a delimited text file.

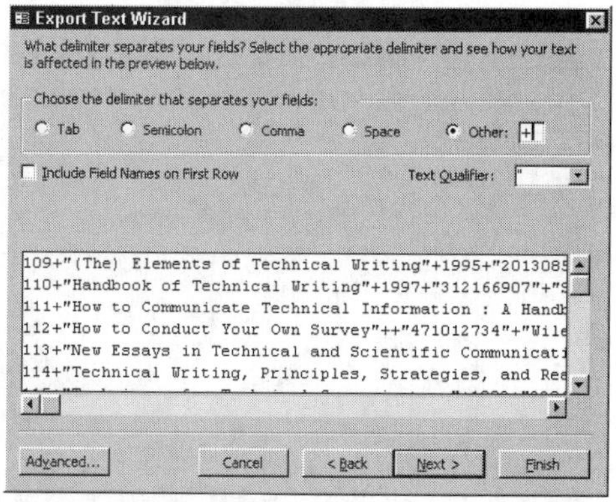

Figure 12.32 Click a delimiter option that will separate your fields.

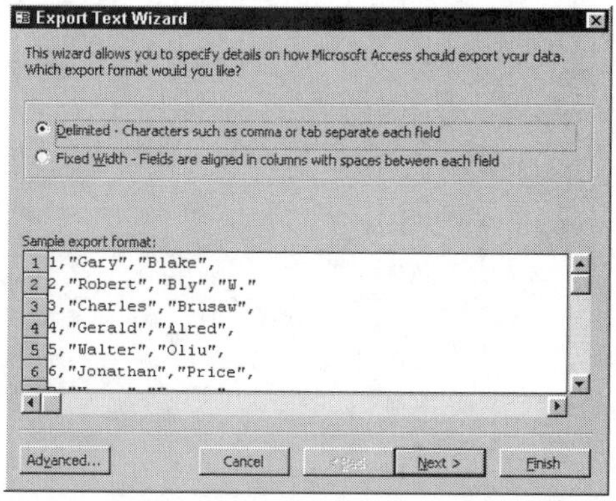

Figure 12.33 The Export Text Wizard helps you translate Access tables to text files.

5. Click Save.

The first screen of the Export Text Wizard appears (**Figure 12.31**). Click Next.

6. Select the character you want to use to separate your fields (**Figure 12.32**).

Your options are a comma (the default choice), a tab, a space, or a semicolon. If you want a custom character, click the Other option button and type your chosen character in the text box. Click Next to continue.

7. Type the name and directory path for your file and click Finish.

Access displays a dialog box confirming that the export was successful.

To export Access data to a fixed width text file:

1. Display the tables in your database, click the table you want to export, and choose File > Export.

2. Navigate to the directory in which you want to save the exported table.

3. Type a name for the file in the File Name text box.

4. Click the Save as type drop-down menu and choose Text Files.

5. Click Save.

The first screen of the Export Text Wizard appears (**Figure 12.33**). Click Next to continue.

(continued on next page)

6. Select the Fixed Width option and click Next (**Figure 12.34**).

A sample of your data appears in the wizard's screen. Field widths are indicated by lines beside the fields' contents.

7. Change a field's width by dragging the arrow at the top of its border to the desired position on the ruler at the top of the pane (**Figure 12.35**). Click Next.

8. Type a name and directory path for your exported file and click Finish.

A dialog box appears indicating that the export was successful.

✔ Tips

■ When you export an Access table to a delimited text file, make sure your records don't contain the delimiting character! A single stray comma, semicolon, or space in your table can cause the target program to read the field boundaries incorrectly and store information in the wrong fields.

■ Most database and spreadsheet programs can import delimited text files, though you should check your program's documentation (or ask the user who's receiving your exported file) to determine whether the program requires delimited or fixed width files.

■ You can also export your Access database to a previous version of Access. If your clients or collaborators haven't upgraded to Access 2000, you can save your files in an older format for Access or even other database programs, such as dBASE and Paradox.

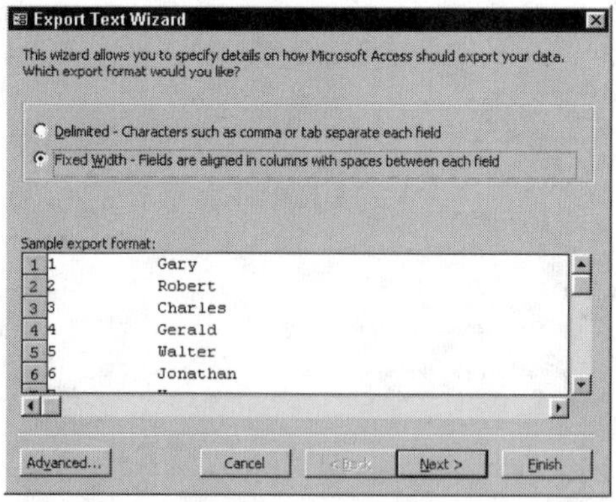

Figure 12.34 Choose the Fixed Width option button to have Access export your data to a text file with invariable field sizes.

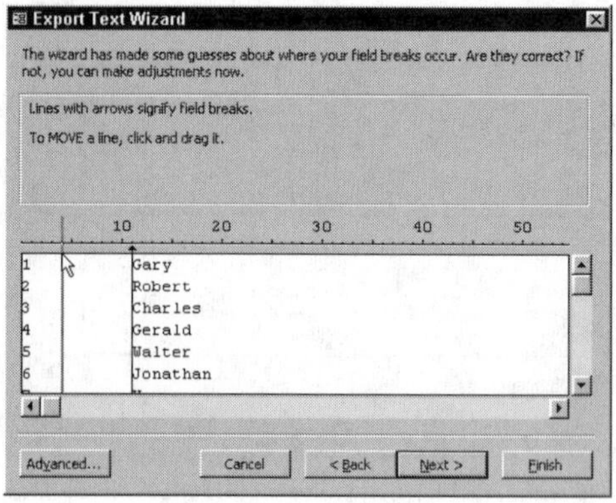

Figure 12.35 Change a field's width by dragging its border in the preview of your table's layout.

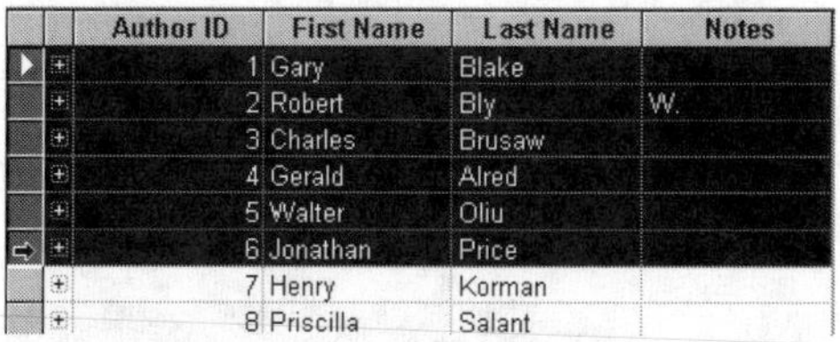

Figure 12.36 Use the row selectors to copy the records you want to paste in another application.

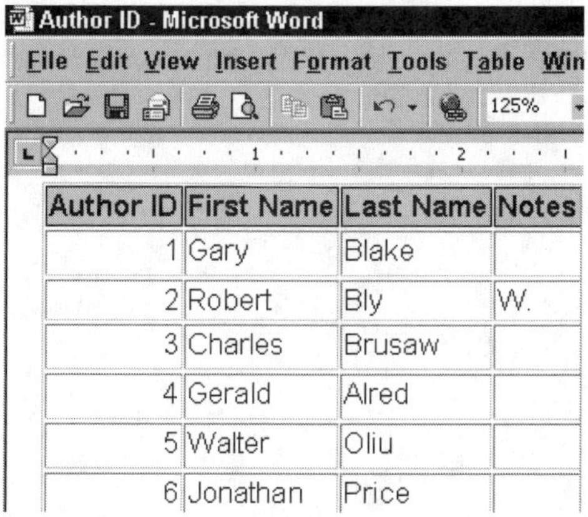

Figure 12.37 Your pasted records appear as a table in Word.

Copying Data to Another Program

Access has many powerful tools and techniques you can use to transfer data or receive it from a variety of other programs, but there may be times when all you want to do is copy a few records in a table and paste them into another document. Because Access uses standard Windows cutting and pasting, it's easy to copy only a few records.

To copy data to a word processing document:

1. Open in Datasheet view the table (or query) with the records you want to copy.

2. Click the row selector of the first record you want to copy data from and drag the mouse pointer until you've highlighted every record you want to copy (**Figure 12.36**).

   The rows you select must be adjacent to each other in the table.

3. Choose Edit > Copy.

4. Open the target file, select the location where you want the records to appear, and choose Edit > Paste.

   Your records appear in the target file, formatted as a table (**Figure 12.37**).

To copy data to a spreadsheet:

1. Open in Datasheet view the table (or query) containing the values you want to copy.

2. Click the row selector of the first row you want to copy data from and drag the mouse pointer until you've highlighted every record you want to copy.

3. Choose Edit > Copy.

4. Open the target file, click the first cell in which you want your data to appear, and choose Edit > Paste.

   Your records appear in the target spreadsheet (**Figure 12.38**).

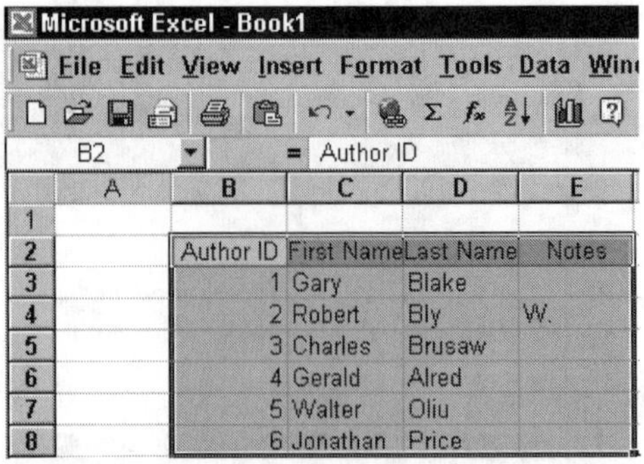

✔ Tips

- To copy all of the values in a field, click that field's column selector.

- If you want to select a few values (in adjacent cells) from a column, click anywhere in the first cell, hold down the Shift key, and click anywhere in the last cell you want to select.

Figure 12.38 Your records appear in the spreadsheet.

		Topic ID	Topic
	+	1	Management
	+	2	Visual
	+	3	Style
	+	4	Interesting
	+	5	Online
	+	6	Editing
	+	8	International
	+	9	Usability
	+	10	Indexing
	+	11	Training
▶	+	17	Travel
	+	18	Political Science
	+	19	Internet
	+	20	Electronic Commerce
→	+	74	Databases
	+	115	General
*		(AutoNumber)	

Figure 12.39 Use the row selectors to choose which records you want to copy and paste into another table.

Copying Data to Another Access Database

Linking and importing tables are powerful features, but they're a bit *too* powerful when all you want to do is copy a few records from a table in one Access database to a table in another. You can use the standard Windows cut-and-paste functions to copy records from one database to another.

To copy data to another Access database:

1. Display the tables in your database, click the table containing the data you want to copy to another Access database, and then click Open to open your table in Datasheet view.

2. Click the row selector of the first record you want to copy, then hold down the Shift key and click the row selector of the last record you want to copy to the other Access database (**Figure 12.39**).

    The selected rows are highlighted. The records you want to copy must be next to each other in the table.

3. Choose Edit > Copy.

4. Choose File > Open and navigate to the directory containing the database with the table you want to paste your records into.

5. Click the name of the database and click Open.

    The first database you opened closes— Access only allows you to have one database open at a time.

(continued on next page)

6. Display the tables in your database, click the name of the table you want to paste the records into, and click the Open toolbar button to open the target table in Datasheet view.

7. Choose Edit > Paste Append.

The records appear at the bottom of your datasheet (**Figure 12.40**).

✔ Tips

■ Be careful to choose Paste Append rather than Paste, as pasting the records you copied will delete every existing record in the target table.

■ You can filter or sort your table to have records you want to copy appear next to each other (See Chapter 7). You can also paste records into a filtered table.

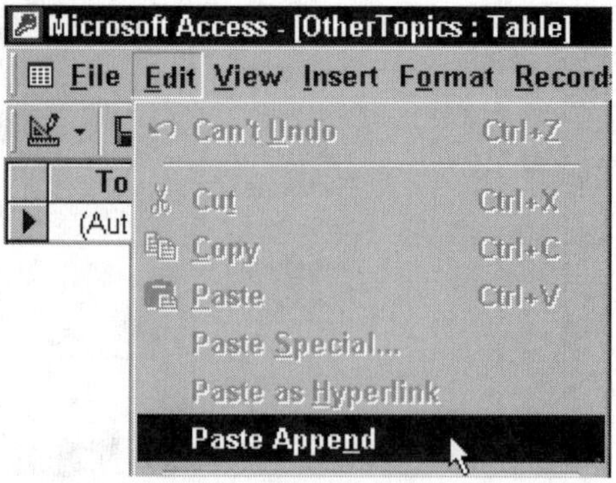

Figure 12.40 Choose Paste Append, and voila! The records appear in their new home.

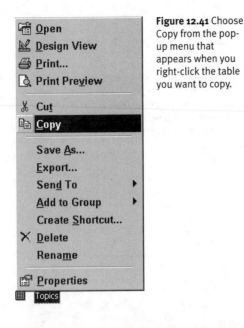

Figure 12.41 Choose Copy from the pop-up menu that appears when you right-click the table you want to copy.

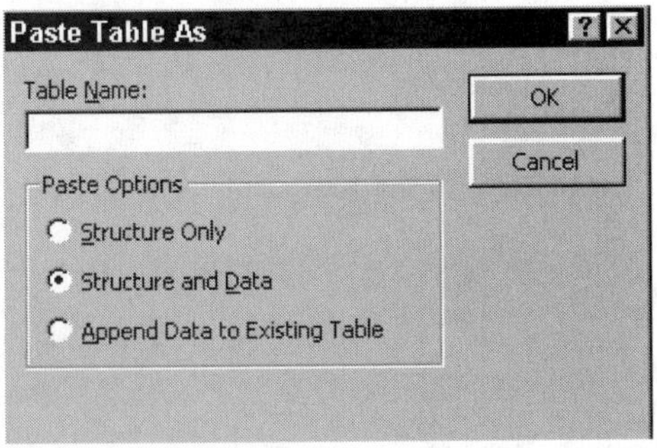

Figure 12.42 The Paste Table As dialog box.

Copying a Table Within a Database

Importing (or linking to) a table from another database or simply copying a few records from one table to another are handy features to have. Another useful ability involves creating a copy of an existing table in the same database. Copying a table within a database offers more flexibility than using the Save As menu option. Save As creates a new copy of your table, both its data and structure, but it doesn't let you copy just the table's structure or append the records in the current table to another table.

When you copy a table, you might not want to transfer the data from the original table to the copy; sometimes just the structure of the table will suffice. For instance, if your database contains a Customers table (with customer contact information for your active customers), you can copy the table to create a separate Leads table that contains contact information for potential customers for another product or service.

To copy a table within a database:

1. Display the tables in your database and right-click the table you want to copy.

2. From the pop-up menu, choose Copy (**Figure 12.41**).

3. Right-click any open spot in the main database window and choose Paste.

   The Paste Table As dialog box appears (**Figure 12.42**).

4. Type the name for your new table in the area provided.

(continued on next page)

5. Select the option button representing the way you want to paste the copy of your table into your database (**Figure 12.43**).

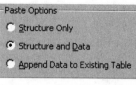

Figure 12.43 Select one of three options when pasting a copy of a table into a database.

◆ Structure and Data (the default option) creates a new table using the copied table's structure and data; that is, an exact duplicate of the copied table, complete with contents.

◆ Structure Only creates a table using just the structure (field names and properties) of the original table as a base.

◆ Append Data to Existing Table appends the copied table's records to another table. In the Paste Table As dialog box, enter the existing table to which you want to append the records. Note that the source and target tables must have identical field names for this option to work.

6. Click OK.

Your new table appears in the main database window.

or

Access appends the records from the table you copied to the table you named in the Paste Table As dialog box.

✔ Tip

■ Copying a table within the same database is a quick way to make a record of how the table looked at a particular time. If you include the date in the copied table name, you'll have an archive of your data within easy reach.

PUBLISHING TO THE WEB

It's no exaggeration to say that the explosive growth in the late 1990s of the World Wide Web, a global network of sites written using the Hypertext Markup Language (HTML), has given companies and individuals an unprecedented freedom to publish information about themselves, their interests, and their products.

Companies can also use Web technologies to make information available over private networks running the same protocol that they use on the Internet. These private networks, or *intranets*, are powerful tools for collecting and disseminating information inside an organization.

One of the many advantages to publishing your Access data to the Web is that you can offer a product catalog that includes information such as your prices, product descriptions, model numbers, and so on, on your public Web site and offer your sales representatives inventory and sales information through a corporate intranet.

Deciding How to Publish

Access gives you three options for publishing information to the Web: *static pages, dynamic pages,* and *data access pages* (a new type of Access database object in Access 2000).

Static Web pages are just that—static. Once you write information to a file, it won't change unless you edit the file's contents using a text editor or Web creation tool.

Dynamic Web pages, specifically Microsoft's *Active Server Pages,* are generated on the fly when the user opens them. The Active Server Page file (which has a *.asp* extension) contains HTML tags, Visual Basic Script (VB Script) code to call ActiveX controls, SQL queries, and a link to your database. When a user opens an .asp file, the Web server (such as Internet Information Server 3.0 or later) links to your database, runs the VB Script code and queries, and combines the results into an HTML file. Because the server runs the queries and code when the user opens the page, the user gets to see the most recent information in the database and if they refresh their browser window, they can see if any new information has been added to the underlying database.

Data Access Pages (referred to simply as *pages* in Access) take the flexibility of dynamic Web pages further by allowing users to interact with the data that was used to create the page. You can create pages to analyze, enter, edit, and review data.

Consider publishing your database objects as static Web pages whenever the information in the HTML document is relatively stable. If the information in your database changes on a regular basis and/or if you want your users to be able to view your data as it stands when they request the information, you should use a dynamic Web page. If you want to allow your users to interact with your data (and potentially add to it) over the Web, you should publish your data on a data access page.

There are significant restrictions when publishing information to the Web, however. For instance, to publish Active Server Pages you must have access to a server that supports them. Here are some packages you can use to host your .asp files:

◆ Microsoft's Internet Information Server (IIS) version 2.0 and later with Internet Database Connector of ActiveX Server on Windows NT 4.0 or later.

◆ Microsoft Personal Web Server on Windows 95/98 or Windows NT Workstation 4.0 or later.

You can publish data access pages on any of those platforms, although you'll need to use Microsoft Internet Explorer 4.0 or later to view them. Designing data access pages requires Internet Explorer 5.0 (which comes with Office 2000) or later installed.

DECIDING HOW TO PUBLISH

Publishing Static Web Pages

Creating a static Web page is quite easy with Access. You simply export the database object you want to publish to an HTML file.

You can create more than just a simple Web page using a template when you export your database object to an HTML file. Much like AutoFormats for forms or reports, a template dresses up your Web page and establishes a uniform design for pages on your network.

To publish a database object as a static Web page:

1. Click the object you want to publish as a static Web page and choose File > Export. The Export Form To navigation window appears (**Figure 13.1**).

2. Navigate to the directory in which you want to publish the static page and type a name for the page in the File name text box.

3. Click the Save as type drop-down menu button (**Figure 13.2**), choose HTML Documents, and click Save.

4. In the HTML Output Options dialog box (**Figure 13.3**), click Browse, navigate to the directory containing the template you want to use for your Web page, and click OK.

   Access publishes your object as a static Web page.

✔ Tips

■ You can publish any of your tables, queries, forms, and reports as static Web documents.

■ In our installation of Access, the built-in templates are located in C:\Program Files\MicrosoftOffice\Templates\1033\Webs\.

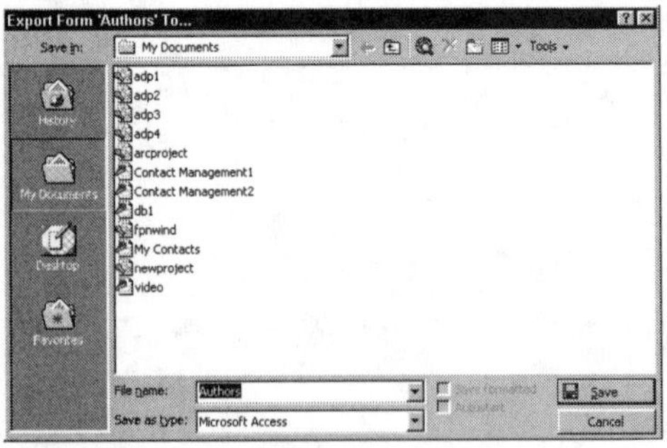

Figure 13.1 You use the Export dialog box to save your documents as static Web pages.

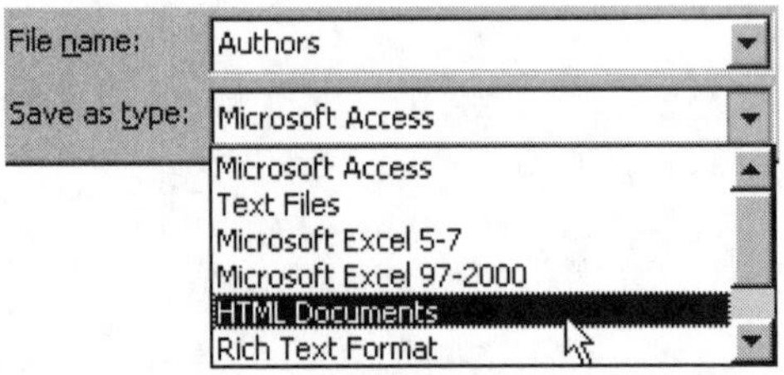

Figure 13.2 Choose HTML Documents from the Save as type drop-down menu.

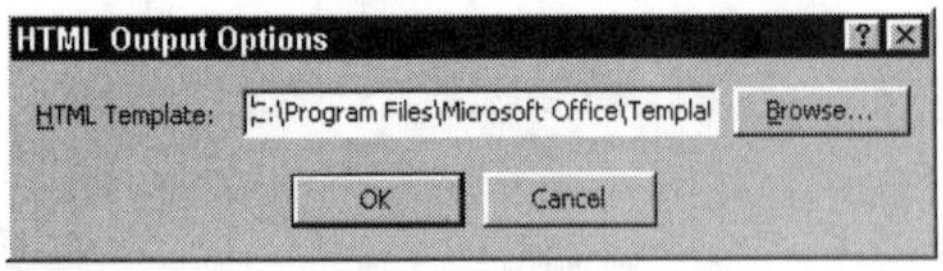

Figure 13.3 Select a template for your Web page from the HTML Output Options dialog box.

Figure 13.4 The Export navigation window also helps you create dynamic Web page.

Figure 13.5 Select Microsoft Active Server Pages from the list of file types.

Figure 13.6 Choose a template to apply to your data access page.

Publishing Dynamic Pages

Publishing your database objects as dynamic Web pages is very similar to publishing them as static pages, although you need to make a few more decisions about where the data will come from and what identification and password (if any) the user will need to enter to open the page.

To publish dynamic pages:

1. Click the object you want to publish as a dynamic page and choose File > Export.
   The Export Table To navigation window appears (**Figure 13.4**).

2. Navigate to the directory in which you want to publish the dynamic page, and type a name for the page in the File name text box.

3. Click the Save as type drop-down menu button (**Figure 13.5**), choose Microsoft Active Server Pages, and click Save.

4. In the HTML Output Options dialog box, click Browse, navigate to the directory containing the template you want to use for your Web page (**Figure 13.6**), and click OK.

   In our installation of Access the built-in templates are located in C:\Program Files\MicrosoftOffice\Templates\1033\Webs\. In the final release, the directory will probably be named C:\Program Files\Microsoft Office\Templates\Webs.

5. In the Data Source Name text box of the ASP Output Options dialog box (**Figure 13.7**), type the name of the object supplying the data for your .asp page.

6. Type a user name and password (if desired) to limit the availability of your page.

(continued on next page)

7. Type the URL (Uniform Resource Locator, or Web address) of your dynamic page.

8. Type the number of minutes for the server to wait before closing the connection with computers requesting the .asp file.

If your server slows down due to increased traffic, try decreasing the time from the default of five minutes to three minutes.

8. Click OK.

Access publishes your object as a dynamic Web page.

✔ Tip

■ To publish Active Server Pages, you need to create the. asp file on a system running Internet Information Server 3.0 or higher and Access. You can also use Microsoft Personal Web Server on Windows 95/98 and Windows NT 4.0 or later. You can verify your system is running these programs by opening the Start menu and looking for Microsoft IIS or Microsoft Personal Web Server under Programs.

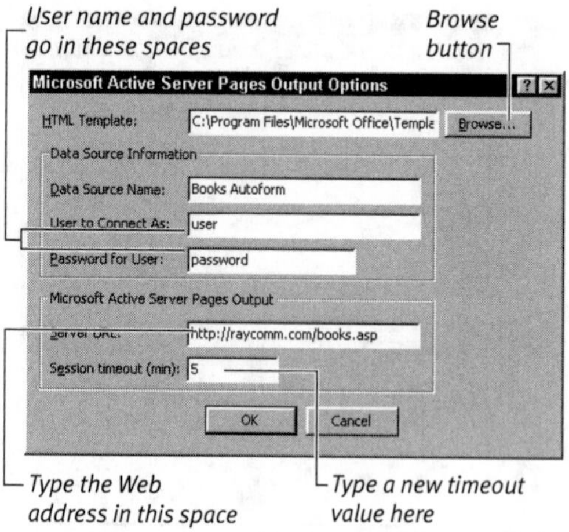

User name and password go in these spaces   *Browse button*

Type the Web address in this space   *Type a new timeout value here*

Figure 13.7 The HTML Output Options dialog box, with a few questions for you.

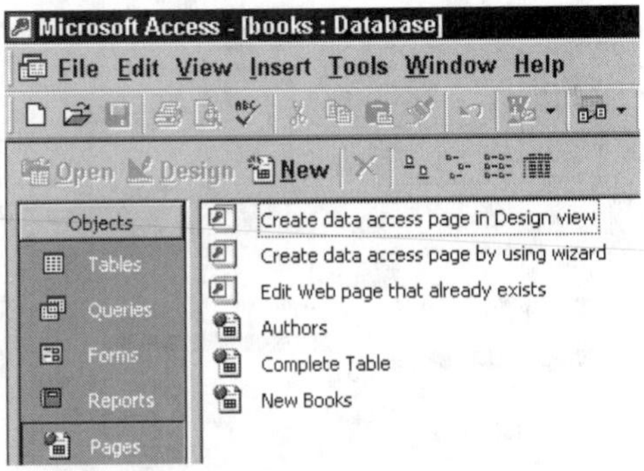

Figure 13.8 The data access pages and wizards in your database.

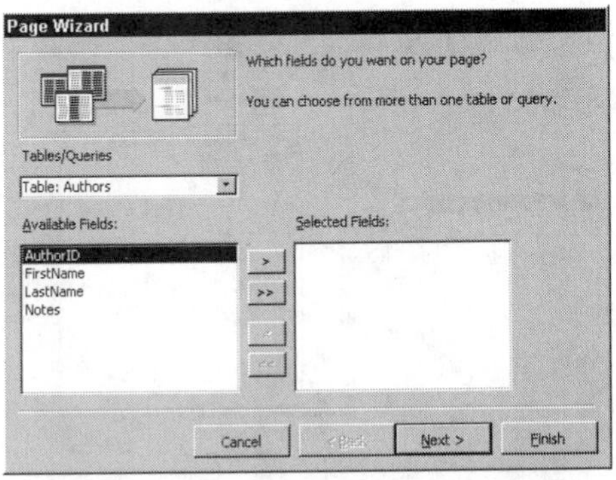

Figure 13.9 The first screen from the Page Wizard.

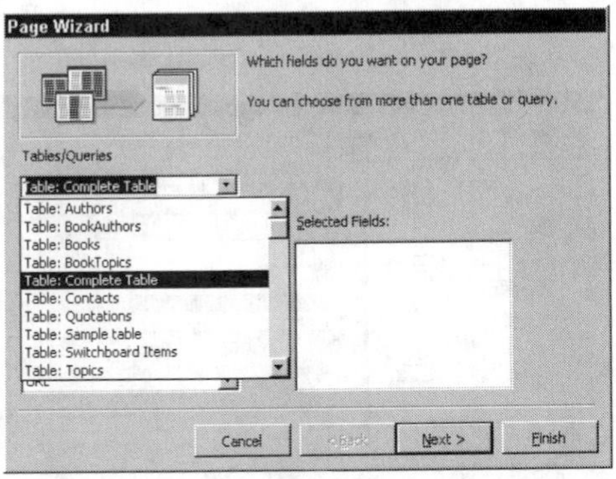

Figure 13.10 Choose the first table or query from which you want to select fields for your page.

Publishing Data Access Pages

One of the new features in Access 2000 is the *data access page*, usually referred to as a *page*. Data access pages are objects into which users can enter data over an intranet or the Internet. Users can also view and analyze data from the database you make available to them.

Pages have quite a bit in common with reports, which we covered in Chapter 6. As with reports, you can group records in your data access pages to present your records in an order that illustrates your data's central message (for that page, at least). For example, you can group your data access pages to present a list of books by copyright year, followed by the publisher within each year.

Pages are also like forms in that your users can enter data into your database through them. You can even add pivot tables to your pages so your users can analyze your data with the most powerful data viewing tool in Access.

To create a data access page:

1. Open the database in which you want to create a data access page, and click Pages.
   The pages (and associated wizards) appear in the main database window (**Figure 13.8**).

2. Double-click "Create data access page by using wizard."
   The Page Wizard appears (**Figure 13.9**).

3. From the Tables/Queries drop-down menu, choose the table or query from which you'd like to add fields (**Figure 13.10**).

   (continued on next page)

4. Click the > button to add a field to the Selected Fields pane (**Figure 13.11**).

You can add fields from more than one table or query to your page.

5. Click Next.

The grouping screen of the Page Wizard appears.

6. Click the name of the first field (if any) you want to use to group data in your page and click the > button to assign it as a grouping field. Click Next when you're done adding grouping fields.

Your grouping field appears in the header of the sample page in the right-hand pane of the wizard screen (**Figure 13.12**).

7. Click the drop-down menu in the first text area and choose the field containing the values you'd like to sort your records by (**Figure 13.13**).

8. Click the Sort Order button to toggle between sorting the field in ascending or descending order. Click Next when you're done adding sort fields.

9. Type a name for your page in the space provided and click Finish.

✔ Tips

- Access automatically sorts records in your data access page by the contents of your grouping fields. Adding a second grouping field to the list creates another grouping level below the one you added first. That is, the records in your page will be grouped based on the values in the first field, followed by the values in the second field. You can sort records in your pages by the values in up to four fields.

- You can change the priority of your grouping fields using the up arrow and down arrow buttons on the grouping screen of the Page Wizard.

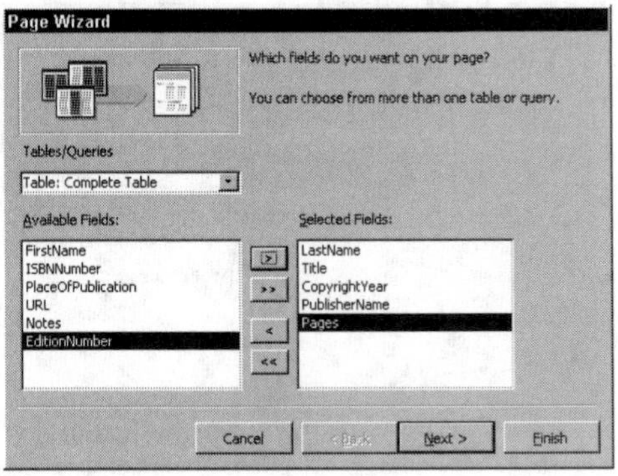

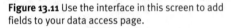

Figure 13.11 Use the interface in this screen to add fields to your data access page.

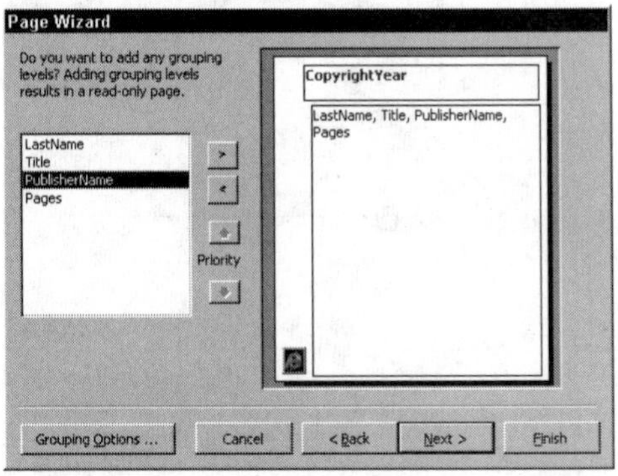

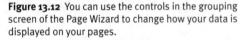

Figure 13.12 You can use the controls in the grouping screen of the Page Wizard to change how your data is displayed on your pages.

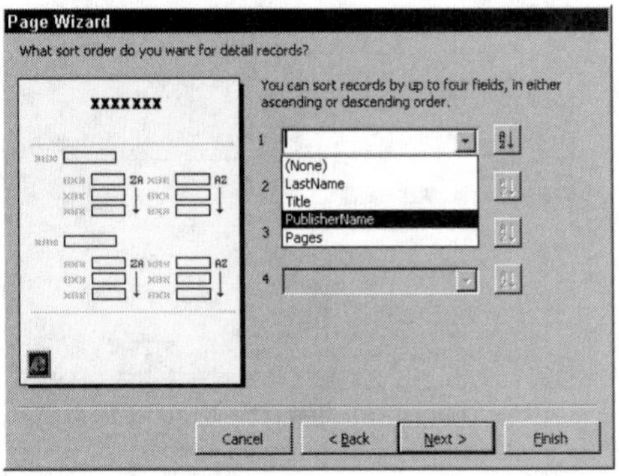

Figure 13.13 Sort the records in your data access page.

Figure 13.14 Clicking the Field List toolbar button displays the field-bearing objects in your database.

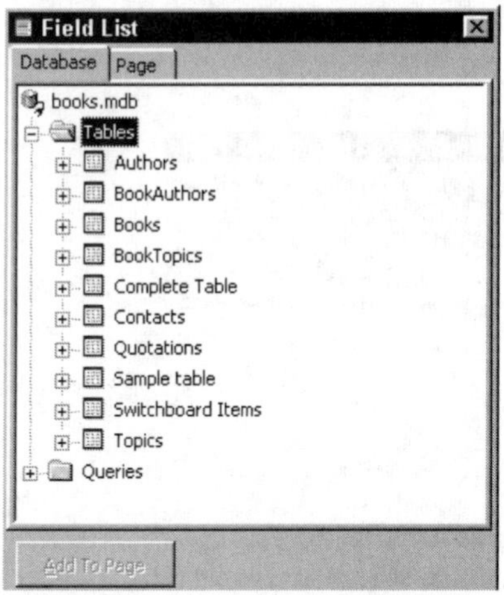

Figure 13.15 Select the type of object you want to draw fields from.

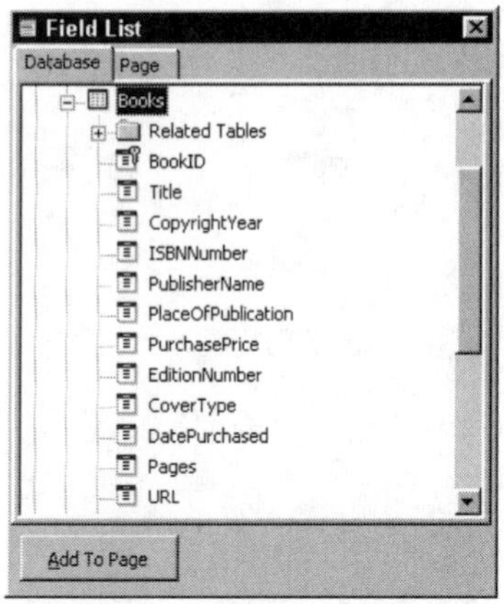

Figure 13.16 Select the table or query containing the fields you want to add.

To add a field to your data access page:

1. In Design view, open the data access page to which you want to add a field.

2. Click the Field List toolbar button (**Figure 13.14**).

3. In the Field List dialog box, double-click the type of object containing the field you want to add (in this case, either Tables or Queries).

   The list of tables (or queries) appears (**Figure 13.15**).

4. Double-click the table (or query) containing the field you want to add.

   The list of fields in the table (or query) appears (**Figure 13.16**).

5. Click the field you want to add and click Add to Page.

   The field appears in the page.

6. Click the Close button to stop adding fields to the page.

   (continued on next page)

To add a title to your data access page:

1. In Design view, open the page to which you want to add a title.

2. Click "Click here and type title text" at the top of the page and type a title for your page (**Figure 13.17**).

3. Choose File > Save.

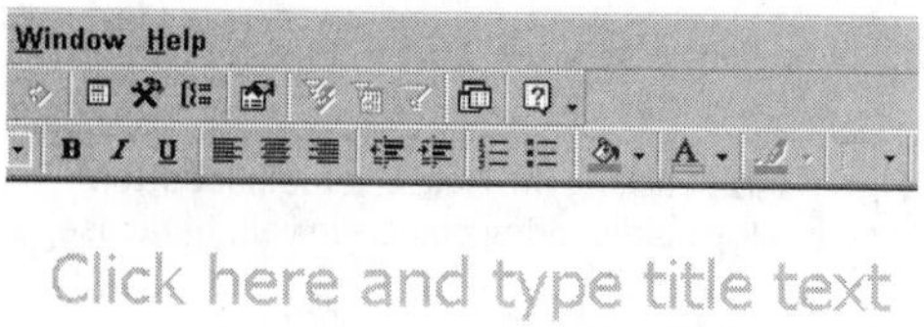

To add body text to your data access page:

1. In Design view, open the page to which you want to add body text.

2. Click the text reading "Click here and type body text" and type the text that will appear in the body of your page (**Figure 13.18**). Choose File > Save.

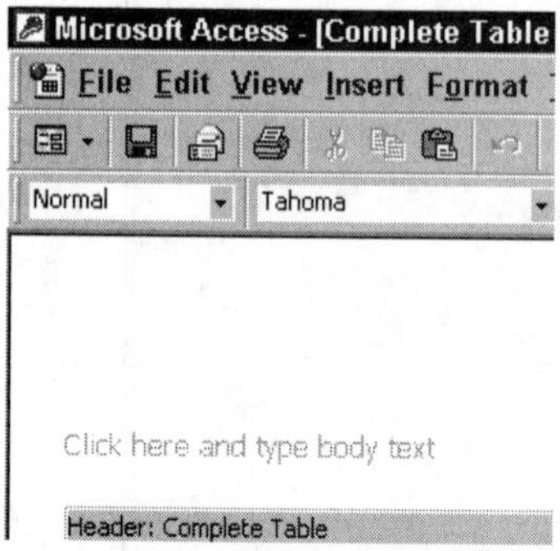

Figure 13.17 Click the text at the top of the page to add a title to the page.

Figure 13.18 Add body text to your page.

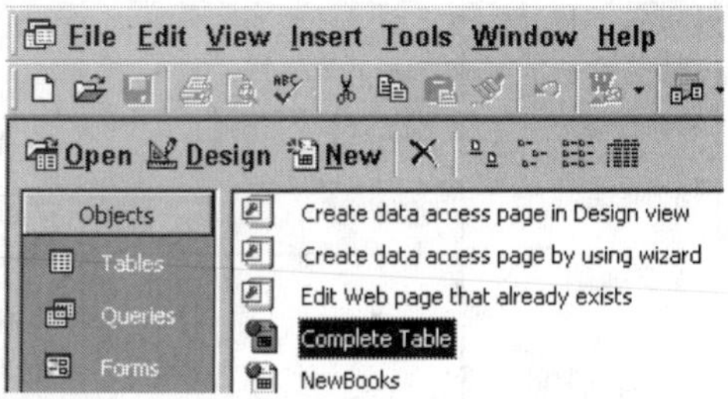

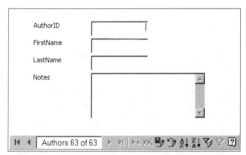

Figure 13.19 The Open toolbar button lets you view the data through your data access page.

AuthorID

FirstName

LastName

Notes

Authors 63 of 63

Figure 13.20 Your data access page appears with the insertion point in the first field.

Viewing and Modifying Data

Data access pages are easy to create and they make it easy for you and your users to view, enter, and modify data in your database, whether it's over the Internet or on your organization's intranet.

To view data using a data access page:

1. Display the data access pages in your database, click the page you want to view, and click Open (**Figure 13.19**).

   Your data access page appears in Page view, displaying values from the first record in the page's data collection.

2. Click the > button on the navigation bar to move to the next record in your data collection.

To enter data using a data access page:

1. In Page view, open the page you want to use to enter your data.

2. Click the New Record button ▸ on the navigation bar.

   A blank record appears in the body of the data access page. The insertion point, represented by a blinking cursor, appears in the first field (**Figure 13.20**).

3. Type the value for the field into the text area provided and press Tab.

   The insertion point moves to the next field. Press Tab when the insertion point is in the last field to create new record.

4. Choose File > Save to save your data.

To modify data using a data access page:

1. In Page view, open the page containing the data you want to modify.

2. Navigate to the record you want to modify using the navigation bar at the bottom of the page.

3. Click the field containing the data you want to modify and edit it (**Figure 13.21**).

4. Choose File > Save to save your changes.

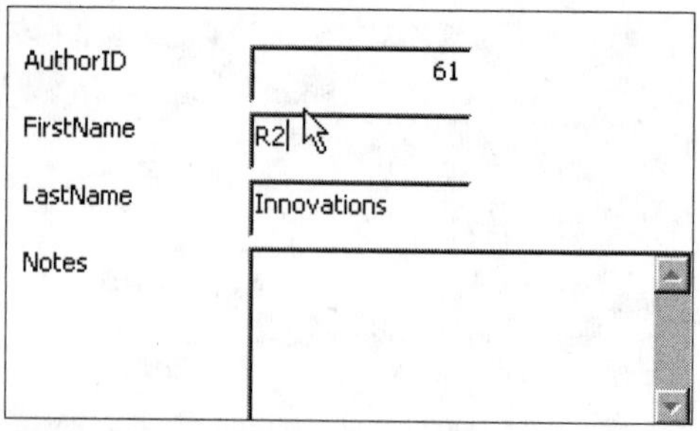

To delete a record:

1. Open the page containing the record you want to delete.

2. Display the record you want to delete and click the Delete Record navigation bar button ✖.

✔ Tips

■ Users must have an Office 2000 license on their machines in order to to open a data access page.

■ Users can only add, delete, or modify records in data access pages based on tables. If want to show your users the entire contents of a table but don't want them be able to to make any changes, just create a query including every field in your table and base your data access page on that query.

Figure 13.21 The insertion point appears in the first field in the new record.

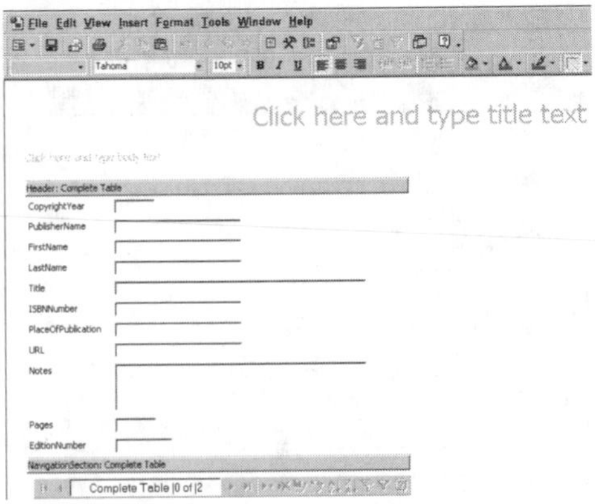

Figure 13.22 A data access page in Design view.

Figure 13.23 Clicking the Promote toolbar button establishes the field you selected as a grouping field.

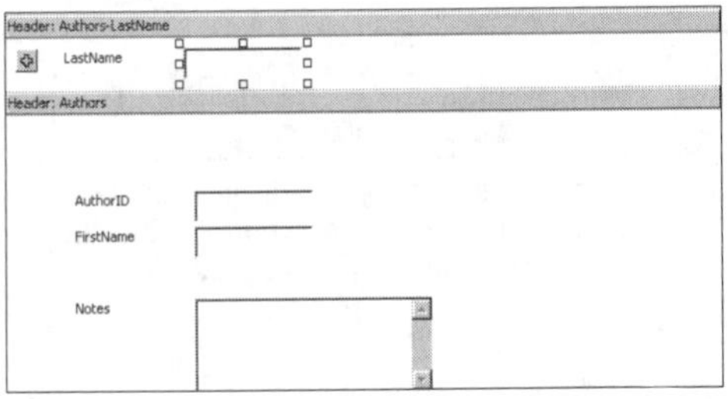

Figure 13.24 Access creates a new section of your data access page and places the grouping field there.

Changing Grouping Levels in a Page

Once you've created a data access page, you can modify it to change its appearance, to allow data entry, or to include a pivot table in the page.

Modifying a data access page is very similar to modifying a form or report—you can add fields, change their location and appearance on the page, and create controls like list boxes, combo boxes, and option buttons to facilitate data entry. You can use the features discussed in Chapter 4 and Chapter 6 to modify your data access pages.

Adding, deleting, or changing grouping levels reorganizes how your data appears in the page. You should change grouping levels whenever you want to change the emphasis of your pages. For instance, you can group sales data by product, and then change the grouping levels to display the same data by sales representative.

To add a grouping level to a data access page:

1. In Design view, display the data access page to which you want to add a grouping level (**Figure 13.22**).

   For this example, we want to group data about books in our library by their copyright years.

2. Click the field by which you want to group your page's records.

3. Click the Promote toolbar button (**Figure 13.23**).

   The field disappears from the page area it was in and moves to a new section at the top of the page (**Figure 13.24**).

   (continued on next page)

4. Choose View > Page View.

Your page displays the values in the grouped field (**Figure 13.25**).

To display the items in a group:

1. In Page view, open the data access page containing the data group you want to display.

In this case, we opened the data access page that displays our library's contents. This page is grouped by copyright year, so it shows the years present in the table providing data for the page. In other words, the page allows you to display books published in 1983 (the "1983 group"), books published in 1987 (the "1987 group"), and so forth.

2. Click the Expand control next to the data group you want to expand.

For this example, we expanded the 1989 group. When you expand a group, the Expand control changes to a Contract control and the first record in the group appears (**Figure 13.26**).

You can use the local navigation bar to move among the records in that group.

3. Click the Contract control to hide the contents of the group you opened.

The group shrinks, returning the data access page to the state seen in **Figure 13.25**.

✔ Tip

■ If you want your users to be able to add, modify, or delete data via a data access page, you may not group your data.

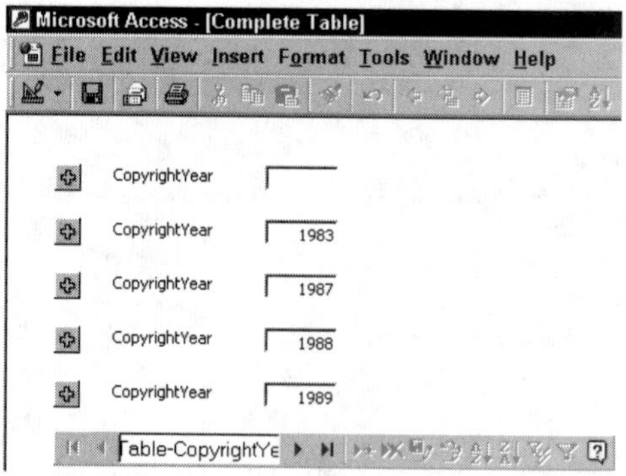

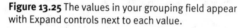

Figure 13.25 The values in your grouping field appear with Expand controls next to each value.

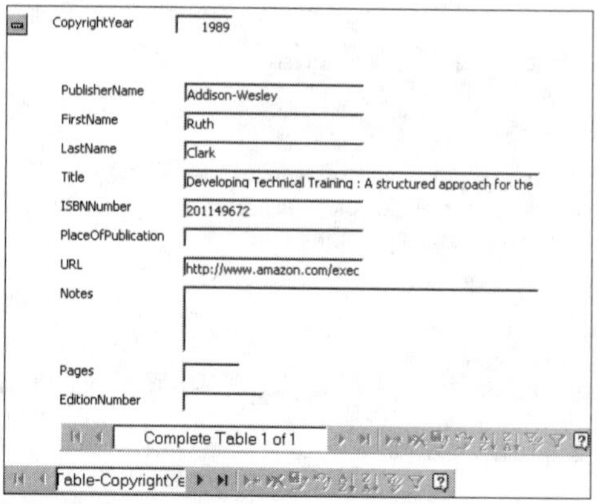

Figure 13.26 Expanding a group displays the records in that group. Click the Contract control to hide the records and only display the grouping value.

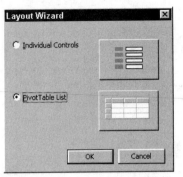

Figure 13.27 The Layout Wizard lets you add the fields from your table or query to your pivot table.

Move to Row Area button

| ProductName ▼ | LastName ▼ | CategoryName |

Figure 13.28 Click the Move to Row Area toolbar button to move a field from the Column area to the Row area...

LastName ▼	ProductName	▼ CategoryName ▼	CompanyName
⊟ Buchanan	Camembert Pierrot	Dairy Products	Gai pâturage
	Camembert Pierrot	Dairy Products	Gai pâturage
	Chartreuse verte	Beverages	Aux joyeux ecclésiastiques
	Côte de Blaye	Beverages	Aux joyeux ecclésiastiques
	Flatemysost	Dairy Products	Norske Meierier
	Flatemysost	Dairy Products	Norske Meierier
	Flatemysost	Dairy Products	Norske Meierier
	Geitost	Dairy Products	Norske Meierier
	Gorgonzola Telino	Dairy Products	Formaggi Fortini s.r.l.
	Guaraná Fantástica	Beverages	Refrescos Americanas LTD
	Guaraná Fantástica	Beverages	Refrescos Americanas LTD
	Inlagd Sill	Seafood	Svensk Sjöföda AB
	Longlife Tofu	Produce	Tokyo Traders
	Manjimup Dried Apples	Produce	G'day, Mate
	Mozzarella di Giovanni	Dairy Products	Formaggi Fortini s.r.l.
⊟ Callahan	Alice Mutton	Meat/Poultry	Pavlova, Ltd.
	Boston Crab Meat	Seafood	New England Seafood Can
	Camembert Pierrot	Dairy Products	Gai pâturage
	Carnarvon Tigers	Seafood	Pavlova, Ltd.
	Chai	Beverages	Exotic Liquids
	Chartreuse verte	Beverages	Aux joyeux ecclésiastiques

Figure 13.29 ...which pivots your table.

Adding a Pivot Table to a Page

Pivot tables (see Chapter 11), are powerful tools that allow your users to display your data in the manner that best meets their needs. While they're neat tools to play with, the real benefit of pivot tables is that you don't have to anticipate your users' needs. In other words, with pivot tables users can manipulate and filter your data as they see fit.

To add a pivot table to a data access page:

1. In Design view, open your data access page.

2. Click the Field List toolbar button to bring up the Field List dialog box.

3. Open the list of tables (or queries) and click the table or query you want to use as the base for your pivot table and click Add to Page.
   The Layout Wizard appears (**Figure 13.27**).

4. Click the Pivot Table List option button and click OK.
   The table or query appears as a pivot table in your data access page.

To pivot your table:

◆ Click the title bar of the field you want to move and click the Move to Row Area toolbar button (**Figure 13.28**).
   Access moves the field to the row area and recalculates your pivot table (**Figure 13.29**).

or

(continued on next page)

ADDING A PIVOT TABLE TO A PAGE

Click the title bar of the field you want to move and click the Move to Column Area toolbar button (**Figure 13.30**).

Access moves the field to the column area and recalculates your pivot table (**Figure 13.31**).

✔ Tips

- You should add a pivot table to a data access page whenever you want to give users who access your data the flexibility to work with it as if the database was installed on their local system.

- You can change the priority of the fields in your pivot table using the techniques covered in Chapter 11, or by clicking the field whose priority you want to change and clicking either the Promote or Demote toolbar buttons.

Move to Column Area button

Figure 13.30 Click the Move to Column Area toolbar button to move a field from the Row area to the Column area…

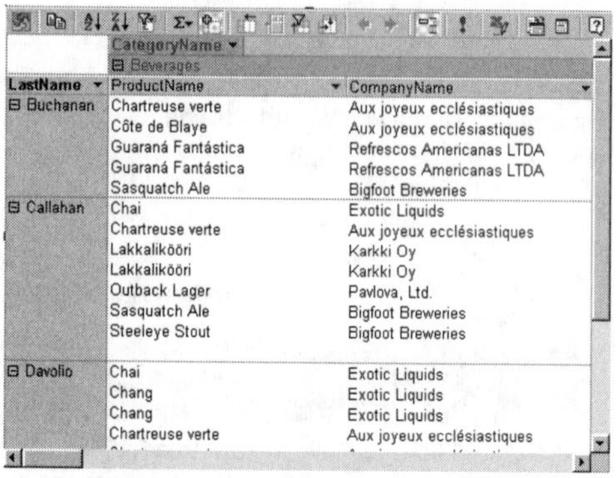

Figure 13.31 …to pivot your table.

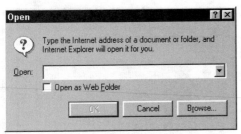

Figure 13.32 Use the Open dialog box to locate the data access page you want to open.

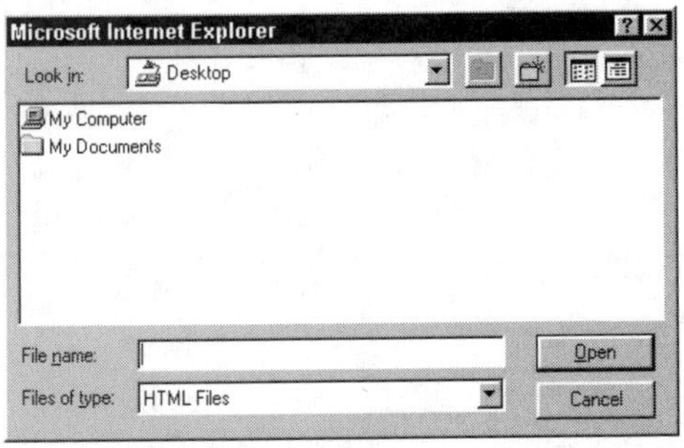

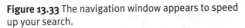

Figure 13.33 The navigation window appears to speed up your search.

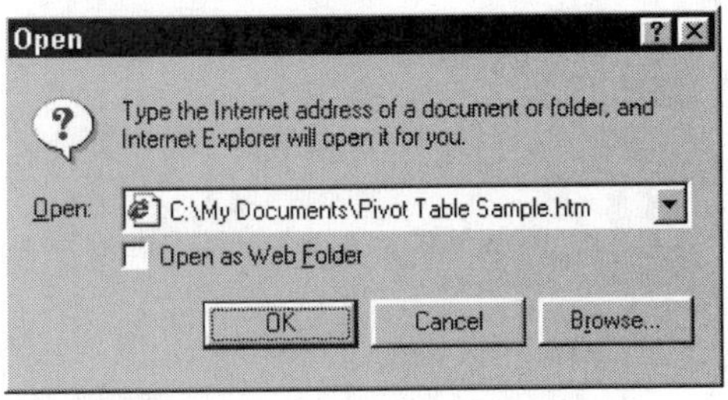

Figure 13.34 The file you selected appears in the Open dialog box.

Viewing a Page in a Web Browser

When you create a data access page, Access stores the HTML file it generates outside the database, but the program establishes a link to the file from the Pages pane of the main database window.

Access stores data access pages as separate files so users can open the objects with Web browsers. As of this writing, you need to use Internet Explorer 4.0 or later to open a data access page. Some features may not work with Version 4.0, so you may need to use Version 4.1 or later. For best results, use Internet Explorer 5.0.

One nice benefit of using data access pages is that you work with them from a Web browser in the same way you'd work with them from inside Access in Page view. You can use the skills you've learned earlier in this chapter to work with data access pages you view from your Web browser.

To view a page in a Web browser:

1. Launch your Web browser.

   For this example, we're using Internet Explorer 5.0.

2. Choose File > Open.

   The Open dialog box appears (**Figure 13.32**).

3. Click Browse.

   The file navigation dialog box appears (**Figure 13.33**).

4. Navigate to the directory containing the data access page you want to view, click it, and then click Open.

   The file (and its complete directory path) appear in the Open dialog box (**Figure 13.34**).

(continued on next page)

5. Click OK.

The page appears in your Web browser (**Figure 13.35**).

✔ Tip

■ If you move a data access page to another directory after it's created, Access will display an error message stating that it can't find the file you want. You can navigate through your directories to locate the file and update the reference, however.

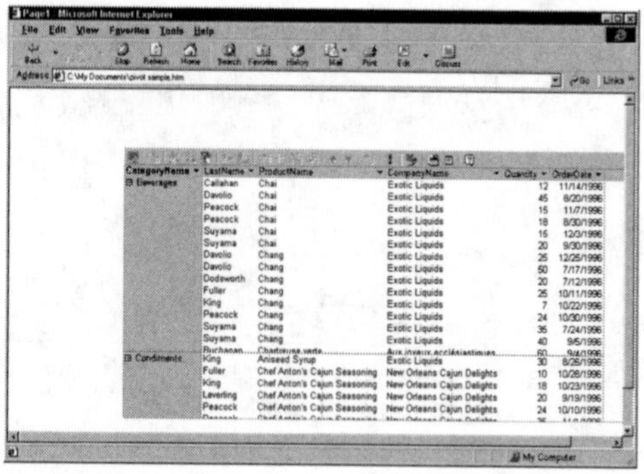

Figure 13.35 The data access page appears in your Web browser.

HONING
YOUR DATABASE

The default Access interface is extremely powerful—you can get to any of the program's commands with the menu system, use built-in toolbars to get at commonly used features more conveniently, and (if you created your database with a wizard) manage your database using a *switchboard*, which is a connected series of forms with controls that open commonly used items in your database.

In this chapter you'll learn how to work with switchboards; how to customize your database's menus, dialog boxes, and toolbars; and how to create macros to automate tasks within your database.

Customizing Switchboards

Access builds a switchboard form for every database you create with a database wizard, but the default configuration may not be quite what you're looking for. If you add forms or other database objects to your database, for instance, you must also add controls to your switchboard to open or redesign those objects. However, you'll be able to open those objects from the main database window as well.

You can also modify your switchboard to change the order of controls on a switchboard page or to create brand new pages. The tool you use to customize your switchboard is the Switchboard Manager, which makes changing your switchboards simple.

To modify an item on a switchboard page:

1. Open your database and choose Tools > Database Utilities > Switchboard Manager.

2. The Switchboard Manager appears with a list of the pages in your switchboard (**Figure 14.1**).

3. Click the page you want to modify and click Edit.

   The Edit Switchboard Page dialog box appears (**Figure 14.2**).

4. Click the item you want to modify and click Edit.

   The Edit Switchboard Item dialog box appears, with the name of the item you selected in the Text text area (**Figure 14.3**).

5. Type new text to identify the control you're modifying.

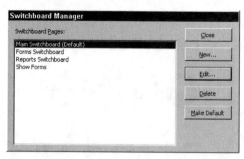

Figure 14.1 The Switchboard Manager lets you make your switchboards easier to use.

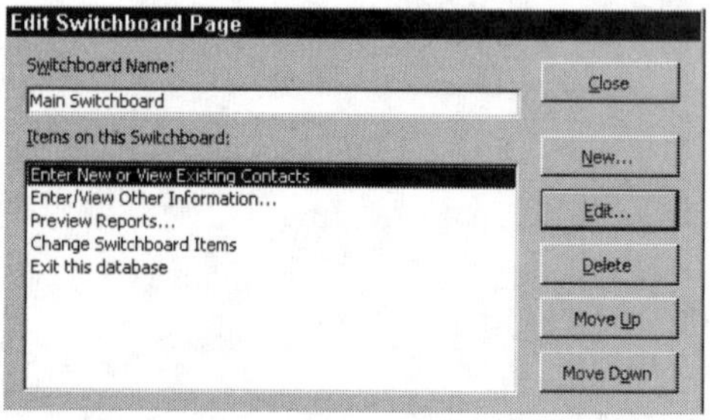

Figure 14.2 One level below the main Switchboard Manager screen you'll find the Edit Switchboard Page dialog box.

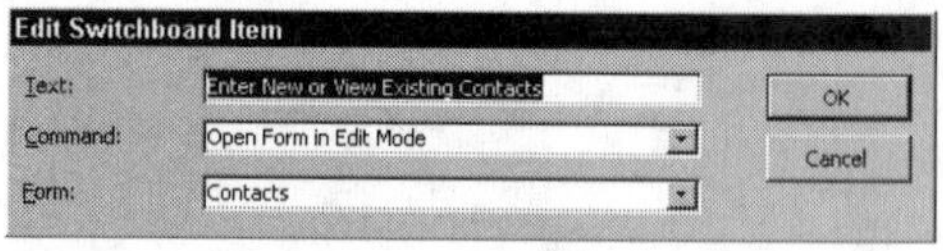

Figure 14.3 To edit an item on a page, open the Edit Switchboard Item dialog box.

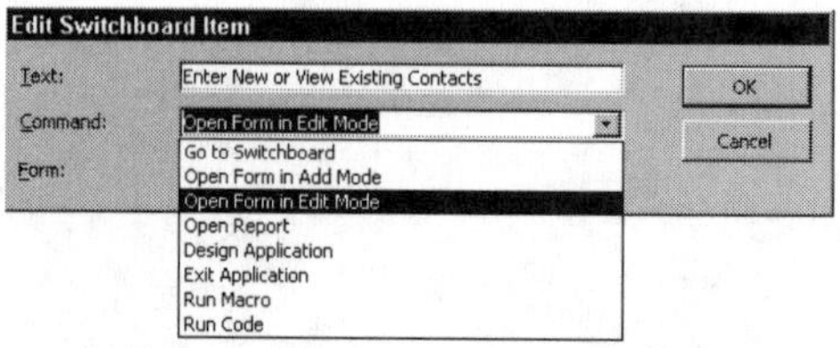

Figure 14.4 You can see the commands available to you by clicking the Command drop-down menu.

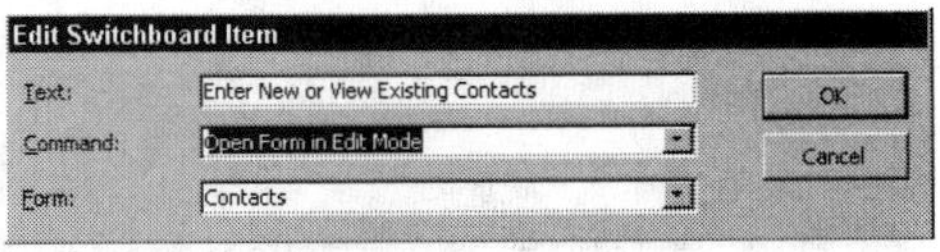

Figure 14.5 The final field in the Edit Switchboard Item dialog box changes depending on what you chose in the Command field.

Edit Switchboard Commands

Go to Switchboard Opens another page in the active switchboard. The third field contains the switchboard page to open when the control is clicked.

Open Form in Add Mode Opens a form in the current database for adding, editing, and viewing records. The third field lists the form to be opened.

Open Form in Edit Mode Opens a form in the current database for editing and viewing records (but not adding). The third field lists the form to be opened.

Open Report Opens a report in Preview mode. The third field lists the report to be opened.

Design Application Opens the Switchboard Manager; there is no third field.

Exit Application Closes the switchboard form; there is no third field.

Run Macro Causes Access to run a macro you created (covered later in this chapter). The third field lists the macro to be run.

Run Code Causes Access to run a Visual Basic code module of your choosing. The third field lists the module to be run.

6. Click the Command drop-down menu button to display the commands available to you and choose the command you want to assign to your control (**Figure 14.4**).

The third (and final) combo box in the Edit Switchboard Item dialog box changes to reflect the command you chose (**Figure 14.5**). For a list of the available commands and the third field that goes along with them, see the "Edit Switchboard Commands" sidebar .

7. Click Close to close the Edit Switchboard Item page, click it again to close the Edit Switchboard Page dialog box, and then click Close a final time to close the Switchboard Manager.

✔ Tips

■ You can add a new page to a switchboard by opening the Switchboard Manager and clicking New to create a new switchboard page.

■ Create a new item on a switchboard page by opening the Switchboard Manager, and displaying the page in which you want to add a new item, and then clicking New.

■ To delete an item from a switchboard page, open the Switchboard Manager, navigate to the item (or page) you want to delete, click the item, and then click Delete.

To change the order of items on a switchboard page:

1. Open the Switchboard Manager and display the page containing the items you want to reorder (**Figure 14.6**).

2. Select the item you want to move and click Move Up to move the item up one spot in the list.

   or

   Click Move Down to move the item down one spot in the list.

   The item changes position in the list.

✔ Tip

- You should change the order of the items on a page to reflect how often you use them. More popular features can appear at the top of the page, less popular ones at the bottom.

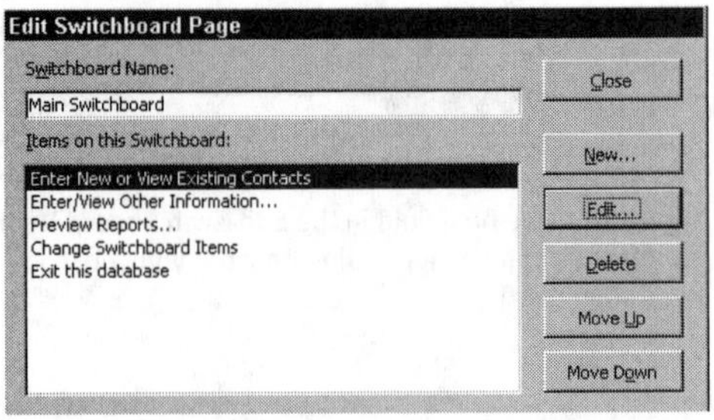

To create a new switchboard:

1. Choose Tools > Database Utilities > Switchboard Manager in a database without an active switchboard (that is, created without using a wizard or where the switchboard has been deleted).

   Access displays a dialog box indicating that it can't find a switchboard form for this database and asks if it should create a new one (**Figure 14.7**).

2. Click Yes.

   Access creates a form named Switchboard and launches the Switchboard Manager (**Figure 14.8**).

   You can add pages and items in the Switchboard Manager at your leisure.

✔ Tip

- Access automatically saves your changes when you close the Switchboard Manager, so you don't need to worry constantly about saving.

Figure 14.6 Open the switchboard page containing the items you want to rearrange.

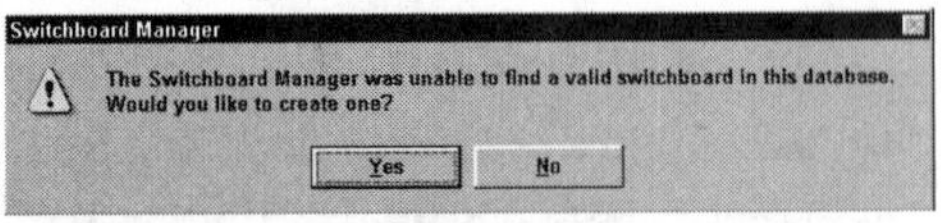

Figure 14.7 If your database didn't come with a switchboard, you can create one.

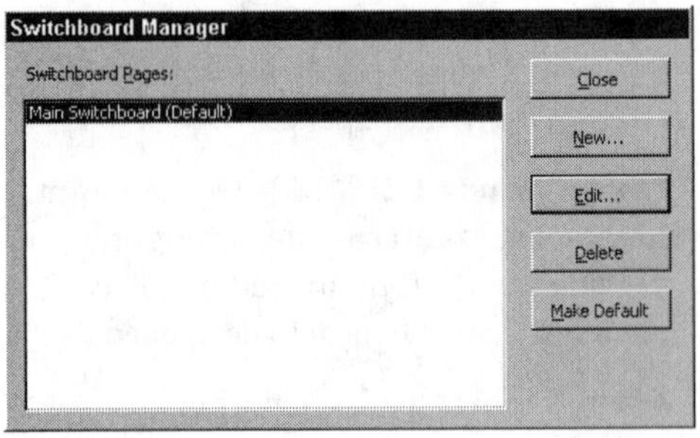

Figure 14.8 Access creates a new switchboard form and opens the Switchboard Manager.

CUSTOMIZING SWITCHBOARDS

Figure 14.9 The Customize dialog box lets you work with your database's toolbars and menus.

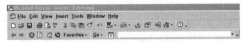

Figure 14.10 Indicate which toolbar you want to appear, and it will!

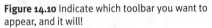

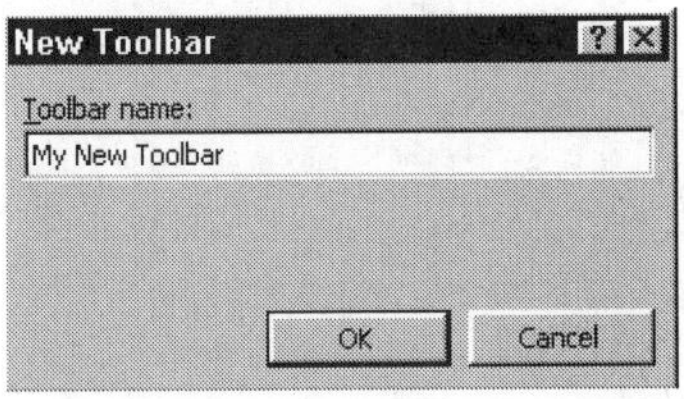

Figure 14.11 The New Toolbar dialog box asks you to name your next creation.

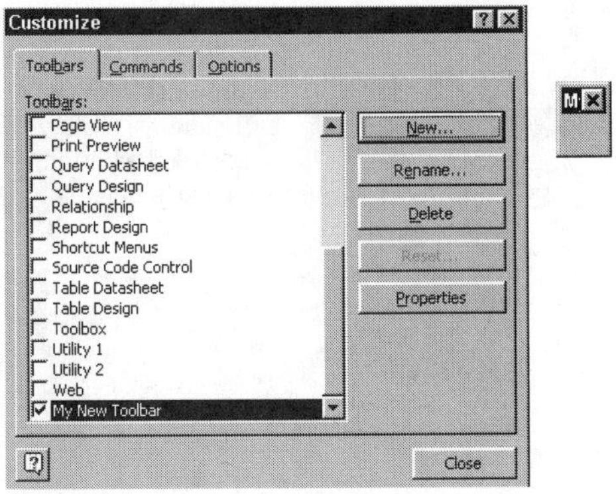

Figure 14.12 Your new toolbar appears immediately in the active window. Because your new toolbar has no buttons on it, it appears quite small.

Customizing Toolbars and Menus

Although Access has an extensive built-in menu and toolbar system, the default versions of the menus and toolbars may not be exactly what you or your users want. It's easy to modify the existing toolbars and menus or create your own.

Choosing menus or toolbars is largely a matter of taste. Microsoft recognized the differences in their design of Access, so many of the functions available from menus, such as saving your work, opening databases, and printing the contents of the active document are also available as toolbar buttons.

You can also create custom toolbars and menus that group menu and toolbar items not normally grouped together in the default interface and you can let users launch macros that you've created specifically for your applications.

To display a toolbar:

1. Choose Tools > Customize.

   The Customize dialog box appears (**Figure 14.9**).

2. Click the Toolbars tab.

3. Select the checkbox next to the toolbar you want to display.

4. The toolbar you clicked appears in the active window (**Figure 14.10**).

✔ Tip

■ You can hide a toolbar by opening the Customize dialog box, clicking the Toolbars tab, and clearing the checkbox next to the toolbar you want to hide.

To create a new toolbar:

1. Choose Tools > Customize and click the Toolbars tab.

2. Click New.

   The New Toolbar dialog box appears (**Figure 14.11**).

3. Type a name for your toolbar and click OK.

   Your new toolbar appears in the active window. Because it has no buttons on it, the toolbar is very small (**Figure 14.12**).

4. Click Close to hide the Customize dialog box.

To add a button to a toolbar:

1. Choose Tools > Customize and click the Toolbars tab.

2. Select the checkbox next to the toolbar on which you want to add a button.

3. Click the Commands tab.

   The list of categories and the buttons within those categories appear in the Customize dialog box (**Figure 14.13**).

4. Choose the category containing the command you want to add.

   The list of commands changes to reflect the category you chose.

5. Drag the button you want to add to the body of the toolbar (**Figure 14.14**).

   The button appears on the toolbar when you release the left mouse button.

✔ Tip

■ To delete a button from a toolbar, just display the toolbar, right-click the button you want to remove and choose Delete from the pop-up menu that appears (**Figure 14.15**).

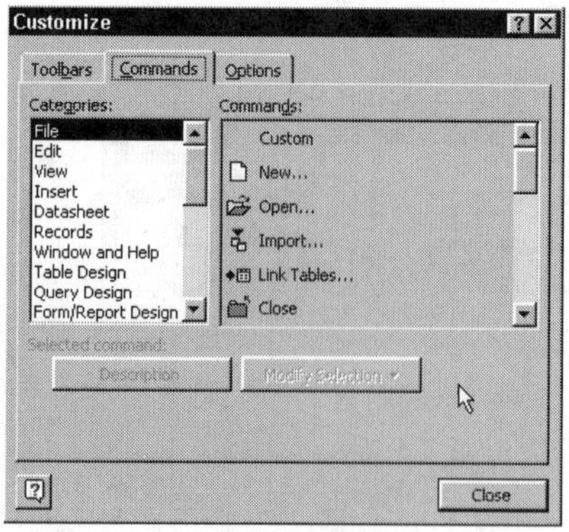

Figure 14.13 Open your toolbar to have Access display your command options...

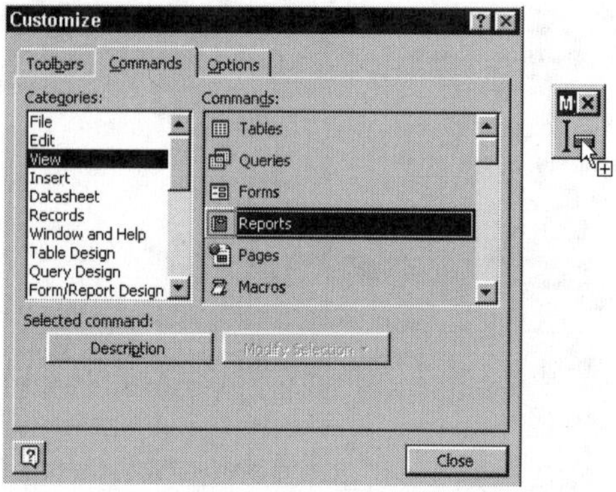

Figure 14.14 ...and drag the button you want to add to your toolbar.

Figure 14.15 To delete a button from a toolbar right-click the button and choose Delete.

Figure 14.16 Choose a new image for your button from the default designs.

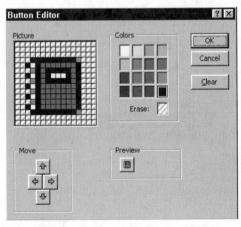

Figure 14.17 Choose which color you want to add to your grid and click the target block.

To change a button's appearance:

1. Choose Tools > Customize and display the toolbar containing the button you want to change.

2. Right-click the button you want to change, choose Change Button Image from the pop-up menu, and choose a new image for your button from the list that appears (**Figure 14.16**).

   The image you chose appears on the button.

To edit a button's appearance:

1. Choose Tools > Customize and display the toolbar containing the button you want to edit.

2. Right-click the button you want to change and choose Edit Button Image from the pop-up menu that appears.

   The Button Editor appears (**Figure 14.17**).

(continued on next page)

3. Click the color that you want to assign to a block in the image grid, and then click the block that you want to change.

   The block in the image grid changes to the color you chose (**Figure 14.18**).

4. Click OK when you're done.

To use text as a button or menu item's image:

1. Choose Tools > Customize and display the menu bar or toolbar with the button whose image you want to display as text.

2. Right-click the button or menu item and choose Text Only from the drop-down menu (**Figure 14.19**).

   Your button or menu item uses its name as its image.

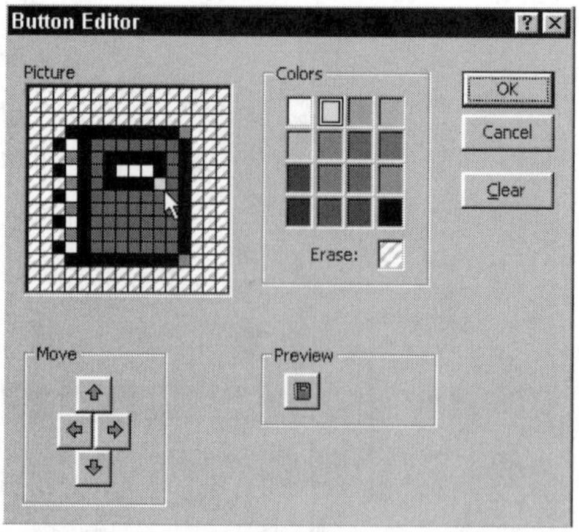

Figure 14.18 The block changes to the color you chose.

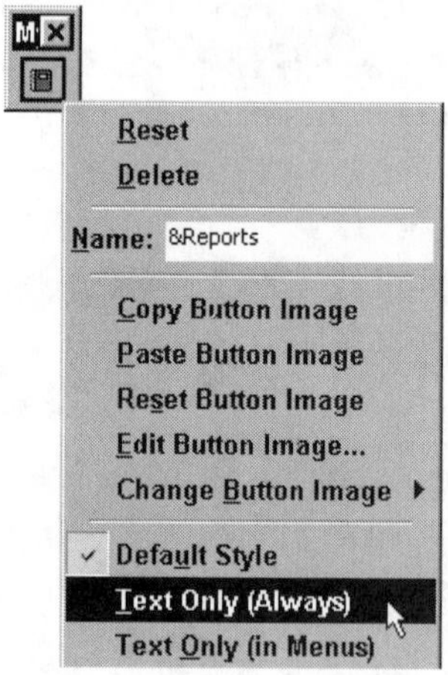

Figure 14.19 You can use a button's name or some other text as its image.

Figure 14.20 Tell Access you want to create a new menu bar...

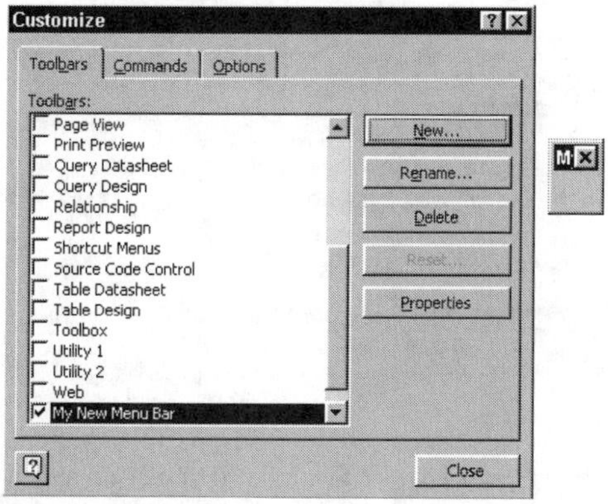

Figure 14.21 ...and Access does the rest.

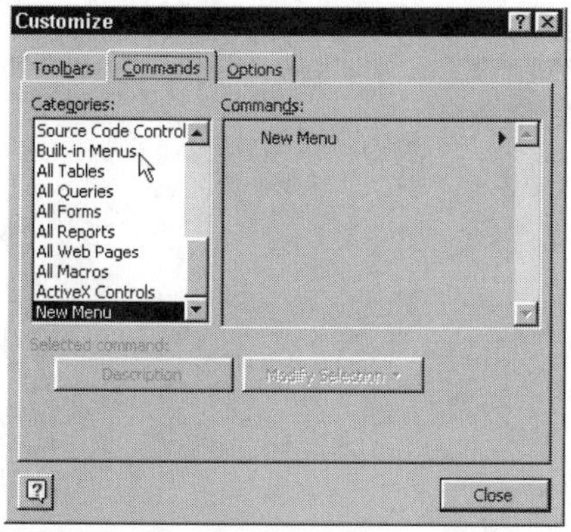

Figure 14.22 Click the Commands tab and select Built-In Menus from the Categories pane to use one of Access's prefab menus.

Creating and Customizing Menus

With Access, you can choose which menus to display, change the make-up of any menu, and create entirely new menus, just as you do with toolbars. Customizing your menus allows you to group the most commonly used menu items and put them in the most effective order.

To create a new menu bar:

1. Choose Tools > Customize and click the Toolbars tab.

2. Select Menu Bar and click New (**Figure 14.20**).

   The New Toolbar dialog box appears.

3. Type a name for your new menu bar in the space provided and click OK.

   Your new menu bar appears next to the dialog box. The new menu bar has no items on it yet, so it is quite small (**Figure 14.21**).

To add a built-in menu to a toolbar or menu:

1. Choose Tools > Customize and display the toolbar or menu to which you want to add a menu.

2. Click the Commands tab and select Built-In Menus from the Categories pane (**Figure 14.22**).

   A built-in menu is a menu that is included with Access, such as the File or Edit menu. The list of existing menus appears in the Commands pane.

   (continued on next page)

3. Drag the menu you want to add to the target toolbar or menu (**Figure 14.23**).

To add a custom menu to a toolbar or menu bar:

1. Choose Tools > Customize and display the toolbar or menu bar to which you want to add a custom menu.

2. Click the Commands tab and click New Menu (**Figure 14.24**).

The New Menu item appears in the Commands pane.

3. Drag the New Menu item from the Commands pane to the target menu bar or toolbar.

The new menu appears on the menu bar (**Figure 14.25**).

To add an item to a menu:

1. Choose Tools > Customize and display the menu bar to which you want to add items.

2. Click the item you want to add to the menu and drag it to the menu's name.

When the new item is over the menu's name, the menu's drop-down section will appear (**Figure 14.26**).

3. Drag the item you want to add to the drop-down section and release the left mouse button (**Figure 14.27**).

✔ Tip

■ Disk space is something to consider when choosing to create a menu bar or toolbar. Because you can add multiple items to the drop-down portion of a menu, you should use menus instead of toolbars whenever space is at a premium.

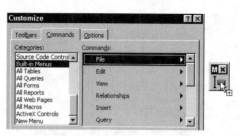

Figure 14.23 Drag the built-in menu to the desired location.

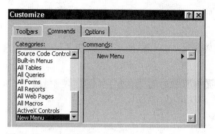

Figure 14.24 The New Menu item appears first in the Customize dialog box...

Figure 14.25 ...and then on your menu bar.

Figure 14.26 Drag a new menu item over a menu header to display the menu's drop-down section.

Figure 14.27 Drop your item into the drop-down section to add it to the menu.

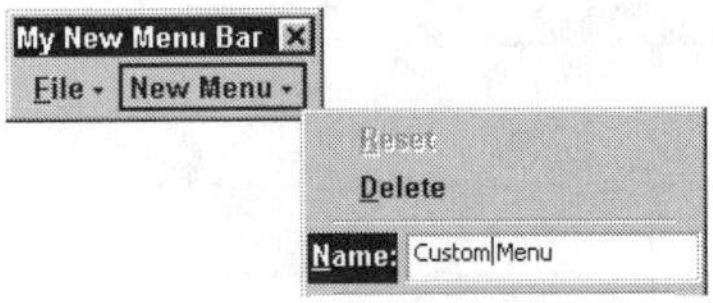

Figure 14.28 Enter a new name for your menu.

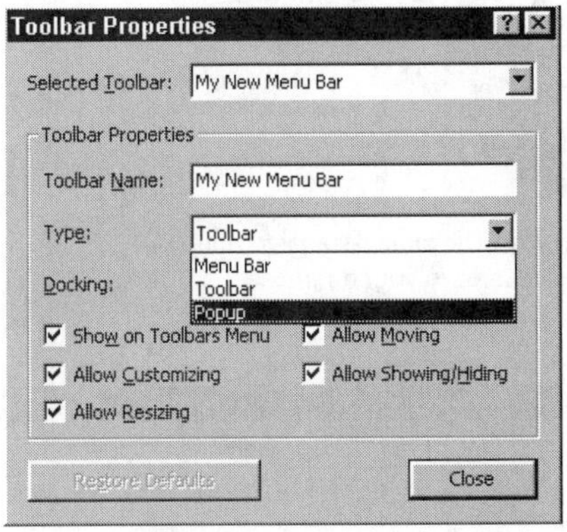

Figure 14.29 Choose Popup from the type list.

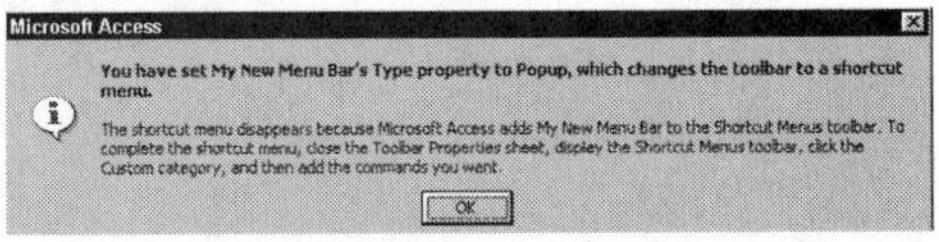

Figure 14.30 Remember that pop-up menus aren't usually accessible from the main database windows.

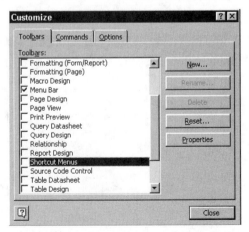

Figure 14.31 You can open your pop-up menus for editing by clicking Shortcut Menus from within the Customize dialog box.

To rename a button, menu, or menu item:

1. Choose Tools > Customize and display the menu bar or toolbar containing the item you want to rename.

2. Right-click the item, type a new name in the Name field of the pop-up menu that appears, and press Enter (**Figure 14.28**). Your item takes on its new name.

To create a pop-up menu:

1. Choose Tools > Customize and click Toolbars.

2. Click the name of the menu or toolbar you want to make into a pop-up menu and click Properties.

3. The Toolbar Properties dialog box appears.

4. Click the Type drop-down menu and choose Popup (**Figure 14.29**).

   A warning box appears, letting you know the pop-up menu will be listed as part of the Shortcut Menus item in the Categories pane of the Customize dialog box (**Figure 14.30**).

5. Click OK, then click Close to redisplay the Customize dialog box.

✔ Tips

- You can edit the pop-up menus in your database by choosing Tools > Customize, clicking the Toolbars tab, and selecting Shortcut Menus (**Figure 14.31**). The pop-up menus in your database appear on the Shortcut Menus menu bar.

CREATING AND CUSTOMIZING MENUS

Writing Macros

Macros are procedures you can write to automate actions that would normally require a potentially lengthy series of steps. If the steps to achieve a result never vary, and differ only in the data used in the procedure, you should consider automating the process with a macro.

Writing a macro in Access is simple. Access provides an interface that allows you to choose the actions you want the macro to perform and set an order for the actions to occur. You can set macros for just about anything including opening forms, printing pages or documents, or launching another program.

Once you've written a macro, you can debug it to make sure every step performs the action you want it to perform. The Macro Single Step dialog box presents the details of your action, its arguments, and any errors in a way that makes tracking the macro and fixing any mistakes quite easy.

To write a macro:

1. Open the database in which you want to create a macro and select Macros from the list in the Objects pane.

    The macros associated with the current database appear (**Figure 14.32**).

2. Click New.

    The Macro Design window appears (**Figure 14.33**).

3. Click the first Action cell and choose the type of action you want this macro to perform (**Figure 14.34**).

    For this example, we chose OpenForm.

    The Action Arguments pane changes the options it displays to reflect the action you chose.

Figure 14.32 The main database window lists the macros in your database.

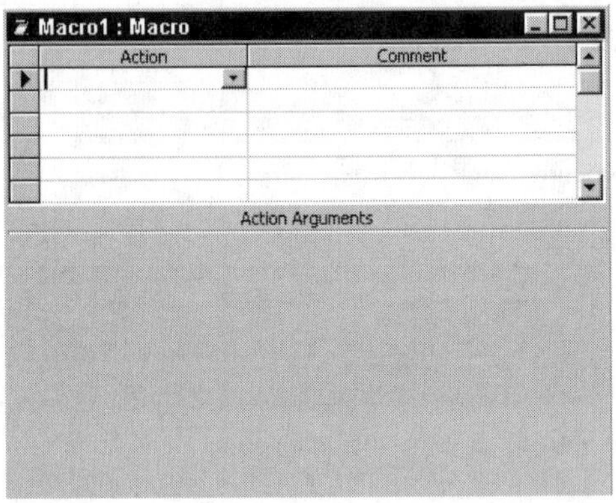

Figure 14.33 The Access Macro Design window.

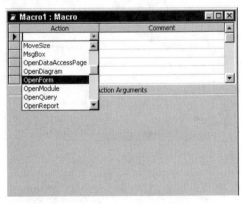

Figure 14.34 You can select an action from a comprehensive list.

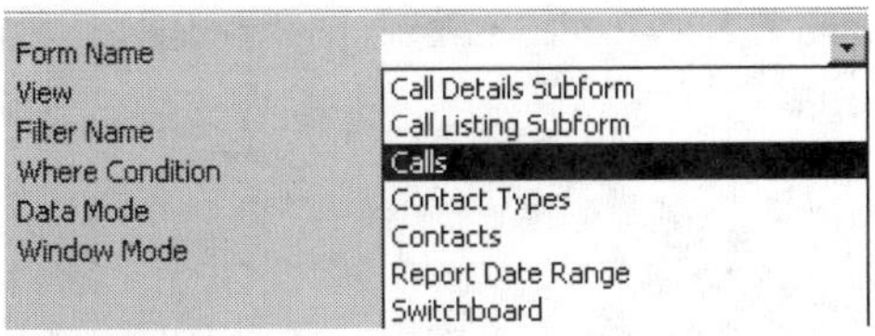

Figure 14.35 Enter the argument(s) the action needs to run.

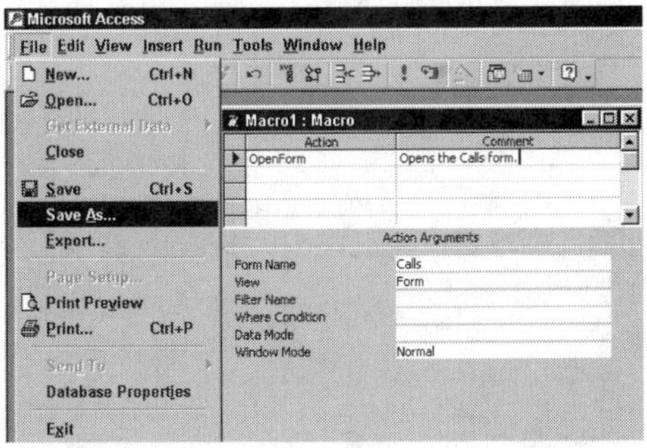

Figure 14.36 Type a name for your macro and click OK.

4. Select an action argument to complete your action.

   In this case, we clicked the Form Name text area, clicked the drop-down menu that appeared, and chose the Calls form (**Figure 14.35**). You don't need to enter anything in the other argument fields for this macro.

5. Type a comment about the action in the Comments field.

   In this example, you might enter the comment "Opens the Calls form."

6. Choose File > Save As (**Figure 14.36**). The Save As dialog box appears.

7. Type a name for your macro in the text area and click OK.

✔ Tips

■ You should enter a comment for every macro you write and consider entering comments for every action in a macro as well. It's much easier to figure out what a macro does if there are comments to guide you, especially if it's been a few months since you last looked at the macro.

■ You can add additional steps to your macro by clicking the next available Action cell and following the steps described in the previous section.

■ You can run your macro by clicking the Run toolbar button while the macro is open in Design view or by double-clicking the macro in the main database window. To run a macro from the main database window, open the main database window and click Macros. Click the macro you want to run and click Run. The macro runs, though you may not see the results if the macro doesn't open another object in the database.

To debug a macro:

1. Click the macro you want to debug and click the Design toolbar button.

   Your macro appears in Design view (**Figure 14.37**).

2. Click the Single Step toolbar button.

3. Click Run.

   The Macro Single Step dialog box appears (**Figure 14.38**), listing the name of the macro, the status of the condition for that particular step, the action name, and the arguments (which form to open, which page to print, and so on).

4. Click Step to execute the next step of the macro.

   or

   Click Halt to stop the macro's execution.

   or

   Click Continue to have Access run the macro to its conclusion without stopping after each step.

   The Macro Single Step dialog box disappears when you reach the end of the macro.

   If there is an error in executing your macro, Access displays a dialog box with details about the error.

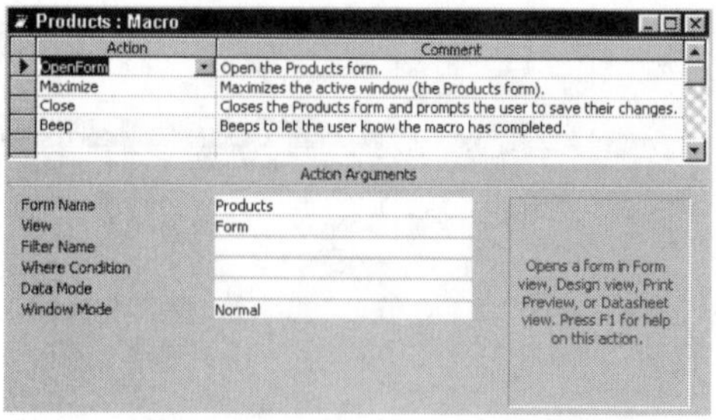

Figure 14.37 To debug a macro, open it in Design view...

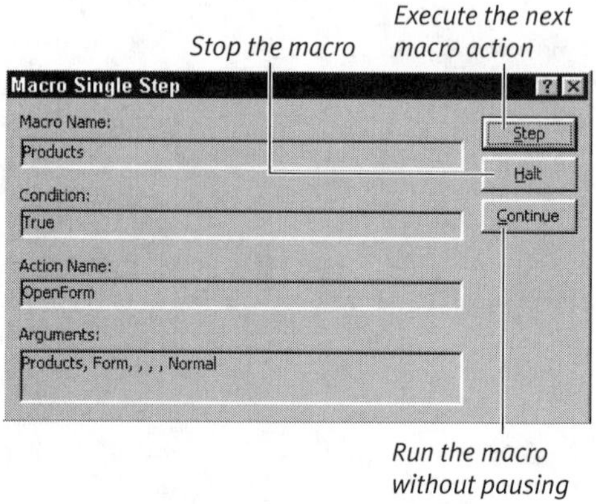

Figure 14.38 ...and click the Single Step toolbar button to display the Single Step dialog box.

Figure 14.39 Turn off the Control Wizards so you can modify your command button yourself.

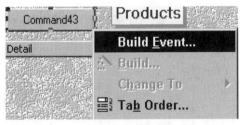

Figure 14.40 Choose Build Event from the button's pop-up menu.

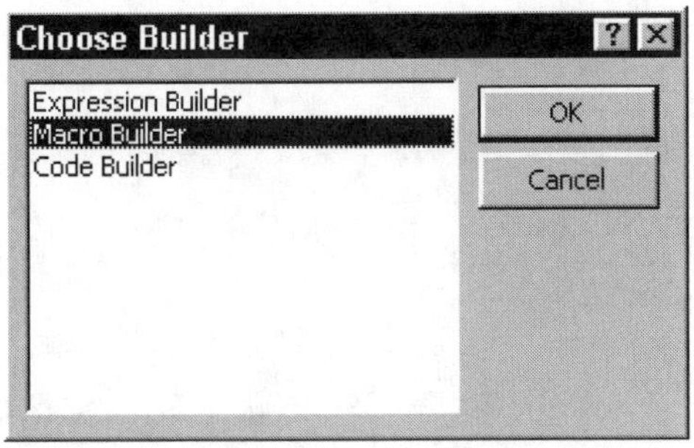

Figure 14.41 The Choose Builder dialog box.

Figure 14.42 Save your work before you go any further.

Customizing Objects with Access Macros

You can run macros from the main database window, but it's often more practical to link them to objects within the database so your users can run the macros by clicking those objects.

In this section, you'll learn how to create a command button that launches a macro. You'll create the command button, and then create a macro that runs when you click the command button.

To customize a database object with macros:

1. In Design view, open the object you want to customize.

   In this case, we opened a form.

2. Click the Toolbox button to display the Toolbox and deselect the Control Wizards toggle button (**Figure 14.39**).

3. Click the Command Button button in the Toolbox and click the spot on the form where you want the command button to appear.

   The command button appears on your form.

4. Right-click the command button and choose Build Event from the pop-up menu (**Figure 14.40**).

   The Choose Builder dialog box appears (**Figure 14.41**).

5. Click Macro Builder and click OK.

   The Save As dialog box appears (**Figure 14.42**).

6. Type a name for your new macro and click OK.

(continued on next page)

7. Create the macro you want your control to run.

We created a macro to open the Products by Category form (**Figure 14.43**).

8. Save your changes and click the close box to close the macro.

The form containing the command button reappears in Design view (**Figure 14.44**).

9. Choose View > Form View.

The form appears in Form view.

10. Click the command button (**Figure 14.45**).

The macro launches and opens the Products by Category form.

✔ Tip

■ You can build events linked to any control you add to your forms.

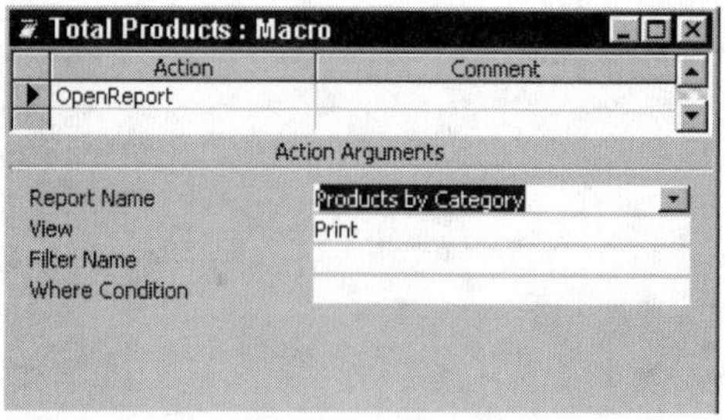

Figure 14.43 Create a macro to launch from your control.

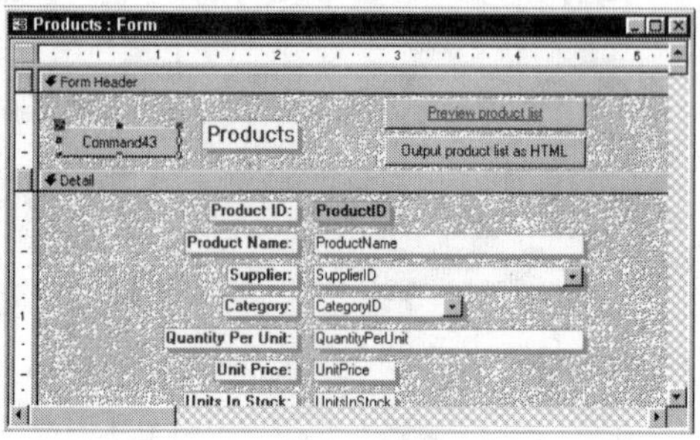

Figure 14.44 Display the form with the command button...

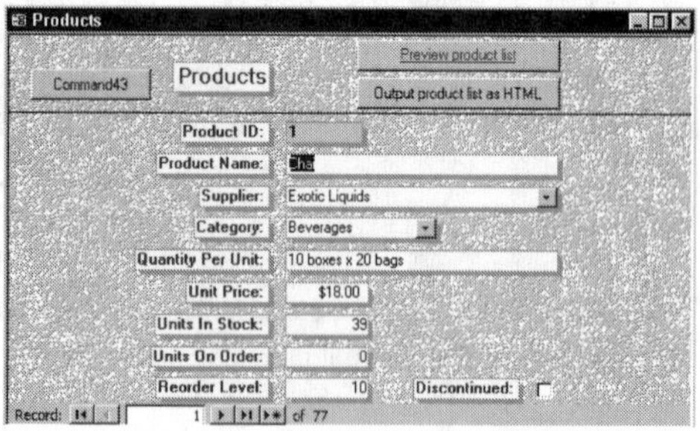

Figure 14.45 ...switch to Form view, and click the button to launch your macro.

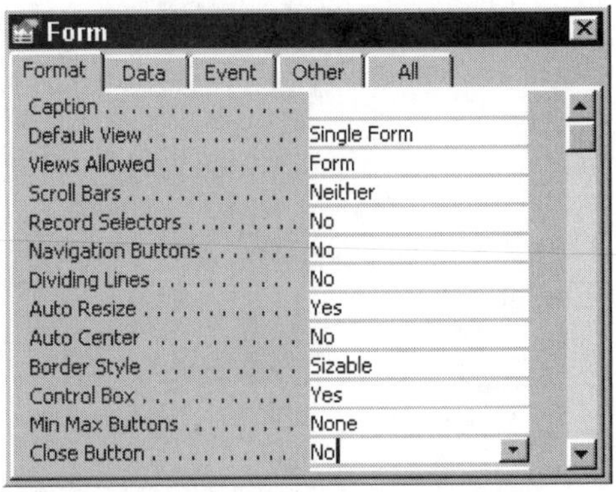

Figure 14.46 To create your own dialog box from a form, display the Format page of the Properties dialog box and change the settings to match those shown here.

Creating Custom Dialog Boxes

Access uses dialog boxes to make it easier for you to perform tasks in your databases. You can create *custom* dialog boxes to pass information to your users and ask them to confirm their choices.

A standard dialog box is simply a blank rectangle with text and controls (such as command buttons) added. So, when you create a custom dialog box, your goal is to create a form without accessories like scroll bars, record selectors, navigation buttons and dividing lines. Once you strip these elements from a form, you're left with a blank rectangle that serves as the base for your custom dialog box.

You should also modify your form so it can only be viewed in Form view. This prevents your users from opening the form in Design view and accidentally changing your dialog box.

To create a custom dialog box:

1. Display the forms in your database and double-click Create form in Design view.
   The form appears.

2. Click Properties and click the Format tab.
   The Format properties of your new form appear in the dialog box (**Figure 14.46**).

3. Click Views Allowed, click the drop-down menu that appears, and choose Form.

4. Click Scroll Bars, click the drop-down menu, and choose Neither.

5. Click Record Selectors, click the drop-down menu, and choose No.

(continued on next page)

6. Click Navigation Buttons, click the drop-down menu, and choose No.

7. Click Dividing Lines, click the drop-down menu, and choose No.

✔ Tip

■ You can leave any or all of the elements you've deleted (navigation buttons, dividing lines, and so on) to give your users more flexibility when using the dialog boxes you create.

Figure 14.47 Open your database in Exclusive mode to ensure that you're the only person working on it.

Figure 14.48 Type the password for your database in the space provided.

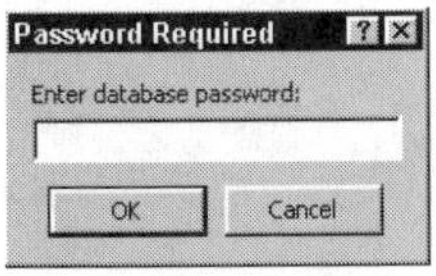

Figure 14.49 Access prompts you to enter the password for your database.

Setting Passwords

Many databases contain information that you don't mind other people seeing. After all, if you can trust them to use your computer, you can trust them with the data on the system, right? Unfortunately, that's not always the case.

If your database contains sensitive information, or if you just want to ensure that only specific users can open the database, you can require users to enter a password to open the database.

To set a password for your database:

1. Start Access, click the database you want to open, click the Open drop-down menu, and choose Open Exclusive (**Figure 14.47**).

    Your database appears in Exclusive mode. Opening a database in Exclusive mode means that you are the only user who can work with the database while you have it open.

2. Choose Tools > Security > Set Database Password.

    The Set Database Password dialog box appears (**Figure 14.48**).

3. Type the password you want to assign your database in the Password text area.

4. Type the password again in the Verify text area.

5. Click OK.

✔ Tips

■   When you open a password-protected database, Access will display a dialog box requesting the database's password (**Figure 14.49**). Type it in the space

(continued on next page)

SETTING PASSWORDS

provided and click OK. If you type the wrong password, Access displays a dialog box informing you of the error. Click OK to get back to the Password Required dialog box.

■ If you forget your password, you won't be able to access your information. Be careful!

■ The best passwords combine numbers and letters in a random pattern. Using a dictionary word or simply substituting numbers for letters like spelling "gopher" as "g0ph3r") isn't enough.

To unset a database password:

1. Open the database you want to remove the password from in Exclusive mode.

2. Choose Tools > Security > Unset Database Password.

   The Unset Database Password dialog box appears (**Figure 14.50**).

3. Type your database's password in the space provided and click OK.

   Access removes your database's password protection.

Figure 14.50 Type the database's password in this dialog box to remove it from the database.

GOING
BEYOND THE BASICS

You have a lot of freedom when you create a database. If you create a database from scratch or modify a wizard-generated database significantly, you could wind up adding unnecessary complications such as tables that contain redundant fields or missing or unneeded relationships, for example. These ultimately make your database run slower than it should. You can use the Performance Analyzer to test your database's performance and suggest ways to improve your design.

If security is a concern, you can go beyond simply setting a password for the entire database. Indeed, you can assign each of your users *permissions*, which limit the ability to view, edit, and delete objects in your database. You can assign permissions individually, assign users to Access-defined *groups* with preset permissions, or create new groups with the permissions you want users of that type to have.

Finally, you can create *projects*, which are special types of files that allow your users to use an Access interface when they work with compatible SQL databases. We don't cover projects in detail, but we do want you to know that they are available. If you'd like more information on working with projects, you should refer to a more advanced text.

Making Your Database Run Faster

Creating databases with Access wizards generates speedy, highly efficient databases. If you create a custom database or add new objects to an existing one, it's possible to create an inefficient information flow in the database.

You can catch those inefficiencies (and get suggestions on how to eliminate them) by running Access's Performance Analyzer. The Performance Analyzer looks at the objects in your database and makes recommendations on how to improve each object's performance. It then generates three types of feedback on your database: Recommendations, Suggestions, and Ideas. The Performance Analyzer can look at every object in your database and select specific object types (like tables, forms, or queries), or even choose which items of a type you want to analyze.

Clicking an item in the Analysis Results list displays information about the proposed optimization in the Analysis Notes box below the list. Suggestion optimizations can trade improved performance in one area for a decreased performance in another. You can click a suggestion in the list and read the entry in the Analysis Notes box to see exactly what those tradeoffs are.

Figure 15.01 The Performance Analyzer recommends ways to make your database run faster.

To analyze your database's performance:

1. Choose Tools > Analyze > Performance. The Performance Analyzer appears (**Figure 15.01**).

2. Click the tab representing the first type of object you want to analyze.

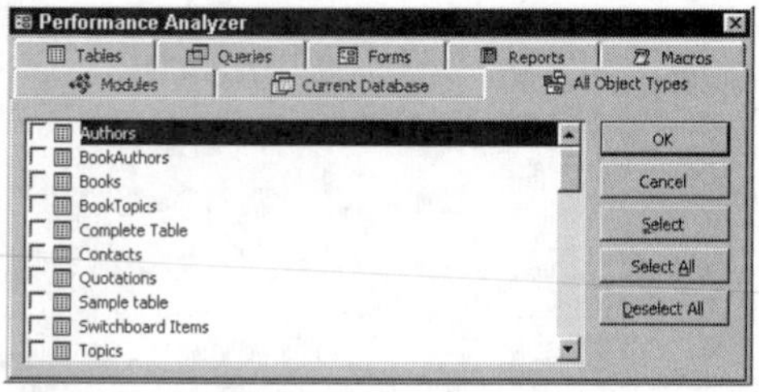

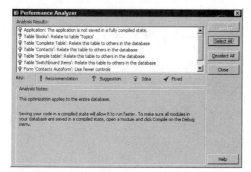

Figure 15.02 Click All Objects for the most comprehensive review of your database.

Figure 15.03 Feedback from the Analyzer: Recommendations, Suggestions, and Ideas.

The list of objects of that type appear. We clicked the All Objects tab (**Figure 15.02**).

3. Click Select All to select every object in your database.

   or

   Choose individual objects to analyze by selecting the checkbox next to their names in the Performance Analyzer's central pane.

4. Click OK to open the Analysis Results (**Figure 15.03**).

5. Click the change you want to make and click Optimize.

✔ Tips

- The first time you run the Performance Analyzer on your database, you should analyze the performance of every object in your database.

- Access performs Recommendation and Suggestion optimizations automatically, but you'll need to implement Idea optimizations yourself by following the directions in the Analysis Notes box.

- If your database starts to run slowly, you should definitely run the Performance Analyzer to rule out any design problems that might be contributing to the slowness.

Controlling Permissions for Multi-User Databases

Password-protecting your database is an important step toward securing your data, but Access also allows you to assign *permissions* to specific users or groups of users within your database. These permissions can apply to tasks like viewing certain types of objects, and changing the database's structure.

Access lets you use the User-Level Security Wizard to create user accounts and assign those users to pre-defined groups, although you can also create groups of your own and give members of your custom groups any combination of permissions.

You should create user groups for any database that that will be worked on by those without full administrator privileges (that is, the privilege to view, add, delete, and modify any element of your database). For instance, you should create at least one other Administrator account to ensure that someone will have the required permissions if your database requires structural changes while you're away. You can do the same for backup operators, who would make archival copies of your database.

Wherever necessary, you can create custom groups to assign users permissions beyond those of any single predefined group. For example, if two data-entry clerks occasionally need to run queries, you can give them additional permissions as members of a new group.

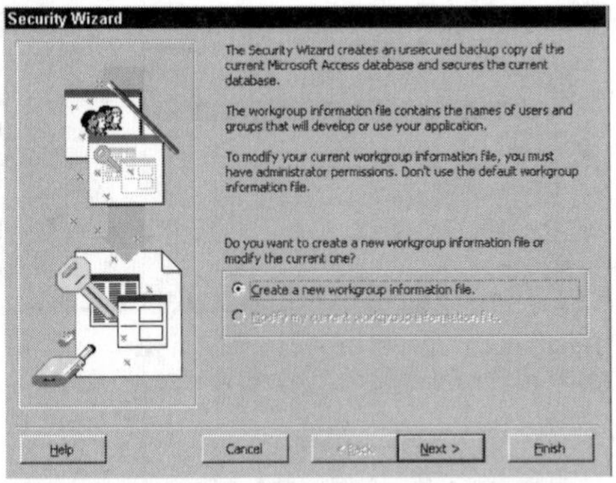

Figure 15.04 The User-Level Security Wizard makes it easy to add and delete accounts.

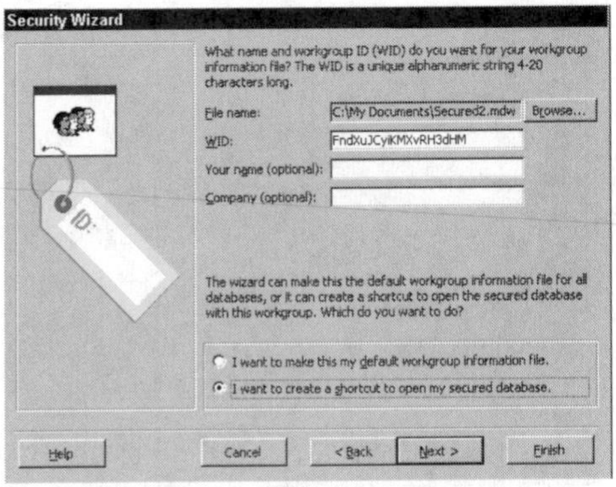

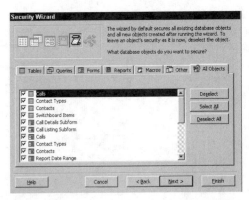

Figure 15.05 The next screen gives you room to type both your name and your organization's name.

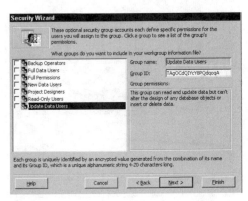

Figure 15.06 It's the best policy to secure every object in your database.

Figure 15.07 Select which built-in groups you want to add to your database.

To assign permissions for multi-user databases:

1. Choose Tools > Security > User-Level Security Wizard.

    The User-Level Security Wizard appears (**Figure 15.04**).

2. Click Next.

    or

    If your database already has some permissions set, and you want to modify the existing permissions, select the "Modify my current workgroup information file" option.

3. In the next screen (**Figure 15.05**), type your name and your organization's name in the spaces provided.

4. Click the "I want to make this my default workgroup information file." to assign these accounts and permissions to all of your databases.

    or

    Click the "I want to create a shortcut to open my secured database." option to assign these accounts and permissions to this database only.

5. In the next screen (**Figure 15.06**), click the All Objects tab, click Select All, and click Next.

6. In the next screen, type a password for your Visual Basic code modules (which are like macros, but written in VBA) and click Next.

7. From the list of groups Access generates **Figure 15.07**), select the checkboxes next to the name of any group you want to add to your database and click Next.

    For this example, we added Backup Operators and Update Data Users.

(continued on next page)

8. The next screen (**Figure 15.08**) asks if you want to assign any permissions to the Users group, which includes everyone who can open your database. You should take the time to grant specific permissions to anyone who needs to work with your database, so accepting the default setting and assigning the Users group no permissions is the best course of action.

9. In the next screen (**Figure 15.9**), type the name of a new user and the password for that user in the spaces provided and click Add this user to the list.

10. If the account you want to work with doesn't appear in the Group or user name box, click the drop-down menu button at the right edge of the Group or user name text area and choose it from the list that appears (**Figure 15.10**).

11. Select the check boxes next to the names of any groups you want to make this user a member of and click Next. The final wizard screen appears.

12. Type the name of the unsecured copy of your database in the space provided.

    Access creates an unsecured version of your database so you'll have a freely-accessible backup copy of your data in case you forget your administrator's password. You should keep the unprotected copy in a secure location to prevent unauthorized use.

13. Click Finish.

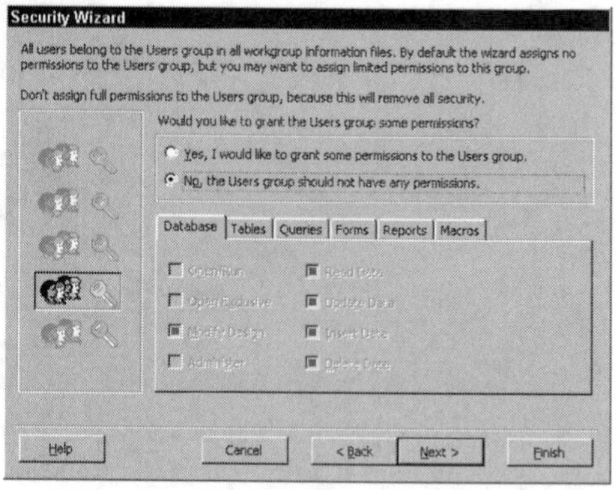

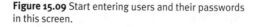

Figure 15.08 Grant the Users group no permissions to ensure the most security for your database.

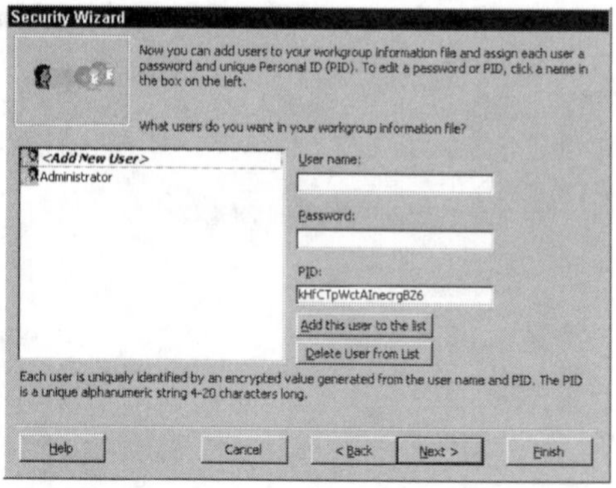

Figure 15.09 Start entering users and their passwords in this screen.

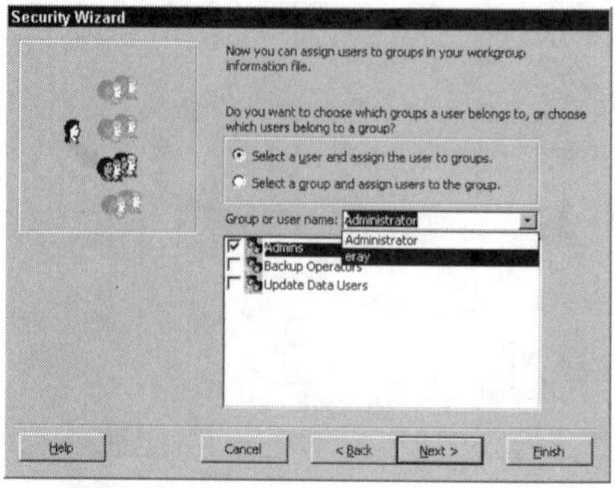

Figure 15.10 Choose the account you want to work on by clicking the drop-down menu and displaying the list of accounts available.

Figure 15.11 The New User/Group dialog box.

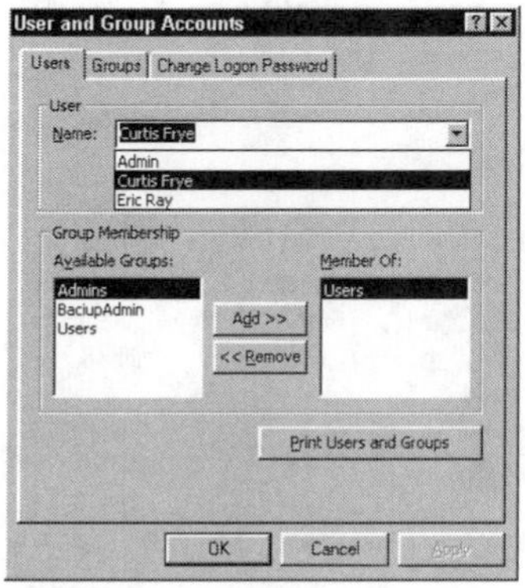

Figure 15.12 Your new account appears in the drop-down list.

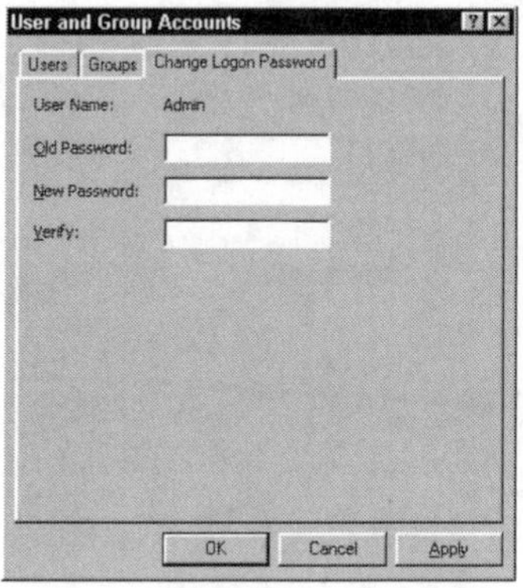

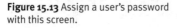

Figure 15.13 Assign a user's password with this screen.

To create a new user account:

1. Choose Tools > Security > User and Group Accounts.

2. When the New User/Group dialog box appears (**Figure 15.11**), click the Users tab and click New.

3. Type the user's name and the user's database ID in the spaces provided, and then click OK.

    Access creates the new account.

4. In the User and Group Accounts dialog box, click the Name drop-down menu (**Figure 15.12**).

    The account you created appears in the list.

To assign a user a password:

1. Choose Tools > Security > User and Group Accounts.

    The User and Group Accounts window appears.

2. Click the Users tab, click the drop-down menu in the Name text area, and choose the user you want to assign a password to.

3. Click the Change Logon Password tab to bring up the Change Logon Password page (**Figure 15.13**).

4. Type the user's old password (if any), and type the new password twice to verify its spelling. Click Apply.

To assign a user to a group:

1. Choose Tools > Security > User and Group Accounts.

    The User and Group Accounts window appears.

2. Click the Users tab, click the drop-down menu in the Name text area, and choose

(continued on next page)

the user that you want to assign to a group.

The user's name appears in the Name box, the available groups appear in the Available Groups pane, and the groups that user is a member of appear in the Member Of pane (**Figure 15.14**).

3. Click the name of the group you want to add the user to and click Add.

   The group appears in the Member Of pane (**Figure 15.15**).

4. Click OK.

To remove a user from a group:

1. Choose Tools > Security > User and Group Accounts.

   The User and Group Accounts window appears.

2. Click the Users tab, click the drop-down menu in the Name text area, and choose the user that you want to remove from a group.

   The user's name appears in the Name box, and the available groups appear in the Available Groups pane. The Member Of pane contains the groups that the user belongs to.

3. Click the name of the group you want to remove the user from and click Remove.

   The group disappears from the Member Of pane (**Figure 15.16**).

4. Click OK.

✔ Tip

■ You should delete a user's account as soon as that person no longer requires permission to use your database, regardless of whether the user remains with the company or has moved on.

Figure 15.14 Determine which group you want to make the user a member of.

Figure 15.15 Click Add to put your user in a new group.

Figure 15.16 Select the group you want to remove the user from.

Figure 15.17 List the group in your database.

Figure 15.18 Enter the name of your new group here.

To create a custom group:

1. Choose Tools > Security > User and Group Accounts.

2. Click Groups to bring up the Groups window (**Figure 15.17**).

   Click New, and the The New User/Group dialog box appears (**Figure 15.18**).

3. Type the name of your new group and an identifier for the group in the spaces provided.

   In this case, we typed the group's name again.

4. Click OK.

   The group you just created appears in the Group list.

✔ Tip

■ If you create a new group, always leave users in the new group assigned to their previous groups as well, even if you believe the new group has all the permissions it needs. Leaving a user's name in its old group ensures that you haven't accidentally left out any permissions that the user needed when you initially created the new group.

CONTROLLING PERMISSIONS FOR MULTI-USERS

Upgrading to Projects

A Microsoft Access project (identified in file lists with an *.adp* extension) is a new type of Access file that lets you use an Access interface for a Microsoft SQL Server database. You should create a project whenever you need to give experienced Access users the means to work with an SQL database. Rather than learn a new interface, your users can rely on their Access skills to work with the data in the SQL database.

An Access project only contains presentation-oriented or HTML-based database objects: forms, reports, pages, macros, and Visual Basic code modules. Unlike a Microsoft Access database, an Access project doesn't contain any data or data definition-based objects, that is, objects that derive their contents from data in your database, such as tables or queries. Those data-defined objects are maintained in the SQL Server database.

You can choose to create a project but not link it to an existing SQL database. For instance, if you plan to link to a future SQL database, you can create a freestanding project and link to the database when it's available.

You can create a project connected to a database running on any of the following SQL servers:

◆ SQL Server 7.0 on Windows NT 4.0 or later (with Windows NT Service Pack 4 or later and Windows 95 or later).

◆ Microsoft Data Engine (MSDE) on Windows NT 4.0 or later and Windows 95 or later.

◆ SQL Server 6.5 on Windows NT 4.0 or later (with SQL Server Service Pack 5 or later).

Figure 15.19 Select the Access database wizards, pages, and projects option.

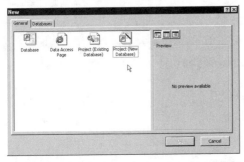

Figure 15.20 Click the General tab and create a project for a new database.

Figure 15.21 Click Create to open the Data Link Properties dialog box.

To create a freestanding project:

1. Launch Access.

2. Select the Access database wizards, pages, and projects option and click OK (**Figure 15.19**).

3. In the New window (**Figure 15.20**), click the General tab and click Project (New Database).

4. Click OK to bring up the File New Database window (**Figure 15.21**).

5. Type the name of your new project in the File Name text area.

6. Click Create.
   The Data Link Properties dialog box appears.

7. Click Cancel.
   Access creates your project.

✔ Tip

■ You can open the New window by choosing File > New or clicking the New toolbar button.

To create a project that's linked to a database:

1. Launch Access.

2. Click the Access database wizards, pages, and projects option button and click OK.
   The New window appears.

3. Click the General tab, click Project (Existing Database) and click OK.
   The File New Database window appears.

4. Type the name of your new project in the File Name text area.

(continued on next page)

UPGRADING TO PROJECTS

5. Click Create.

The Data Link Properties dialog box appears (**Figure 15.22**).

6. Type (or select from the drop-down menu) the name of your server in the "Select or enter a server name" text area.

7. Select the option button representing the login information your database will require.

8. Type a user name and password to limit your database's availability.

9. Type the name of the database you want to use as the base for your project, and then click OK.

Access creates your project.

✔ Tip

■ You can convert an existing Access database to an SQL database by running the Upsizing Wizard, which you can launch by choosing Tools > Database Utilities > Upsizing Wizard.

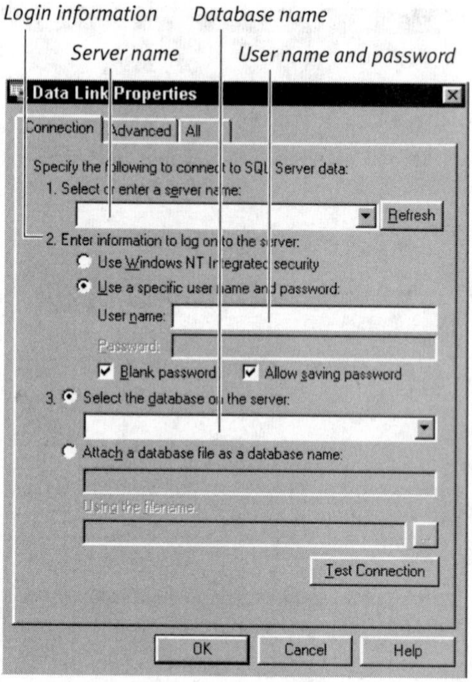

Login information   *Database name*

Server name   *User name and password*

Figure 15.22 The Data Link Properties dialog box.

SETTING OPTIONS AND PREFERENCES

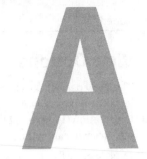

You can control how Access displays your information and responds to your actions. For instance, you can open objects in your database with a single instead of double click.

There are eight pages in the Options dialog box; browse them and familiarize yourself with options and settings. Go ahead and experiment—you can always change back to your previous settings.

View Options

The View page of the Options dialog box lets you change how Access presents your information (**Figure A.1**). The categories of changes you can make are:

Show Select which of the six types of available objects you want to display in your database windows. The default setting is to show every object type except Hidden and System Objects.

Show in macro design These two options determine whether Access automatically displays the Name and Conditions columns when you view a macro in Design view. Select the appropriate checkbox if you want Access to show those columns.

Click options in database window Pick whether database objects should open with one click or two.

Dual font support This checkbox specifies a backup font your users' systems will use to display text in your database if they don't have the font you used on your system. Once you select the Use substitute font checkbox, you can choose (or type) the name of the font you want to assign as the backup. If you don't assign a backup font, Access will use your system's default font instead, which is usually Arial.

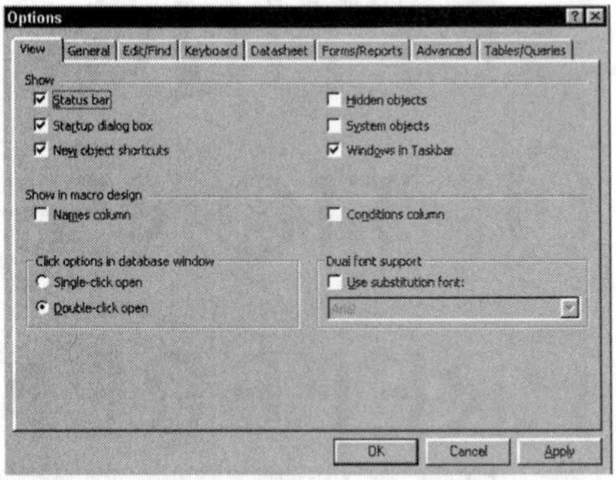

Figure A.1 The View page of the Options dialog box.

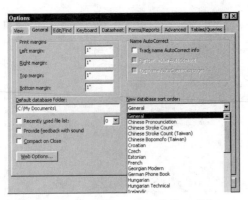

Figure A.2 The General page of the Options dialog box.

General Options

The General page of the Options dialog box allows you to specify how Access handles and presents data throughout your database (**Figure A.2**).

Print margins Use the combo boxes to set the margins for any document you print from your database. The default setting is a one-inch margin on all four sides.

Name AutoCorrect In previous versions of Access, if you changed the name of a field after you'd created queries or other objects that used the field's name, those dependent objects no longer functioned properly. Select Track name AutoCorrect info to maintain a history of field name changes. Select Perform name AutoCorrect to automatically update field references in objects referencing that field; selecting Log name AutoCorrect changes has Access write its changes to disk.

New database sort order This combo box contains a list of languages and character sets Access can use to sort the contents of your database.

Default database folder This is the directory Access looks in first when you ask it to open or save a file.

Recently used file list Select this checkbox to get a list of recently opened files to appear in the File menu. The default list size is 4.

Provide feedback with sound Selecting this checkbox lets you hear as well as see the Office Assistant.

Compact on close This option lets Access optimize your database by removing references to deleted objects and rewriting the database to disk using the least possible space.

Web Options This brings up the Web options screen, which displays choices for hyperlink appearance.

Edit and Find Options

Options on the Edit/Find page of the
Options dialog box dictate the way Access
searches for and filters information in your
tables and query results (**Figure A.3**).
You can also choose which actions (like
deletions and record changes) Access asks
you to confirm.

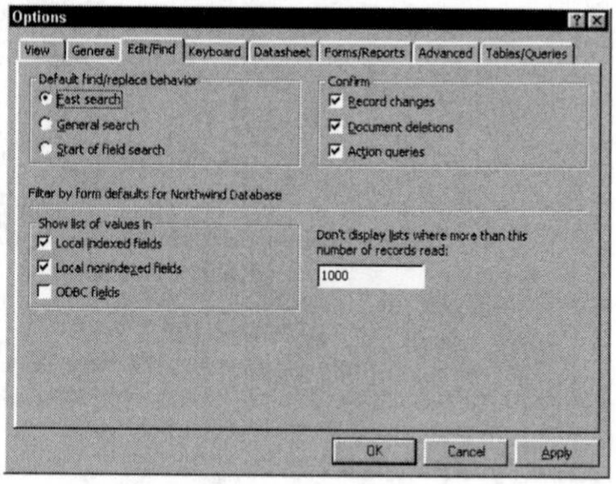

Default find/replace behavior This
option group allows you choose which
method Access uses to search for values in
your tables and query results. Fast search
(the default) is the best choice.

Confirm This series of checkboxes tells
Access whether or not to display a confirma-
tion dialog box when you delete an object,
change records, or run action queries.

Filter by form defaults This group of
checkboxes allows you to specify which
values to display in the filter by form results.
You can set defaults for each of your databases separately—the name of the active
database appears in the label. ODBC (Open
Database Connectivity) fields refer to fields
in SQL databases you've linked to your table
or query.

**Don't display lists where more than
this number of records read** This sets the
upper limit of the number of records to be
shown in a table or query results. The default
value is 1000, but you should modify that
limit based on the size of your database and
the capabilities of your system.

Figure A.3 The Edit/Find page of the Options dialog
box.

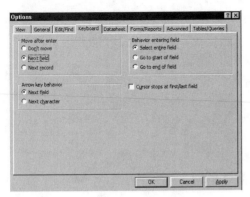

Figure A.4 The Keyboard page of the Options dialog box.

Keyboard Options

You can use the mouse to move among the fields in your tables and forms, but you can also use the keyboard to move from place to place (**Figure A.4**). This page allows you to control how the keyboard moves your cursor in Access.

Move after enter This option group determines how your cursor moves after you press Enter. You can have the cursor move to the next field (the default), the next record, or not at all.

Behavior entering field This option group allows you to pick where the insertion point appears in the field you've moved to: the end of the field, the start of the field, or highlighting the field's contents (the default).

Arrow key behavior This two-option group allows you to choose whether the arrow keys move the cursor to the next field (the default) or to the next character within a field.

Cursor stops at first/last field This checkbox determines whether you can use the keyboard to move beyond the bounds of a record. If you don't select this box, for instance, pressing Tab while in the last field of a record creates a new record and puts the insertion point in the first field of that record.

Datasheet Options

This page of the Options dialog box allows you to change how your datasheets are drawn on the screen (**Figure A.5**). You can pick the color for each element of your datasheet, the font used, and the default width of each cell.

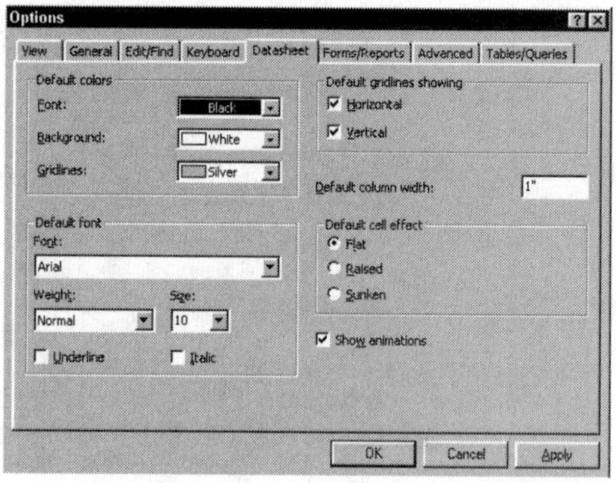

Default colors You can use these drop-down menus to choose the colors for the datasheet's font, background, and gridlines.

Default font The controls in this group allow you to choose the font, size, and weight of the text used in the datasheet. You can also choose to have your text displayed in italics or underlined.

Default gridlines showing These two checkboxes allow you to show or hide the horizontal and vertical gridlines.

Default column width This specifies the standard width of columns in your datasheets. The default value is one inch.

Default cell effect This option group lets you determine whether your cells will be displayed with a flat (the default), raised, or sunken effect.

Show animations Selecting this checkbox has Access run any animations you've included in your datasheets.

Figure A.5 The Datasheet page of the Options dialog box.

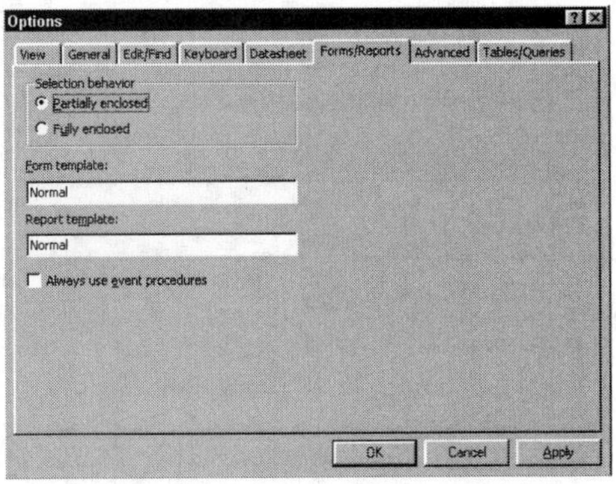

Figure A.6 The Forms/Reports page of the Options dialog box.

Forms/Reports Options

The Forms/Reports page of the Options dialog box allows you to change how you choose items on forms and reports in Design view (**Figure A.6**). You can also choose the default templates used to create your forms and reports.

Selection behavior This option group allows you to choose whether you need to fully enclose an item in your selection loop while working in Design view.

Form template Enter the name of the template to use to create your forms.

Report template Enter the name of the template Access will use to create your reports.

Always use event procedures This checkbox allows you to determine whether Access will use event procedures while in Design view.

Advanced Options

The Advanced page of the Options dialog box lets you change the way Access interacts with other programs, how it opens your database, and how it protects your database from multi-user changes (**Figure A.7**).

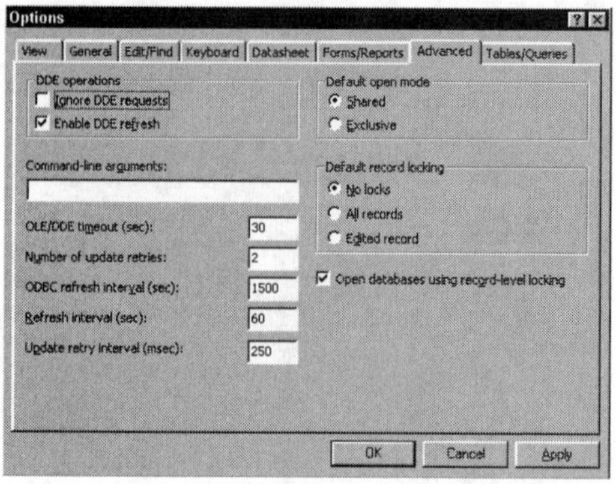

DDE operations DDE (Dynamic Data Exchange) operations look for data in other applications. You can set the Control Source property of a control to use the contents of, for instance, a cell in an Excel spreadsheet.

Command line arguments Adds command line arguments to the instructions Windows uses to run Access. If you wanted Access to open your books database on startup, for example, the command line argument would be books.mdb.

OLE and DDE settings You can enter times for OLE timeouts (how long Access tries to establish a DDE or OLE connection), the number of update retries, ODBC (Open Database Connectivity) refresh intervals, refresh interval, and the update retry interval.

Default open mode This option group determines whether users open Access in shared (the default) or exclusive mode.

Default record locking Choose which records are locked in your database. Locking a record means that only one user at a time can open a record for editing. The default choice is for no locks, but you can also lock the active record or all records in your database.

Open databases using record-level locking This checkbox allows you to turn record-level locking on and off.

Figure A.7 The Advanced page of the Options dialog box.

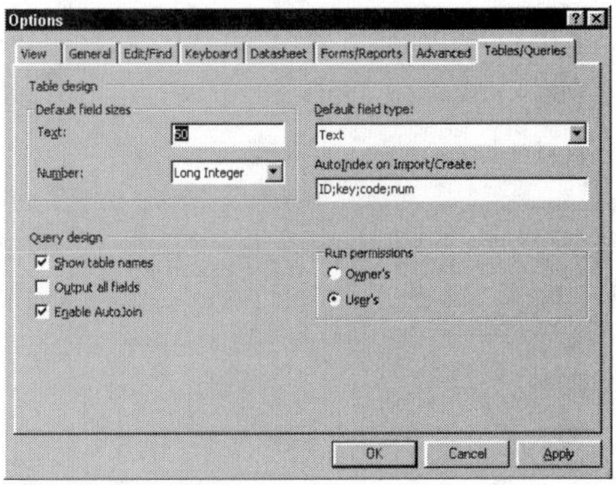

Figure A.8 The Tables/Queries page of the Options dialog box.

Tables/Queries Options

The final page of the Options dialog box allows you to change how you work with your tables and queries (**Figure A.8**).

Default field sizes You can use the drop-down menus to pick the default size for your text fields and number fields. The defaults are for text fields of 50 characters and Long Integer number fields.

Default field type This value determines which data type Access assigns a new field. The default value is text.

Autoindex on Import/Create The values Access uses to index new tables.

Query design Use these checkboxes to select whether your queries show all table names (default is yes) and output all fields (default is no). Enabling AutoJoin lets Access automatically join the tables used in your query. For more information on joins, see Chapter 8.

Run permissions These option buttons specify whether Access requires owner or user permissions to run macros and modules in your database. Owner permissions equate to having administrator privileges; user permissions allow anyone to run queries.

TABLES/QUERIES OPTIONS

APPENDIX B: FIELD TYPES PROPERTIES

This appendix gives you more detailed information on the field data types you first encountered in Chapter 3. This information can help you pick the best data type for any field you add to your tables; if you need to change the range of values an existing field holds, you can find the best replacement here as well.

Table B.1

Basic Access Data Types		
TYPE	DESCRIPTION	SIZE
Text	Text or combinations of text and numbers, such as addresses; numbers not subject to calculations, such as phone numbers or postal codes.	Up to 255 characters.
Memo	Lengthy text and numbers, such as notes or descriptions.	Up to 64,000 characters.
Number	Numeric data to be used for mathematical calculations, except money (use Currency type). Set the FieldSize property to define the specific Number type.	1, 2, 4, or 8 bytes. 16 bytes for Replication ID (GUID) only.
Date/Time	Dates and times.	8 bytes.
Currency	Currency values. You can also use the Currency data type to prevent rounding off during calculations.	8 bytes.
AutoNumber	Unique sequential or random numbers automatically inserted when a record is added.	4 bytes.
Yes/No	Fields that will contain only one of two values, such as Yes/No, True/False, On/Off..	1 bit.
OLE Object	Objects created in other programs using the OLE protocol.	Up to 1 gigabyte (limited by disk space).
Hyperlink	Field that stores a link to another object in your database, another file on your computer, or an address on the World Wide Web.	Up to 64,000 characters.
Lookup Wizard	Creates a field that allows you to choose a value from another table or from a list of values using a combo box.	The size of the primary key in the lookup field(s). Typically 4 bytes.

Table B.2

Number Data Subtypes

SETTING	DESCRIPTION	DECIMAL PRECISION	STORAGE SIZE
Byte	Stores whole numbers from 0 to 255.	None	1 byte
Integer	Stores whole numbers from –32,768 to 32,767.	None	2 bytes
Long Integer	Stores whole numbers from –2,147,483,648 to 2,147,483,647. This is the default subtype.	None	4 bytes
Single	Stores numbers from –3.402823E38 to –1.401298E–45 for negative values and from 1.401298E–45 to 3.402823E38 for positive values.	7	4 bytes
Double	Stores numbers from –1.79769313486231E308 to –4.94065645841247E–324 for negative values and from 1.79769313486231E308 to 4.94065645841247E–324 for positive values.	15	8 bytes

Table B.3

Date/Time Data Subtypes

SETTING	DESCRIPTION
General Date	The default setting. For date only, no time is displayed; for time only, no date is displayed. This setting is a combination of the Short Date and Long Time settings. Example: 5/30/99, 11:02:00 PM.
Long Date	Example: Sunday, May 30, 1999.
Medium Date	Example: 30-May-99.
Short Date	Example: 5/30/99. The Short Date setting assumes that dates between 1/1/00 and 12/31/29 are twenty-first-century dates (between 2000 and 2029) and that dates between 1/1/30 and 12/31/99 are twentieth-century dates (between 1930 and 1999).
Long Time	Example: 2:59:18 PM.
Medium Time	Example: 2:59 PM.
Short Time	Example: 14:59.

Table B.4

Currency Data Subtypes

SETTING	DESCRIPTION
General Number	(Default) Displays the number as entered.
Currency	Inserts a separator every three places to the left of the decimal point. Negative values are displayed in parentheses. The default number of decimal places is 2.
Fixed	Displays at least one digit. The default number of decimal places is 2.
Standard	Displays the number as entered, adding a separator every three places to the left of the decimal point. The default number of decimal places is 2.
Percent	Multiplies the value by 100 and appends a percent sign (%). The default number of decimal places is 2.
Scientific	Use standard scientific notation. Example: 1.25E10

6 0 4 5